DUBLIN FROM DOWNING STREET

JOHN PECK

Dublin
from Downing Street

To mourn a mischief that is past and gone
Is the next way to draw new mischief on.

SHAKESPEARE, *Othello*

GILL AND MACMILLAN

First published 1978 by
Gill and Macmillan Ltd
15/17 Eden Quay
Dublin 1
with associated companies in
London and Basingstoke
New York, Melbourne, Delhi, Johannesburg

7171 0872 4

Printed and bound in Great Britain by
Bristol Typesetting Co. Ltd, Barton Manor, St Philips, Bristol

For Mariska
who shared it all, endured it all,
and made it all worth while.

Contents

Preface

IN THIS book I have described, with their causes and their consequences, some of the things that happened during the three years that I served as British Ambassador in Dublin. It was during this time that after three days of rioting the Chancery of the Embassy was burnt. Out of this disaster there sprang the resolve of the British and Irish governments to work together in the common duty of enabling the people of the whole of Ireland to live in peace. Since then there has been a far worse tragedy—the violent death in July 1976 of the newly-appointed British Ambassador to Dublin, Mr Christopher Ewart-Biggs. But the tragedy was made bearable by the strengthened determination of both peoples not to be distracted by it from the quest for peace, and above all by the compassion and the courage of his widow, Jane. I hope that this book will make some contribution to the search for understanding.

I write from the viewpoint of an English-speaking European, a private English citizen living in Ireland. I have not consulted or sought the help of anyone, either British or Irish, who is or was in an official position. The opinions expressed, the conclusions drawn, and the suggestions I have ventured to make are exclusively my own, and they commit nobody but myself.

This is a very personal account of public matters, and its pages are interspersed with notes of some of the things that seemed relevant on the way to Dublin from Downing Street. I have not tried to convey a message, but if there were one, it would be this. There is nothing unique or insoluble about the problems of this island. In the end Christian charity allied to common sense, courage and the broader vision will triumph over bigotry and its blood-brother, brutality. And even in the most sombre parts of the journey there is always some light and love and laughter for those who try to notice and to care.

I

EARLY that morning the telephone rang. It was Christopher Aliaga-Kelly, a distinguished businessman from Cork, who had become a close friend. We were due to meet for lunch at the Stephen's Green Club.

'About our lunch.'

'Yes, are you snowed up in Cork?'

'No, I'm in Dublin, but are you worried about trouble if you are seen at the Club?'

'I'll chance it, but what about you? Do you mind being seen with me?'

'No, I'll chance it too.'

It was the morning of Monday 31 January 1972. Dublin lay under deep snow. Roads and streets were iced up. The airport was closed. My wife Mariska had to use the official Daimler for some appointment so I drove my own car the seven miles from Glencairn, the Ambassador's official residence, to the Chancery in Merrion Square. The atmosphere in Dublin could have been cut with a knife. Late on the previous evening the news had come through that thirteen young civilians had been killed by British paratroops in Derry. In Dublin the thirteen dead were everywhere—the huge headlines, a sort of hush, a vast sullenness. In mid-morning the Foreign Office telephoned from London. A ministerial meeting arranged for Wednesday 2 February, which I had been instructed to attend some weeks previously, was being put forward to Tuesday the first. Could I be there by mid-day? Yes I could, but did I have to go? Things smelt bad in Dublin. Yes, I did have to go—this really was important.

The only possible way was to take the British Rail night

boat to Holyhead, so somewhat reluctantly I was booked on that. Then I drove off for lunch with Christopher.

There was no trouble at the Club, but Peter Evans, my Information Secretary, on duty over lunch, telephoned. 'You had better bring the car to the back entrance to Chancery after lunch. Students from Trinity are beginning to picket the front, and there might be problems.'

As I drove unobserved along Merrion Square to the back lane, I saw an orderly file of students walking round in a circle in the street, carrying placards with predictable slogans about the thirteen dead of the previous day, with the words 'Bloody Sunday' prominent. My room was on the first floor, looking out on the square. More students arrived and started throwing snowballs at the Embassy and shouting slogans and abuse. Then they started putting stones in the snowballs. Then they dispensed with the snow.

I had intended to have an office meeting to make our dispositions for what was evidently going to be a substantial riot. We closed the shutters, but the din was by now so tremendous that serious discussion was impossible. We made the normal demand for protection to the Irish Department of Foreign Affairs.

I was now face to face with a hateful dilemma. I had to be in two places at the same time. At this point I telephoned the Foreign Office. 'Listen to this,' I said, and held out the telephone for them to hear the din. 'Do you still want me to leave Dublin?' But I had to go. Ministers really did require my presence, and I patently had something to tell them.

In the precarious security situation inherent in the British presence in Dublin and the over-riding need to keep relations between the two governments as near to normal as possible, it was a cardinal rule that Her Majesty's Representative did not risk violence to his own person—an unheroic role, but whereas a few broken windows could be shrugged off with a protest, insult, injury, or abduction could not and were thus to be avoided if possible. (That is why the British Ambassador in Ireland never flies his flag on his car.) The staff were well trained in riot drill, and nobody knew at that point how far what was then only a noisy student demonstration would go. Mariska, in Glencairn, was strongly guarded and had strong nerves, so I supposed that I would be more use next day in London than in Dublin.

At around 4.30 pm we closed the office. There was a danger that the demonstrators would block the back lane and we wanted to get the girls out and everybody back home before dark, and anyway the din outside made work impossible. I drove myself back to Glencairn, to be greeted by the news that Dr Patrick Hillery, the Minister for Foreign Affairs, wanted to see me, so I piled into the police car with the detectives and went back into Dublin. On the police radio we heard that Sinn Féin had now taken over from the students, and workers from the factories were marching on Merrion Square. Heavy police reinforcements were being called in.

The Irish government had recalled their Ambassador from London after Bloody Sunday, making the ultimate gesture short of breaking off diplomatic relations. Dr Hillery wanted to tell me that he was going off on a tour of European and transatlantic capitals to explain the Irish viewpoint on the North and Bloody Sunday. I said I had been called to London but expected to return, pointed out that there was a considerable demonstration in progress outside the Embassy and said that I expected everything necessary to be done to protect it. He was evidently not protesting to me about Derry, and I had nothing to protest to him about. I went home to collect my bag, and then to the night boat for Holyhead.

At Holyhead next morning I could see nobody selling newspapers, but in the breakfast car in the train someone had obviously found them, for at a neighbouring table I could just see the headline 'British Embassy in Flames'. When the train stopped in Bangor I bought every paper in sight and read how the mob in Merrion Square had attacked the Chancery, and also the Passport Office and Commercial Departments in their separate buildings, mainly with petrol bombs. The police had defended all three buildings vigorously, no serious damage had been done, the crowds had been dispersed, and all was quiet.

In the train I wrote down in a little notebook the main points which I should need to make in London about the political scene in Dublin. Bloody Sunday had unleashed a wave of fury and exasperation the like of which I had never encountered in my life, in Egypt or Cyprus or anywhere else. Hatred of the British was intense. The promise of an enquiry into the conduct of the paratroops in Derry would be of little use; what is believed serves for truth, and however eminent and painstaking the person conducting the enquiry might be, the fact that he was British would guarantee to the Irish that he would whitewash the Army. Someone had summed it up: 'We are all IRA now'. One consequence would be that whereas up till then it had been hard enough to get an Irish jury to convict anyone charged with a crime that was remotely anti-British, it would now be impossible. The already shaky position of Jack Lynch, the Irish Taoiseach (Prime Minister) was now extremely precarious, and the threat posed by the IRA to democratic institutions in the Republic would now be far more serious. In other words, Bloody Sunday heavily accentuated and accelerated developments in Ireland to which we had already been calling attention.

As regards the North, it would now be impossible to persuade the leaders of the Catholic minority to return to Stormont as then constituted. Paradoxically, however, there were people in Dublin who claimed there was a growing belief among moderate and well-to-do Protestants that reunification was the only answer. Meanwhile, a major question agitating the Irish government was in what circumstances did we see internment ending, this being the biggest single issue causing the violence?

The only hope that Irish politicians could see lay in a package deal which could first be discussed between British and Irish Ministers on the basis of mutual respect and understanding, such as had marked the Treaty negotiations of 1921. The sort of items on which they would want to negotiate were:

1. An interpretation of the offer made by Reginald Maudling (then Home Secretary) that there should be a guaranteed permanent place for Catholic leaders in the Stormont Cabinet.

2. Recognition by Her Majesty's Government that crushing the Provisional IRA solved nothing, and that the key to the security situation was political.

3. Talks with the Irish government about phasing out internment.

4. An expression of hope by HMG that reunification could come about by democratic means.

To this summary, which was of course a distillation of the views increasingly pressed upon us during the previous weeks, I added my personal view that despite the reactions of the previous day (i.e. Monday) to Bloody Sunday, there was a desperate desire in the Irish government for friendly collaboration with us.

From Euston Station I went straight to the Foreign Office. The news from Dublin was that there had been small petrol fires, but that the Embassy was functioning. Mariska and all the Embassy families were safe. Within a few minutes I was in 10 Downing Street with the Prime Minister, Mr Edward Heath. I spent the rest of the day, until late at night, either in meetings with Ministers and officials, or in the House of Commons, or on the telephone to Dublin. The situation there during the day was quiet. The Embassy staff had worked all day; Mariska was careful to be seen shopping and going about her normal business; there had been a peaceful demonstration outside the gates of Glencairn; the Irish government had refused to bring in troops to protect the Embassy (As someone in Protocol said : 'What could they do except shoot, and do you think they would shoot our people to protect you after Bloody Sunday?'); sandbags to protect the ground floor doors and windows could not be obtained as nobody would do any work for the Embassy; Dublin airport was handling no British aircraft or mail; the following day, Wednesday, had been proclaimed a day of national mourning for all the dead in Northern Ireland; there would probably be more demonstrations in the evening but the Dublin police were doing all they could.

In London, the Lord Chief Justice, Lord Widgery, had been appointed to enquire into the events of Bloody Sunday. Bernadette Devlin, MP, had pulled Mr Maudling's hair in the House of Commons. Ministers were principally worried about another civil rights march which was to take place the following Sunday in Newry, with the danger that the tragedy in Derry might be repeated.

Late that night I rang up Mariska. She was safe in Glencairn

and very calm. The news from Merrion Square was bad, but
elsewhere things were quiet and none of the Embassy families
seemed to be in danger.

The next morning, Wednesday 2 February, I went in to the
Foreign Office early and telephoned Dublin again. Things
were much worse. Mariska's diary for the previous day reads:
'Leopardstown demonstration at gates. After lunch I went to
Stillorgan shopping. Mixed-up woman came to offer me sym-
pathy. Looked at TV. 5,000 people in front of Embassy.
Gelignite. Passport Office burnt out. Chancery abandoned.
Father rang up. More bombs, door gone.'

I talked to Peter Evans, as the Chancery telephone was still
working. The front door of the Chancery had been blown up
by a small gelignite bomb which had badly injured one of the
policemen trying to protect the building, and petrol bombs
had been hurled in. David Blatherwick, the First Secretary,
and the security guard on duty had been sweeping the burning
petrol out with buckets of water and brooms. The building
could no longer be defended. The mob was not satisfied and
clearly intended to destroy the place. The national day of
mourning meant that the factories would be shut and the pubs
open. The police fought hard and many had been burnt by
petrol, but they were outnumbered. The staff were destroying
the files and essential equipment and would then have to
evacuate the building. I could only agree, and said I would be
back as soon as the Prime Minister consented; I asked Peter to
tell Mariska I hoped to be back by six.

The Prime Minister readily agreed to my plea that the
remaining business for which I had been called to London
should be concluded by lunchtime. The only problem was how
to get back to Dublin. No aircraft from London were being
accepted there. Train and boat would not get me to Dublin
until the following morning. Number Ten got the Ministry
of Defence to work. I suggested a helicopter, as the grounds
at Glencairn made a perfect landing place, but the sea crossing
from Anglesea was too long for a single-engined helicopter,
and the only available large machine was in Sussex. I then
suggested that I should be sent in a small RAF jet to Baldonnel
military airfield on the outskirts of Dublin, and the Irish
Chargé d'Affaires, in the absence of his withdrawn Ambassador,

should be requested to obtain clearance for the flight. (He had already received a vigorous protest over the damage to the Embassy on the previous days and had promised full compensation.) I then went in to the meeting.

During the meeting word came that the Irish authorities had given clearance for the flight, which would leave Northolt at 4.00 pm. The Prime Minister suggested that I should travel in a large aircraft, which could then be used to evacuate the Embassy women and children. I was very dubious about this. To begin with, I was not sure whether Baldonnel could handle a large plane or whether it would be allowed to stay overnight. But besides that, I did not believe that the families were in immediate danger as the hate object seemed to be the Embassy itself. We could not, in any case, have organised the evacuation on a day when movement in Dublin was unwise, if not impossible. So the Prime Minister gave me full responsibility and discretion to handle this—and indeed the entire immediate situation in Dublin—as I thought fit; in fact, in retrospect, it is an odd and not unflattering fact that throughout that week I was not given any precise instructions at all. It was a matter of playing everything by ear.

I left Number Ten with the good wishes and encouragement of the Ministers present, took off from Northolt at 4.00 pm as planned, and immediately rose into dense cloud from which we emerged at 5.15 to see the runway lights of Baldonnel immediately below. Darkness was falling. It was as filthy an evening as I have known, with a gale and heavy driving rain. The solitary figure of Colonel Swann, the Officer Commanding the Irish Air Force, was standing among pools of water to greet me. Hugh McCann, the Permanent Secretary to the Department of Foreign Affairs, wanted to speak on the telephone. 'John, I'm glad you're back, but I'm afraid your Embassy is in flames and there is nothing we can do to save it. Glencairn is all right. Please keep absolutely clear of the middle of town'. I said I would like to see the Taoiseach the next day and proposed to call at noon. Two carloads of detectives were waiting for me, the large black Daimler, which had always been the most observable and ostentatious car in Dublin, having been relegated to the obscurity of its garage. We rode to Glencairn, and, as promised, I walked in to the library as the radio signalled six.

Mariska, our American house guest Wenda, our son Nicholas and his friend Sandra were there. All the domestic staff were in the house, and what seemed to be a large number of uniformed and plain-clothes policemen were close by. As always, the great floodlights on the tower were maintaining a pool of light around Glencairn.

I telephoned round the Embassy staff and called for a staff meeting at 10.00 the following morning. There was nothing to do but await developments.

We did not have long to wait. The police superintendent in charge asked to see me urgently. The Embassy was now destroyed, and headquarters had just sent word that the mob was now on the way to attack Glencairn. The police did not know whether they were strong enough to hold it against heavy attack, and the place must be evacuated immediately.

We refused to be stampeded. We told the domestic staff who lived nearby that it would be better if they went home for the night. A young French couple who worked for us were finding themselves a little out of their depth in this Anglo-Irish situation, but they owned a car so we sent them off to find a hotel. I rang up a friendly diplomat who lived not far away, further out of Dublin, and he instantly agreed to have Mariska and Wenda to stay for the night and longer if need be. They then packed.

Mariska defends with perfect feminine logic her selection of items to pack in this emergency. It included her evening dresses, all her bras, one pair of gold slippers, no day clothes and no shoes. As she says, she only took the irreplaceable. By the same logic, into my Sunbeam Rapier Nicholas and Sandra packed the scrapbooks, Mariska's tapestries, our Churchilliana, and other household gods until the car was full. Mariska could not drive, so Wenda did, with a detective in a squad car to guide her.

Nicholas was a student at Trinity College at the time, but he had been advised by his tutor that it would be wise to keep clear of College for a while. Special Branch had also advised him to avoid his regular lodgings and I was not going to let him and Sandra stay in Glencairn, so they roared off up the drive in his venerable Volkswagen to doss down with friends somewhere.

Meanwhile I was having a slight difference of opinion with the Superintendent of Police. I said that I had evacuated Glencairn as requested but did not intend to leave myself until I had to. What would I do in that case? Well, there was only one short meadow to cross and then I could be over the wall into Leopardstown Hospital's grounds, from where I could easily escape. After some thought he agreed, provided one of his own men came with me as I might otherwise be shot by the police. Brian, my admirable young butler, who had already sent his wife somewhere safe, flatly refused to leave me in Glencairn, so we put a table with a lot of glasses and bottles of Paddy (whiskey) in the portico and asked the senior police officers to dispense them according to the needs of the men when they came off duty. I sat down at the head of the desolate table still laid for my departed family and Brian served me a large and lonely dinner.

Afterwards I rang up Mariska to confirm that she had arrived safely and tell her that all was well at Glencairn, and then went out to rejoin the police in the portico. It was still a very dirty night. I was in the middle of a Paddy when a young policeman whizzed round the corner of the house and skidded to a breathless halt before his chief, 'Sir, Sir, the donkeys are on the lawn'. Sure enough, in the confusion somebody had left the meadow gate open, and my three donkeys were happily munching their way across the grass. The Superintendent and I looked at each other.

'Is all quiet?'

'Yes.'

'Can you call up HQ and confirm no trouble is on the way?' There was none.

'So at the moment your men have nothing much to do?'

'No.'

'All right—Donkey Drive.'

So some of the defenders of Glencairn were formed into a special task force, and gently and effectively we shepherded the donkeys, who usually preferred to take their own decisions, back into the meadow. Another Paddy.

I went into the library and the telephone rang.

'Is that the Ambassador?'

'Yes.'

'Ten Downing Street here. The Prime Minister wants a word.'

It was indeed the Prime Minister. Mr Heath wanted to ask whether I was safely back and how things were—a thoughtful gesture which helped a lot during a somewhat taut evening. I gave him a brief report, leaving out the bit about the donkeys, and he wished us all luck. I rang Mariska once more, went to bed and slept peacefully. It had been a long day. How it came about that my Embassy had been burnt because British parachutists had killed thirteen British subjects on British soil is another story altogether.

Next morning all the staff came to Glencairn and we reviewed the situation. Chancery was destroyed. The Commercial Department had been bombed and damaged by fire and water, and was unusable. The Passport Office was wrecked. We had lost, or had destroyed, all our classified files, cypher equipment, teleprinters and telephones. In other words, we were out of action.

There was only one thing to do. The Embassy had to be back in operation, and be known to be back in operation, at the earliest moment. The only possible way was to cram the essentials into Glencairn itself and make the house the Chancery. On the ground floor Mariska gave up the large and small drawing-rooms, the small study with the original strong room leading off it (where we had stored the drink), leaving only the dining-room and the library for the family. Upstairs we gave up four bedrooms and the old chapel which Mariska had restored into a charming little writing-room. Owing to the geography of the house the remaining private rooms and the offices were sandwiched between each other. The only access to the library was through the registry; my office was converted each evening to its proper role of main drawing-room (largely by folding up the card table which served as my desk); the bedrooms resounded to the tramp of passing feet, and such was the pressure of work during that year that some members of the staff were there every weekend and far into most nights. Our personal privacy was intermittent and precarious. When we retired a year later, Chancery was still there.

The single telephone line to the house was our sole contact with the outside world, and there was no interior switchboard. An urgent call from the Foreign Office might therefore have to wait until Annie the cook had finished placing her order with the local butcher.

In a clear moment we telephoned to Foreign Office Administration who instantly agreed to send me a strong team to deal with all our accommodation, security, communications and transport needs. Meantime we were able to set up a new cypher link.

Having arranged to see the Taoiseach, Jack Lynch, at noon, I had to decide what to say, which meant deciding instantly what to do. We pieced together the events of the previous day. The crowd had been assembling in Merrion Square throughout the day, and by mid-afternoon there were estimated to be some 35,000 people in the square. Many of them were curious onlookers, but many others wanted to be in at the kill while the hard core organised the attack. It is clear from the photographs that young men swarmed up on the first-floor balcony of the house next door, smashed the shutters of my room, poured in petrol and started the fire. The police and fire brigades were hopelessly outnumbered. The crowds would not let the fire engines through, or cut their hoses. There were in all about 4,500 police in county Dublin, and half of them had been drafted to Merrion Square. They fought on as long as they could, and many were burnt by bottles of burning petrol which were lobbed from the rear of the crowd and fell short. In the closing stages it was feared that there were gelignite bombs inside the burning building, and all the police could do was to form a semi-circle round the blazing entrance and keep the crowds back from danger. It was apparently at this moment that British television picked up the story and thus gave the damaging and totally erroneous impression that the Dublin police had stood and done nothing but watch the Embassy burn.

There was nothing I could do about the fire except repeat our protests and demands for compensation. What disturbed me was that when the flames had died down a mob had gone on the rampage through the city. They had not, as had been feared, taken off after Glencairn or Embassy families, but had stormed through the streets smashing indiscriminately shop fronts and windows, including some in a maternity hospital. For all I knew the next Sunday's civil rights march in Newry could produce another bloodbath and consequent riots, and the next time could be worse.

From every point of view it seemed to me essential to lower the temperature. The burning of the Embassy was, up to that time, the biggest single outrage perpetrated against the British presence in the Republic and there was no occasion to mince words about it. But I saw it also as the explosion of a national rage deeply and widely felt, on which a precarious government was unable to clamp down, and which was likely to carry its own punishment with it. I also believed that, with the passage of time, Bloody Sunday and the Day the Embassy was Burnt would merge into a single event, marking what I hoped would be the lowest point in Anglo-Irish relations. For my part my anger was cold-blooded.

In this mood I drove in to look at the still smouldering ruins with the awful smell of sodden plaster and charred wood which I have always associated with London in the blitz. I was televised and interviewed in the wreckage, and again on the steps of Government Buildings where I saw Jack Lynch. I had no script or prepared statement and I cannot remember exactly what I said, but judging by both Irish and English reactions, whatever it was had a steadying and reassuring effect. The main point which I stressed in a retort to a needling journalist was, 'Well, I'm still here, aren't I?'

With the Taoiseach I did most of the talking. We were both correct, courteous and forward-looking. On the immediate situation I said that for administrative reasons I was sending back to England all those members of the Embassy staff who could do no work without their offices, keeping an essential political nucleus in Glencairn. Their wives and children would go with them. I had been particularly concerned with the apparently complete breakdown of public order after the fire, and for that reason I intended to send home *all* the Embassy women and children, except my wife who would presumably be adequately protected in Glencairn. However, to spare the government further humiliation I intended to include them all in the one evacuation party and give no publicity to the fact that all the women and children were being sent to safety. Having said this, I discussed the future with the Taoiseach in an informal and more relaxed manner, and it was clear to me that our working relationship was not impaired.

I then returned to Glencairn. As I had arranged, Mariska had returned from her temporary refuge, and all the household staff were back from the village. This may be the moment to mention that between Bloody Sunday and our final departure, not a single member of the indoor or outdoor staff of Glencairn left our service, except one old lady whom the years overtook.

We carried out my threat and promise to Jack Lynch forty-eight hours after I made it. In a blaze of publicity the Embassy wives and children assembled at Dublin Airport, and were evacuated to England. Nobody spotted that there were substantially more wives than husbands, so my undertaking was exactly carried out. A week later the political climate was so transformed that we allowed the wives and children to trickle back, without any fuss or ceremony.

But first we had to face the tensest moment—the civil rights march in Newry, one week after Bloody Sunday, four days after the fire. It could have been a carbon copy of the Derry disaster, but it passed off without incident. We all breathed again.

2

IF your Embassy has just been burnt down, and especially if it is the first time ever that this has happened to a British Ambassador in a European country, it is reasonable to ask, 'Why Me, how did I come to be here? How, as a historic event, did the fire happen?'

I had become personally involved towards the end of 1969. Since 1966 I had been an Assistant Under-Secretary of State in the Foreign Office. I had begun my career in the Home Civil Service in 1936, switched to the Diplomatic Service in 1946, serving mainly abroad, in Holland, the Suez Canal Zone, Cyprus, New York, Strasbourg and Senegal. Now the end of the road was in sight. One more foreign post was possible before I reached the compulsory retiring age of sixty—assuming that I did not get thrown out earlier, for the Foreign Office was not very happily placed at that time. In a shrinking Diplomatic Service the Foreign and Commonwealth Offices had just been merged and there were now fewer posts to fill than there were men to fill them. Thirty senior members of the Foreign and Commonwealth Services had already been retired before their time and nobody felt safe. For the survivors, prospects of promotion were not bright and preferment tended to go to those who had special qualifications for particular posts.

Mariska and I talked the situation over and decided to wait and see. If I were offered a post outside Western Europe without promotion, I would decline it, retire, and take my chance of finding another job. Otherwise I would soldier on. Naturally, I said nothing of this to the Administration, who were only too eager to find someone who would retire without being actually pushed. Mariska and I were acquiring the accoutrements of middle age and could hear the jangle of time's winged chariot—the declining years of two surviving but very aged parents; our eldest son Michael's blissfully happy marriage which brought us two enchanting grandchildren; Nicholas, bitterly disillusioned with an Oxford to which he had gone with the highest hopes and much promise, keeping strange company but still turning back to Mummy and Daddy before it was too late; our refuge from the world, a tumbledown shack on three acres of hill and valley in Provence; and our marriage, after thirty years of selfishness, stupidity and as much incompatibility as the day we met, miraculously surviving. Mentally and in all respects I felt as strong and in tune as ever. I wanted badly to have one final fling to show what Mariska and I could really do with our last diplomatic mission.

One evening in November 1969 Denis Greenhill, the Head of the Foreign Office, sent for me.

'The Secretary of State has approved the proposal that you should take over Dublin next spring. Would you accept? It must of course be confidential until the Irish Government agrees, but you can tell Mariska. Peter (Wilkinson, Chief of Administration) will give you all the details.'

I was delighted. It did not mean promotion, and I knew nothing of Ireland, but it seemed as good a post as I could hope for. Mariska was happy too. I told Peter Wilkinson and we had a preliminary talk about dates and details, but until an appointment such as this is made public there is not much that can be done inside or outside the office. Then a few days later I met my namesake Ted Peck in the passage. He was a Deputy Under-Secretary and thus a member of the Board that would have recommended me for the Dublin post. As we did a good deal of work together I said, 'I gather I am on the move.'

'Are you happy about it?'

'Very.'

'Does Mariska mind?'

'What about? She's delighted.'

'You don't mind about the threat?'

'What threat?'

'Do you mean you haven't been told? It's simply that in these troubled times the Irish government think Her Majesty's Representative might be the object of unwelcome attentions so they give him armed protection all day and all night wherever he goes in Ireland. You might want to discuss it with Mariska.'

We duly discussed it, but we had had all this before—protection and perhaps the threat in the Suez Canal Zone, and the threat without the protection in Cyprus. Anyway, if there was a threat it was better to have the protection. Mariska's reaction was to be highly amused. 'That will fix your private life,' said she. On which cheerful note we waited until the appointment was announced, and prepared to set forth for territory as mysterious and unknown to us, geographically, politically and diplomatically, as any that had gone before.

While a new posting is still confidential it is quite in order to take a look at a book published each year by Her Majesty's Stationery Office, entitled *The Diplomatic Service List. An Official Year Book*, in order to see who your new colleagues in the Embassy are going to be. Here I instantly ran into the first of that long list of anomalies in Anglo-Irish affairs, the end of which I have still not reached. When I tried to look up Dublin I could not find it, until I discovered that according to this official publication Ireland is not a foreign country. The British Embassy, Dublin will be found tucked away between New Delhi and Kingston, Jamaica, under 'List of British Representatives in the Commonwealth, and the Republic of Ireland'.

Ireland had left the Commonwealth in 1949 and become a foreign country like any other, except for a series of anomalous arrangements which create a unique relationship with Britain. Incredibly, up to 1965, when the two Services were merged, the Dublin Embassy could only be staffed by the Commonwealth Service. From 1965 onwards a member of the Foreign Service could be posted to Dublin but up to October 1968 the Embassy could only report to the Commonwealth Office. From October 1968 onwards the Dublin Embassy reported to the combined Foreign and Commonwealth Office. My predecessor, Sir Andrew Gilchrist, was the first Ambassador from the Foreign Service to be posted to Dublin by the Commonwealth Office. Thus, only in October 1968, nineteen years after Ireland had left the Commonwealth, had the Republic of Ireland, in official eyes, taken its place among the other independent sovereign states of Western Europe. The Dublin Embassy had begun to report to the Western European Department of the Foreign Office, and the year book still only grudgingly recognised the fact.

To the detached observer these may seem minor administrative or verbal changes, rather like carving up and shuffling government departments such as Environment, or Trade and Industry. In fact, the implications were considerable. During their first fifteen months of responsibility for relations with the Republic of Ireland, the staff of the Foreign Office had discovered that they knew very little about it. The reason was that the traditions and requirements of the Foreign Office and the Commonwealth Office had been different. The Foreign Office dealt with the world that is truly foreign—independent nations which might be stronger or weaker than Britain, friendly or hostile, but which were in any case wholly detached. The Commonwealth Office dealt with former British colonies which recognised the British Sovereign as their own Head of State or at least as the Head of Commonwealth; countries which were in varying degrees influenced by British traditions, and possibly still financially or administratively dependent on Britain; where, as befits a member of the family, a good deal could be taken for granted. But since the Foreign Office could take nothing for granted, they naturally needed to know a great deal more about personalities, politics, the springs of power, economic and financial policies, attitudes to Europe and so on. It was understandable but in my opinion unfortunate that although the Republic had long since severed its connection with the Commonwealth, the Dublin Embassy had continued to be treated, where administration and chains of responsibility were concerned, as though it were a High Commission in an ex-colony. This misinterpreted the unique relationship that exists between Ireland and Britain.

There is no independent state in the world, inside or outside the Commonwealth, with which Britain has such an intimate relationship, whether in personal or family ties, general harmony of interests throughout the world, commerce, culture or history. There is virtually a common currency and a common travel area; no passports are needed to travel to and fro, and an Irishman living in England can vote in a general election or settle and work there without any special permit, just as an English person can settle and work in the Republic. And no other country lays formal claim to six British counties which themselves have only been formally different from the rest of Ireland for the last fifty of the eight hundred years of Anglo-Irish history. There is therefore a very great temptation for Britain to treat Ireland as though it were a member of the Commonwealth—regardless of the history of the Treaty negotiations and the Civil War—or even to forget entirely that Ireland is independent. We called this the Isle of Wight syndrome.

We had not been long in Ireland when the wife of a very distinguished British ex-soldier, retired from public life, said to Mariska, 'Tell me, my dear, what is it like now, living in Government House?' 'I'm afraid I wouldn't know,' Mariska answered very gently. 'The President moved in before we came here.'

Unofficially, from friends, acquaintances and comparative strangers who had heard I was going to Dublin, I was told all about Ireland. I learned how lucky I was to be given that nice quiet Embassy where, traditionally, old faithfuls were put out to grass. There would be wonderful riding, racing, hunting, shooting, fishing and golf. I would not need to worry much about the Irish and there really were some nice ones, some people said. But London seemed to be well stocked with the nephews and nieces of somebody or other whose place had been burnt down in the Troubles, and they were able to warn me that the Irish were untrustworthy, idle and irresponsible. They kept hens in the kitchen. Irish women never cleaned their jewellery.

I was told, too, about the Anglo-Irish, or the Ascendancy, sometimes referred to as the West Britons. These, it appeared, were rich and Protestant, pillars of the Church of Ireland, living in large properties surrounded by high walls. They did not mingle with the native Irish and generally conducted themselves as though Independence had never happened. Provided the natives were not actively hostile, the British Ambassador could have a most agreeable time in their company.

I wish I could say I was making this up, but the fact is that every word of this nonsense was uttered either to Mariska or to me in and around London and the Home Counties in the year 1970 AD.

From the world of the arts—music, theatre, literature—I gathered that Dublin was one of the most civilised and congenial capitals in Europe, that Mariska and I would find ourselves among kindred spirits, that we should never want for good company and good conversation and that we could not fail to enjoy ourselves.

I made a tentative note to accept as gospel truth everything I was told about Ireland, and to put these great verities through my mental sieve when I actually got there.

My official briefing had its surprises too.

In the Foreign Office, before I was posted to Dublin, I had been the Under-Secretary responsible for, among other things, the direction of the Official Overseas Information Services. This meant that I had to have at least a nodding acquaintance with all those events which the government needed to have promoted, publicised or explained away. Not unnaturally, these had included the very violent rioting and destruction in Northern Ireland which had erupted in 1968 and had continued ever since. At that time, the early spring of 1970, Ireland had been partitioned for fifty years. Since the Easter Rising in Dublin in 1916, there had been (i) a war between Britain and Ireland, technically a civil war since Ireland was an integral part of the United Kingdom; today this would be called a national liberation movement; (ii) a peace treaty granting independence and dominion status to Ireland (the 'Irish Free State'), signed in December 1921 and followed by the Free State Act which became British law in December 1922; (iii) civil war in the Irish Free State between the Irish Army, loyal to the Provisional Government which had signed the Treaty, and the Republican Army which rejected it, ending in victory for the Treaty Party by 1923; (iv) rejection of an all-Ireland Free State by the Six Counties which retained their separate parliament, set up at Stormont and opened by King George V in June 1921; (v) The abandonment of the projected Boundary Commission, intended to remove anomalies and injustices to the minority, by agreement with the Irish authorities in 1925; (vi) sporadic and minor outbreaks of shootings and bombings carried out by the defeated Irish Republican Army North and

South of the Border and in Britain, before, during and after the Second World War.

Theoretically the IRA had sprouted a political wing, called Sinn Féin, which was legitimate in a free democracy, while retaining its military wing which was not. In practice, nobody was fooled by the switching of civilian hats and military caps, since it was the same men who wore both. Under either head-gear they did not recognise the Border and whatever they did was designed to bring the Six Counties into a united independent Irish republic. After a number of 'military' fiascos they had fallen more and more under left-wing ideological influence, and had mainly disappeared, behind the scenes or underground, when the real trouble in the North began. Naturally enough, since the aim of Sinn Féin/The IRA was to regain the lost counties for Ireland their base was in the Republic of Ireland; but because conditions in the North were so different from those in the South, and because fragmentation is the most persistent of genes in Irish political heredity, it did not follow that anything Sinn Féin/The IRA did in the North was attributable to a central command in the Republic—or for that matter, vice versa.

The real trouble in the North began in 1968 when the worm turned, and civil rights became an issue. Ireland had been divided along the worst possible border. Northern Ireland could have comprised either three overwhelmingly Protestant counties in which the Catholic minority would have been so impotent that a little Christian charity could not have threatened the political and financial domination of the Protestant majority; or it could have comprised all nine counties of the Province of Ulster, in which case the proportion of Catholics would have been sufficient to ensure an element of political ecumenism. As it was, the Catholic minority had the worst of every world. Not only had they been forced to live in an artificial new entity carved out of what they had always considered to be a single country; but living under what its first Prime Minister, Sir James Craig, called 'a Protestant government for a Protestant people', within a border so drawn that by Westminster rules nothing but a Protestant government could ever be elected, they were helpless spectators of a process whereby jobs, houses, electoral boundaries and local government could all be fiddled to their disadvantage, and all in the name of democracy and loyalty.

In 1968 the Catholics had had enough of being second class citizens and another of the recurring, cyclical waves of unrest broke loose. But on this occasion things were different, for Westminster sat up for the first time in fifty years and asked just what was going on in Northern Ireland. The results were electrifying. Harold Wilson's Labour government insisted upon basic reforms being introduced by the Northern Ireland government and 'responded to the requests of the Northern Ireland government for military assistance in Londonderry and Belfast in order to restore law and order. They emphasise again that troops will be withdrawn when law and order has (sic) been restored'. (The full text of the historic Downing Street Declaration of 19 August 1969, from which this quotation is taken, is in Appendix I.) The Army were welcomed as protectors, if not liberators, by the Catholic minority. Nine years later they are still there, in greater strength and spread all over the Six Counties.

In February 1970 I paid a two-day visit to Belfast and had an intensive round of calls and talks with, among others, Lord Grey, who after a career in the Colonial Service had been appointed Governor of Northern Ireland in 1968; Major Chichester Clark, who had succeeded Lord O'Neill as Prime Minister of Northern Ireland in 1969; General Sir Ian Freeland, the G.O.C. British Troops in Northern Ireland, and others. I was accompanied for most of the time by Oliver Wright, who had been appointed by the Home Office in 1969 as United Kingdom Representative to the Northern Ireland Government, and was colloquially referred to as 'our man in Belfast'. His appointment and title epitomised the confused relationship between Westminster and the government of Northern Ireland. The source of the problem was succinctly set out by Mr William Whitelaw, nearly three years later when he was Secretary of State for Northern Ireland:

Section 75 of the (Government of Ireland) Act of 1970 saved the sovereign authority over all matters in Northern Ireland. In practice, however, this reserve of power came to be used only in the most limited way. In general the view prevailed that, having established responsible if subordinate institutions in Northern Ireland with certain powers, the United Kingdom Parliament and Government should not lightly supersede or override these powers . . .

What this meant was that a Member of Parliament in Westminster who wanted to ask just what was going on in Northern Ireland had for many years been liable either to have the question disallowed on the grounds that the matter was within the jurisdiction of Stormont, or, if it was allowed, to be fobbed off with this doctrine as an answer. This flight of successive British parliaments and governments from their sovereign responsibilities in Northern Ireland since 1920 is the strongest single reason for the state of affairs today. The body responsible in London was the Home Office, headed by the Home Secretary. There, on British soil, was a subordinate local government administering six fairly minor counties of United Kingdom territory, with a tense security and political situation which Westminster had allowed it to bring upon itself, yet it had appointed to it a special representative of Her Majesty's Government, just as an ambassador might be accredited to a foreign country. The anomaly was compounded by the fact that the Home Secretary, whose responsibility Northern Ireland was, did not appoint (or could not find) a Home civil servant for the post which had to be filled by, of all places, the Foreign Office. Oliver Wright came to Belfast from being Ambassador in Copenhagen, while his successor Ronnie Burroughs went on to be Ambassador in Algiers. They both played an important role in the coming years, not least by bringing a broader vision to men wearing the blinkers of history.

I came back to London uneasy and unsettled, mainly, I think, because everyone I met in Belfast seemed uneasy and unsettled too, uncertain whether they were sitting on a volcano or treading a quicksand. I met no Catholics.

In spite of everything it was impossible not to feel a sneaking sympathy for the Protestants in Northern Ireland. For nearly fifty years they had been sitting pretty behind a border designed to give them perpetual power. The police force and especially its reserve, the B Specials, were in effect the instrument of the ruling party. The convention of non-interference by the Westminster parliament had left them with a free hand to gerrymander electoral boundaries and ensure that Protestants got the lions' share of the houses and the jobs. They operated a Westminster-type system, with Members of Parliament and Ministers, in which the magic word democracy could be invoked to justify anything they wanted. They could proclaim their loyalty and flaunt the flag without ever having to ask themselves what they were loyal to.

Then suddenly their political paradise fell apart. Within less than eighteen months (starting from October 1968) a Labour government in London was actively exercising its sovereign power in Northern Ireland. Reforms of the major scandals were being forced upon Stormont. Its police force, the Royal Ulster Constabulary, was headed by an Englishman and the B Specials were disbanded. The British Army was inexorably playing a more and more important role in security and moreover was treating all rioters, gunmen and thugs alike. More damaging in the long run, television was showing the British electorate what Belfast and Derry were like, and by displaying the tension helped to heighten it.

The picture of the situation disclosed and the reforms that ensued could not be attributed to Catholic or Republican or Communist propaganda. The evidence was dispassionately and meticulously sifted, assembled and assessed, in three weighty documents, The Report of the Commission on Disturbances in Northern Ireland (Cameron Report), drawn up in September 1969; the Report of the Advisory Committee on Police in Northern Ireland (Hunt Report) drawn up in October 1969, and the Report of the Tribunal of Enquiry on Violence and Civil Disturbances in Northern Ireland in 1969 (Scarman Report) of April 1972. The two devastating documents of 1969 constituted for me the factual background briefing about the North at the time I went to Dublin. It is hardly surprising that a certain malaise was apparent when I went to Northern Ireland in February 1970.

The Home Office and the British authorities in Northern Ireland were very kind and patient, but a small question remained. How did all this concern the Foreign Office and the British Embassy in Dublin?

My mind turned back fifteen years, to Cyprus. The EOKA

B

gunmen, under the guidance of the political Archbishop Makarios, were trying to force Britain to hand over the colony to Greece, in the face of stern but non-violent resistance from Turkey. Their weapons were smuggled guns and home-made bombs and the British Army had been called in to help to restore law and order. This was a British Colony, the responsibility of the Colonial Office. It was useless to point out that the murder and destruction were part of an age-old conflict between Greece and Turkey, that it was an international and not a colonial affair, and that by whatever means law and order were going to be restored it would happen outside Cyprus. Northern Ireland was not even a colony, since it had been incorporated in the metropolitan power in 1800 and only given limited autonomy in 1920. The Home Office was very clear that this was an internal affair.

On the other hand the Foreign Office's main concern regarding Ireland was the yearly butter wrangle. The British government set a limit to the amount of butter that was to be imported from Denmark, Ireland and New Zealand, and every year each country complained that it was not being given its fair share. There would be long negotiations between officials who could not agree and would have to refer the matter to Ministers, and in the end the whole thing would be settled for another year. This year, 1970, the Irish were being particularly difficult, and I gathered that they were led by an unusually tough Minister for Agriculture, Mr Neil Blaney. Of course it all ended in agreement, and there was the usual government lunch at Lancaster House, to which I was invited as Ambassador-Designate. There I had my first and last conversation with Neil Blaney. He was pleasant but he struck me as a bit dour—in fact he conformed exactly to my mental picture of a typical Northern Irishman, which indeed he is, from Donegal. (People sometimes forget that the most northerly county of Ireland is in the Republic, that for part of its erratic course the Border runs due north and south, and that Northern Ireland comprises only six of the nine counties which form the Province of Ulster.) Within two months Mr Blaney had been dismissed from the government, arrested on charges concerning the supply of arms to the North, acquitted, and had retired to the back benches of the Dáil (parliament).

At the lunch there was the usual enquiry whether I had any Irish ancestry. I said no, we thought the name Peck was Norman, originally spelt Peche, but whether we fished, grew peaches, or were simple sinners depended on which French accent you chose. The Irish speakers pointed out that the Gaelic word for sin was paca, so they would fear the worst.

Apart from this annual butter affair, the Irish Republic was largely left to its own devices. This is borne out by the Cameron Report on the 1969 disturbances, which in its 236 paragraphs and twelve appendices, devotes a single paragraph to the Republic. It reads thus :

(149) The fears and apprehensions felt widely among Unionists have solid and substantial basis both in the past and even in the present. From the setting up of the Constitution of Northern Ireland there had been an absence of full recognition by the Republic and the attitude of the Roman Catholic Hierarchy in Northern Ireland has been ambiguous. Among a proportion of Catholics there had been opposition to the Constitution as well as a degree of hostility towards Great Britain. IRA attacks have continued and Irish Republican Army activity is still undoubted. The steady decline of Protestant population in the south, the influence of Roman Catholic doctrines there on Government, displayed in matters of censorship, restrictions on birth control and other health matters, as well as difficulties which arise over the Church's attitude to mixed marriages—all these factors tend to feed these fears as illustrative of what might be expected if Catholic political domination were to be achieved. (At the same time, it should be recognised that among a certain proportion of Unionists it was a matter of satisfaction that Catholics in Northern Ireland should have held themselves aloof from the community and thus accentuated the appearance of division and provide justification for a policy of sectarian and political discrimination.)

The Republic is not mentioned in the Summary of Conclusions.

And yet there had been two significant indications that Britain should look south of the Border. First, in speech after speech during the violent second half of 1969, Mr Lynch, the Taoiseach and leader of the Fianna Fáil party, insisted that the reunification of Ireland could provide the only permanent solution to the problem of the North. Secondly, in December 1969 the IRA/Sinn Féin, following the fissile tradition of their ancestors, split yet again. The movement had become increasingly Marxist and had abandoned military training and preparedness to the point where it could do nothing to help the beleaguered Catholics in Belfast and Derry. The traditional, nationalist, militarist elements broke away, to form the 'Provisional' IRA and Provisional Sinn Féin, and since that time the Provisionals have been the principal exponents of the vicious, indiscriminate murder, maiming and destruction. Both movements have a structure North and South, and a high proportion of the membership is from the North, but nominally, at any rate, the headquarters are in Dublin; the directives emanate from there, and the aim of both branches—reunification—is shared by many Irishmen who wholly reject and despise IRA methods. It is therefore the Irish government and people who, in British eyes at least, incur most of the odium that the IRA provokes. Could this really be an exclusively internal Home Office affair and could the police and the Army restore law and order if it were treated as such?

However, in early 1970 the implications of these developments were still unclear and the Foreign Office was not unduly concerned. There seemed no reason to suppose that Northern Ireland would loom very large in the life of the British Embassy in Dublin. We had been there twenty-seven days when we discovered that other people had other ideas.

Before we left London a small matter had to be disposed of in the Foreign Office. When an Ambassador receives a new posting News Department like to collect as much material as they can about his tastes and interests, in order to pave the way with some friendly publicity. Others too were interested to know more about Mariska and myself, since the arrival of a new Ambassador is always an event. So gradually the awful truth leaked out, and I had to explain to increasingly incredulous questioners that, no, I didn't ride, hunt, go racing, shoot, fish, or play golf; no, I had no drop of Irish blood and yes, my wife was Hungarian. To questions about religion I replied simply and truthfully that I was an ecumenical Christian. Then

I admitted one day in desperation that I could sail a boat. Even that was stretching veracity to its limits, since my sailing experience consisted of occasionally messing around in a dinghy on a warm day, so I was a little concerned to discover on arriving in Dublin that my fame as a yachtsman had preceded me. However, the thing solved itself. A kind friend offered to take me out in his boat on a calm summer's evening and I accepted with pleasure. But my faithful and ever-present Special Branch escort said that we should remain within the confines of Dun Laoghaire harbour, with one of their number at the end of each harbour wall; if we went out into the open waters of Dublin Bay a police launch or helicopter would have to be in attendance. We had a nice sail, but the word got round that sailing with His Excellency presented problems.

3

WE arrived in Dublin on 9 April 1970. We had had very mixed accounts of the Residence, Glencairn. We heard that it had been built by an ex-Tammany Hall boss called Croker and looked it, being a massive and hideous pile in Victorian Scottish Baronial, but it was said to have handsome grounds and good furniture and pictures. It lay seven miles south-east of Dublin, near the village of Sandyford. With a police motor-cyclist leading us and the black squad car behind us—the escort car, without which I could not move until the day I left the Embassy in Dublin—we came to Glencairn. We emerged from the green canyon of the winding drive, with its twelve foot high walls of trimmed evergreens, and the house came into view. Mariska's reaction was improbable : 'What a dear little castle'.

But she was right. Glencairn had all the right towers and battlements and stained glass and mullion windows, and was built of massive granite without and mahogany within. But rather than dominate its setting, it conveyed a strange intimacy as if it had been built by craftsmen with loving care—as indeed it had, in 1905. We became deeply attached to its unique and dotty charm.

We soon explored its thirty-eight acres of grounds. There were some formal gardens near the house and a walled vegetable garden, but the elegantly trimmed shrubs that lined the long drive concealed a jungle in which ivy was strangling magnificent trees and trailing over decomposing mowing machines, mouldering bedsteads, old motor tyres, piles of beer cans, miscellaneous metal objects rusted beyond identification, and everywhere, above and below the soil, thick strata of broken bottles and smashed crockery. We were living on a rubbish dump. Most of the estate was meadow land, let out for grazing, and there was a once-beautiful glen where a little stream fed a chain of three artificial pools. But the dams had broken, the pools were silted up, and the channels lost in trees that had fallen across them many years before. In the glen too, ivy was busily taking its lethal toll.

We decided that while the British Ambassador might not be addicted to the sports and pastimes traditional to Ireland, there was no need for him to live in a rural slum. We set ourselves to the task of making Glencairn into something clean and open and lighthearted—two years to do the work and one to enjoy it. Dwellers round about, and all who had known or worked in Glencairn, were highly amused—and generous with their approval when, to their amazement, the plan was completed, on time, with results that surpassed our own expectations. I may qualify for the *Guinness Book of Records* as the first Ambassador to persuade his government that the official Embassy transport should include a tractor.

Mariska, meanwhile, was going through the house like a feudal typhoon, starting, as is her wont, by bringing some badly needed dignity into the domestic staff's quarters. That part of the Department of the Environment which looks after Embassies always seems to alternate between pennilessness and a surplus of money, and we evidently hit a good phase. Luckily Glencairn was in any case due for a lot of replacements, and Mariska was able to dispense with much of her pet hate—excessive acres of glazed chintz. Nearly two years later it was all done to her satisfaction, when circumstances in the first week of February 1972 forced us to reorganise the entire house for a very different purpose.

We had had all this before.

When we arrived in Dakar in 1962, to take up my post as Ambassador to Senegal and Mauritania, the Head of Chancery was a young man called Michael Palliser. If ever anyone was destined to rise with breathtaking speed to the top of the tree it was Michael—indeed, he since has—and we were extremely lucky to have him and his delightful wife Marie to initiate us into Senegalese life and politics for the four weeks before they were posted home, he to be promoted and she to have a baby.

They showed us round the house. The Residence was built

in the colonial style of the area in the nineteenth century—concrete walls two or three feet thick embodying large chunks of laterite rock, and a pitched roof of tiles exported from Marseilles. It was an exact square, with rooms leading off a central tiled hall and bedrooms leading off a gallery supported by stone pillars in the hall. The dining-room and drawing-room opened on to a recently built terrace on the south side, above which a narrow enclosed verandah ran the length of the house. On the west side was a walled area embracing the garages, servants' quarters, washhouse and back entrance. The grounds extended some hundred yards by forty, and in them was the one-storey Chancery building and a hard tennis court. A small area between the main gate and the front door had been put down to grass with various flowering shrubs—hibiscus, rose-de-Chine and others. There were some good trees, notably some flamboyants (flame of the forest) and frangipani, by the terrace, and large quantities of the common crimson bougainvillia. The whole stood on a plateau of crumbled laterite with pockets of silver sand, the edges of which fell steeply away to the sea and were heavily eroded.

It must once have been lovely.

For six months Senegal is hot and dry. For six months it is hot and wet. We arrived at the end of the rainy season. The trees were green and fresh but all the rest was brown dust eroded by the rains, the ornamentation being thirty-seven old oil drums in varying stages of decomposition, containing some dispirited ferns and oddments. There were stories that once it had all been carefully tended and we found some evidence to support the legends. Buried here and there in the dust were little cones of cement set out in rows or rectangles, and we asked old inhabitants of Dakar if they had any idea what their nature or purpose might be.

Once upon a time, they said, many years ago, there was a much loved Consul General whose breakfast, lunch, tea and dinner never varied from day to day nor differed greatly from each other, the menu being almost exclusively brandy and Perrier water. His manners and his manner never faltered, and his bearing grew more correct and his posture more erect as the day wore on. The resulting accumulation of Perrier bottles was prodigious, and the problem of their disposal was becoming insoluble. Then one day somebody conceived the idea of using them for edging paths and flower beds. Foundations of cement were laid and the conical hollow at the base of each bottle was filled with mortar. These little cones were all that survived after the paths and the flowerbeds were lost in the sand. For all I know people may still be digging them up, and if anyone wonders what they are, the elders of Dakar may still be recounting their story about this legendary figure whom they loved so much because he was such a perfect *gentleman.*

It was obvious that while our predecessors had begun the process they had not had time to remove all traces of the era in which 'anything would do for Africa'. There is always a time lag between a policy change of attitude and its trans-lation into such basic details as mattresses and garden hose pipes. Mariska and I let fly. The rusting oil drums in the grounds were matched by the squalor in which Her Majesty's Representative was apparently expected to keep his servants (and the Senegalese are the cleanest of people) and by our prize exhibit—the mattress in one of the guest bedrooms. This bore unmistakeable evidence of the incontinence of dogs or infants, which it had had ample time to endure since it bore, under the imprint signifying that it was Government Property, the date 1912.

Three years later the Residence was a show place and we had problems with a travel agency who wanted to give several busloads of tourists off a cruise ship a tour of the garden.

So much for houses, but what about the job? I am often asked what an Ambassador does. Perhaps the Queen's Com-mission will explain :

ELIZABETH THE SECOND, by the Grace of God of the United Kingdom of Great Britain and Northern Ireland and of Her other Realms and Territories Queen, Head of the Commonwealth, Defender of the Faith, &c, &c, &c.

To All and Singular to whom these Presents shall come, Greetings ! Whereas it appears to Us expedient to nominate some Person of approved Wisdom, Loyalty, Diligence and Circumspection to represent Us in the character of Our Ambassador Extraordinary and Plenipotentiary at Dublin; Now Know Ye that We, reposing especial trust and confidence in the discretion and faithfulness of Our Trusty and Well-beloved John Howard Peck, Esquire, Companion of Our Most Distinguished Order of Saint Michael and Saint George, have nominated, constituted and appointed, as We do by these Presents nominate, constitute and appoint him the said John Howard Peck to be Our Ambassador Extraordinary and Plenipotentiary at Dublin as aforesaid. Giving and Granting to him in that character all Power and Authority to do and perform all proper acts, matters and things which may be desirable or necessary for the promotion of relations of friendship, good understanding and harmonious intercourse between Our Realm and the Republic of Ireland, and for the protection and furtherance of the interests confided to his care; by the diligent and discreet accomplishment of which acts, matters and things aforementioned he shall gain Our approval and show himself worthy of Our high confidence. And We therefore request all those whom it may concern to receive and acknowledge Our said Trusty and Well-beloved John Howard Peck as such Ambassador Extraordinary and Plenipotentiary as aforesaid and freely to communicate with him upon all matters which may appertain to the objects of the high Mission whereto he is hereby appointed.

Given at Our Court of Saint James's, the Ninth day of April One Thousand Nine Hundred and Seventy in the Nineteenth Year of Our Reign.

BY HER MAJESTY'S COMMAND.

In practice, a British Ambassador has two roles. The major one is to conduct diplomatic business with the government to which he is accredited, and establish all the political, commercial and social contacts that go with it. The minor one is to be a sort of figurehead for the British community, inviting them to the annual Queen's Birthday Party, giving them advice and guidance in times of crisis, and generally being seen to be the Queen's Representative. The Ambassadress, besides being concerned in all this, usually becomes involved with the British community in charitable work, church activities, and so on, depending upon local circumstances. This community is usually distinct, closely knit and intensely patriotic. In my nomadic life I have observed certain trends in the pattern of patriotism and loyalty. First, the further away from London, the more intense the sentiment is. Secondly, the longer the time since the original colonisation, emigration or settlement, the further back in history the image of the home land is fixed. Moreover, this tendency is not confined to the British. Just as the Daughters of the British Empire inhabiting our earliest colonies are proud of their connection, however remote, with an England which died with Queen Victoria, so Americans or Australians of Irish origin have difficulty in comprehending that a nostalgic devotion to the cause of an idealised IRA in 1916 is irrelevant to the aims, and still more the methods, of the IRA of the 1970s.

In Ireland nothing, least of all the British community, seems distinct and closely knit. As an independent sovereign state the Republic is barely half a century old; there are families, originally of non-Irish stock, who have been living in Ireland, even in the same home, for eight hundred years, and yet have retained a non-Irish personality. The British community includes many who at the time of Independence kept the British nationality that they inherited, whether or not they took Irish nationality as well (for anyone, in both North and South, who has even one grandparent born in Ireland, can claim Irish nationality.) It also includes Englishmen who married Irish girls and came to live in Ireland; Irishmen who married English girls; Irishmen who from the habit of generations of service in the Army or public life feel British as well as Irish : people without special ties with Ireland who settled there, almost as one might settle in Devon or Dumfries, when Ireland was not a separate state : some who have come to earn a living; and some, like myself, who have chosen to live in Ireland for complex and perhaps inexplicable personal reasons. Some play an active part in agriculture and other sectors of the Irish economy. A few are, virtually, absentee landlords. Many see no contradiction and no difficulty in being loyal British subjects and loyal Irishmen, thus it is dangerous to generalise or apply indiscriminately terms like Anglo-Irish, the Ascendancy, or the West Britons. Some move largely within their own circle, rather like the English who have settled in Spain, Portugal or Malta— the big difference being that in Ireland they put down roots.

In such groups we rarely discussed Irish politics. We made many friends among them.

Officially an Ambassador does not exist until he has presented his credentials to the Head of State, so my first official act, on 17 April 1970, was to present mine to President de Valera. (Even the title was significant, for if we called him the President of Ireland we recognised the Irish claim to the Six Counties whereas if we called him the President of the Irish Republic it was inacceptable to him as he would thereby be admitting *our* claim to the Six Counties. 'President de Valera' left the issue wide open.) The presentation of credentials is an important ceremonial occasion, when a large official car wearing the flags of both countries calls at the Embassy to collect the top-hatted Ambassador, with a very smart motor-cycle escort provided by the Army. There was even a bugler but it turned out that his instrument was for show rather than blow, as there appeared to be some technical hitch about where the mouthpiece had been mislaid.

At the President's Residence, Áras an Uachtaráin, the formal speeches were made and the letters handed over. I had been warned that President de Valera had been seriously ill and was not wholly recovered. But the formalities over, I sat down to the usual informal chat, with this very old gentleman, this ancient enemy of Britain who instantly evoked in my mind the phrase 'all passion spent'. Apart from almost total blindness, which enhanced his natural courtesy and dignity, the only mark that age and illness had left upon him was that from the Olympian height of his ninety years, when history lay spread out before him, his intellect and his reflections like a zoom lens would focus on 1916, 1940 and 1921 with bewildering speed. One opinion he expressed was that at the time of the Treaty negotiations Lloyd George had misread British public opinion and need not have insisted upon Partition, with all the evils that followed from it. He asked about Glencairn and talked of Boss Croker who had built it, quoting with amusement a saying of Boss Croker's: 'If I have two men with equally good claims to a job, I will of course give it to the one who is in my debt'.

The ceremony included inspecting a guard of honour provided by the Irish Army, some of whose members wore medals for service with the United Nations in Cyprus and the Congo. I stopped to ask some of these boys where they had won them—an elementary courtesy which produced an unexpected but significant little item in the *Daily Express* headed 'Envoy Makes Chatty Debut'. The motor cycle escort, some thirty strong, then led the procession back to Glencairn. I had been warned that the officer commanding would then ask me for leave to dismiss, speaking in both English and Irish. He did, so not to be outdone I replied, 'Yes, thank you, good luck to you all. Tá, go raibh míle maith agaibh. Go n'eirí an bóthar libh'. I was then able to slip off from beneath my watchstrap the card with the phonetic spelling of the Irish from which I had been reading.

On 29 April Mariska paid her formal call upon Bean (Mrs) de Valera and was charmed by her. A month later the President made his annual visit to Trinity College's social event of the summer—College Races—to which all Ambassadors were invited. He was sitting chatting, reminiscing about his childhood, when he made some remark about it being his wife's ninety-second birthday in a few days' time. I mentioned this to Mariska, who sent her a little note of good wishes. A few days afterwards, Mariska was out gardening when our butler came panting up to say that the President was on the telephone. 'What president?' asked Mariska, whose years in France taught her that almost any stranger was probably president of something. So when he said 'President de Valera' she rushed in to take the call. 'I'm afraid my wife cannot write many letters now, but she asked me to telephone to thank you for your letter which touched her greatly.' He then talked for some fifteen minutes, about Glencairn, about Ireland, and said he hoped we would be very happy here.

On 20 April I paid my first formal call upon the Taoiseach, Mr Jack Lynch, who had succeeded Séan Lemass as leader of Fianna Fáil in 1966, led it to an election victory with an increased majority in 1969 and now had a majority over Fine Gael and Labour in the Dáil of seven.

The 'formal call' stretched into an informal, wide-ranging chat of some forty-five minutes, in which Jack Lynch mentioned problems that had arisen over settling some of that group of nomads known variously as tinkers, itinerants or travelling people, in which a small Galway town called Rahoon had figured prominently. Later that day a memory began to stir, and after a short rummage at home I unearthed a little booklet I had bought in Oxford forty years earlier, called *Pomes Penyeach* by James Joyce. It included one with the opening line, 'Rain on Rahoon is falling, softly falling.'

I wrote to the Taoiseach :

April 23 1970

I very much appreciated your kindness in granting me so much of your valuable time, and our talk was, for me, very enjoyable and extremely interesting.

You will remember that in the course of our conversation you mentioned that an Irish community had given its name to a phenomenon known as 'Rahoonery'. This stirred some memory which has lain buried for years and you may conceivably be interested to see the attached. I would not myself regard it as one of James Joyce's major contributions to literature, but at any rate he knew about Rahoon!

Jack Lynch replied in his own handwriting :

Dear Ambassador,

Thank you for sending me 'She weeps over Rahoon' by Joyce. I agree with your assessment of it. Apart from its literary merit it is powerfully and tenderly descriptive.

Yours sincerely,
Jack Lynch

While I talked about almost everything with Jack Lynch over the next three years, I think this was our only literary exchange. I do not know what he would say about it; but as far as I am concerned I felt instantly and instinctively that whatever confrontations we might have on the political and diplomatic plane, however much British and Irish policies and interests might clash, we two would be able to deal with our differences without heat and rancour, and without the laborious preliminaries which are so often necessary, and yet so often fail to prevent Anglo-Irish discussions from becoming a dialogue of the deaf. I did not then foresee how important this was going to become.

Ten days later the Minister for Foreign Affairs, Dr Patrick Hillery, gave the customary dinner for an incoming Ambassador, and assembled as guests a representative cross-section of people from political and public life, some of whom became our closest friends. I learned later that at the last minute he had torn up the formal speech of welcome prepared by the Department and substituted an informal and personal impromptu. I replied in the same vein, unscripted, except for a useful remark by André Maurois which I had unearthed for the occasion : 'If in the eyes of an Irishman there is any one being more ridiculous than an Englishman, it is an Englishman who loves Ireland.'

Mariska and I decided not to refuse any serious invitation from whatever quarter. Thanks to the energy and hospitality of the Embassy staff we were quickly introduced to the business community, the leaders of industry and commerce, the judges, the press, the arts, the armed forces, the universities, those who directed the National Gallery, the Zoo, the Royal Dublin Society, the Botanical Gardens, the Dublin City Manager—in fact to Dublin itself and to the heart of Irish public life. Of all the capital cities to which I had been posted, Dublin provided some of the most marked and significant contrasts with London—contrasts whose importance and implications were no less real because they were subtle and not immediately obvious. Dublin could be John Bull's China Shop.

The Foreign Office, having acquired political and administrative control of the Dublin Embassy, had fortunately decided to satisfy their interest in the Republic by posting two officers of the highest quality—Peter Evans as Information Officer and David Blatherwick as Second Secretary in Chancery. They preceded me by a few weeks and it was immediately obvious that we three were on the same wavelength and could work together as a closely-knit team. The Counsellor, Peter Piper, was of the old school and within a few months of retirement— a well-known and well-liked figure in Dublin, in whose house we first met many of our subsequent friends. And in the Commercial Section I had a young and high-spirited staff who happily responded to my insistence that an Embassy did not consist of a series of watertight compartments. When I took over the Dublin Embassy I did not find any passengers on the staff—a situation for which any Head of Mission can be truly thankful.

In the world outside the Embassy Mariska and I found that some thought we had let the side down before we even arrived, by being plain Mr and Mrs; never in Irish history, it seemed, had the representative of the sovereign and his consort been anything but Sir and Lady. The Irish, having no honours system or orders of chivalry, were not disposed to regard it as a studied insult—in fact they could not have cared less. Others were not so sure. It was widely assumed that I must have blotted my copy book and that Dublin was no longer a green pasture but a punishment station. The domestic staff at Glencairn were puzzled but solved their problem by invariably and safely referring to me as His Excellency, while Mariska was known as Her Ladyship Mrs Peck. After a while one of the staff could contain her curiosity no longer and asked Mariska disarmingly whether HE's non-knighthood was due to his marriage to a foreign lady. My foreign lady was indeed an object of interest in traditional circles. She took it all in her stride, pointed out that she, and Dublin, were in good company with Mrs Soames in Paris and Mrs Freeman in Washington (never mind about the subtleties of political appointment), and soon won them over. Anyway, the problems of Mr Ambassador and Her Lady-ship Mrs Peck were resolved in the happiest way possible in June 1971, when I appeared in the Queen's Birthday Honours List as a Knight Commander of the Most Distinguished Order of St Michael and St George.

The only thing that shook Mariska slightly, when she made her first speech to the ladies of the British Legion, was the surprise at and compliments on her excellent English. 'Look,' she said, 'it ought to be good—I have been married to an Englishman for thirty years.'

Many books have been written about the role and duties of Ambassadors, but few about those of Ambassadresses, perhaps because they are harder to define. The diplomatic career has much in common with a trapeze or tight-rope turn in a circus, or running the village store. It should be a husband-and-wife act in which each is dependent on the skill and reliability of the other. If it had not been for Mariska I doubt whether I should have left the Home Civil Service, or whether I should have got where I did as a diplomat. Three parts Hungarian and one part Austrian, born in Vienna, brought up in Paris and

London, trilingual, totally loyal and never totally assimilated, with the same concern for and interest in under-gardeners as Under-Secretaries of State, she was made for the career and largely made mine. Only twice in our married life did her nationality pose problems, once in distasteful circumstances and once hilariously.

At the outbreak of the Second World War Mariska volunteered as a nurse (VAD) and in her Red Cross uniform served long hours during the bombing of London, working in a first aid post in Chelsea; I meanwhile was serving as an Assistant Private Secretary to the Prime Minister Sir Winston Churchill.

At the height of the Blitz a sickening incident occurred. The Commandant of the first aid post sent for Mariska and with tears in her eyes told her that the British Red Cross had demanded her resignation on the grounds that she was not British. Mariska pointed out that she was indeed British by marriage, having previously been stateless. This was not good enough; she had been born in Vienna of Hungarian parents, and anyone not British-born might be a secret collaborator with the Germans. Out she must go.

When they heard of this from one of my colleagues in 10, Downing Street, Winston Churchill and Mrs Churchill were furious. The British Red Cross was addressed in no uncertain terms, but the waves of Number Ten's wrath surged in vain against its adamantine rules. Mariska was deeply hurt, as well she might be, seeing that she had spent all her days and many of her nights in the thick of London's battle. I felt it was an odd moment, when every helper was needed in casualty stations, for any patriotic body to behave like this, and that someone who was good enough for Winston Churchill ought to get by with the British Red Cross. I was brooding on the next move, when Chelsea Borough Council solved the matter very simply, and made the Red Cross look totally ridiculous, by giving Mariska a different uniform and putting her back on the same duties in the same first aid post with the same Commandant.

We heard later that through all this time the Red Cross lady who had defied the Churchills and deeply hurt Mariska retained her Austrian cook.

The absurd episode, or non-event, occurred in New York,

shortly after I took over the British Information Services. Radio Section of BIS got Mariska to make a tape on her life as a British housewife in Cyprus. It was an interesting account with good policy implications, and she carefully prefixed it with her customary lead-in that she was actually Hungarian and British by marriage. This tape was used by a large number of radio stations across America, including one in New Jersey. Hearing it, the local chapter of a women's organisation called the Daughters of the British Empire, which does a great deal of charitable work, invited Mariska to address them in person. She did, and so captivated were they that the President asked her whether she would consent to become a Daughter. She made a suitably polite reply, including a gentle aside about her Hungarian origin, and thought no more about it. Some days later there was an agitated telephone call from the lady in New Jersey.

'It's about your joining the Daughters of the British Empire. You are English, aren't you?'

'No, I told you. I am British by marriage. I am Hungarian.'

'Oh, dear. Weren't either of your parents English?'

'No, I haven't a drop of English blood. Only an English husband.'

'Well, you see, it's all very difficult. We . . .'

'Please don't worry about it. I understand perfectly and actually I never suggested it in the first place. Thank you all the same. Good-bye.'

So Mariska never became a Daughter of the British Empire.

I believe that first impressions of a person or a place are nearly always right, and however much you may have second thoughts you tend to discover in the end that you were right first time. In the same way I believe that an incoming Ambassador and Ambassadress have irrevocably established their identity and their style during their first few weeks in a new post, which means that it all happens before they know their way around and are being guided mainly by instinct and experience. Mariska and I were lucky because we instantly happened to find ourselves attuned to Dublin.

We needed to be. On 6 May 1970, when I had been in Ireland less than a month, Peter Evans woke me at 7.15 am to tell me that Mr Charles Haughey (Minister for Finance) and

Mr Neil Blaney (The Minister for Agriculture I had met at the butter wrangle lunch)—two of the most senior Cabinet members and 'Strongmen' of the ruling Fianna Fáil party—had not only been sacked from the government by the Taoiseach, Jack Lynch, but had actually been arrested on charges of illegally financing and trafficking in arms, and a third Minister, Kevin Boland (Local Government), had resigned in sympathy. It was like saying, of a British Labour government, that Mr Healey and Mr Silkin were behind bars and another Cabinet Minister had resigned. The British government naturally had to be told what was going on and what was likely to happen, particularly as the arms, if any, were presumably destined for the Catholic minority in Northern Ireland. We had a major political crisis on our hands. I had heard or read the political background in London and Belfast. Now I was to see it from Dublin.

The Sinn Féin movement was legal in the Republic so long as the leaders wore their political hats. If they replaced them with military ones, and called themselves the Irish Republican Army, they became illegal and clandestine. When the Provisionals had broken away from the Officials in the previous autumn, the split extended right across the political and military spectrum. The reason for it was the failure of the IRA to take any effective part in protecting and organising the Catholic community in Northern Ireland during the preceding years of violence. Henceforward the movement was to be divided. There were those who thought that republican ideals would best be attained by class warfare with Catholic and Protestant workers allied against the capitalist bosses in Northern Ireland; and there were those who disapproved of the marxist ideological pentration of the movement, and believed that the national patriotic fervour of 1916-22 should be revived and its weapons, the gun and the bomb, brought out once more.

There were at the same time two distinct but intertwined strands of sentiment in the Republic: a desire that Ireland should be reunited, with its accompaning resentment of the British over Partition, and anxiety over the plight of the Catholics in Northern Ireland and a desire to help them.

Now the dream of reunification is written into the Irish

Constitution and is enshrined in the Irish spirit. But just as Winston Churchill once observed that everyone wants to go to heaven but not yet, I did not myself notice any burning desire in Ireland to try and force reunification through tomorrow. A sense of realism was enough to curb such zeal. On the other hand there was a strong national sense of unity and indeed responsibility for the Catholics in Northern Ireland.

The two strands of feeling were brought together by a growing conviction that in the last resort a just society in the North could only be achieved, and preserved, through some form of reunification. By the time the IRA split, the Cameron Commission had already reported on the 'disturbances', the violence, death and destruction, which had taken place in 1968 or earlier in 1969 without IRA direction or incitement, and the Hunt Commission had reported on the state of the Royal Ulster Constabulary. The Unionist government, under Major Chichester Clark, had promised reforms. The 'Downing Street Declaration' had expressed suitable sentiments about equality of treatment and freedom from discrimination. The British Army, presumably a more impartial body than the Royal Ulster Constabulary, had been committed to aid the civil power. Nevertheless there were many Irishmen who were deeply sceptical. While they thought the Labour government in Westminster was doing its best, they could not believe that the Orange Order would ever relinquish its stranglehold, or that any British government would impose its will upon Stormont, or that the British Army would be able to maintain justice and peace between the communities. Dublin therefore somehow had to intervene. Where Irish opinions differed was over method.

To the Provisional IRA it seemed simple. With guns, bombs, any weapons they could lay their hands on, they would renew the war of 1916-21 and claim to protect the Northern Catholics, who, in their turn, would provide the infrastructure and support that the IRA needed. They probably knew that they could not defend the Catholics against a Protestant backlash, but reckoned upon creating a desperate situation in which the Republic would have to make armed intervention. Ultimately they would create a situation in which the British would withdraw in exasperation, and the way would then be open for the reunification of Ireland.

To the majority of Irish people things did not appear so simple. They detested violence and were afraid of it spreading from the North into the Republic. On the other hand, if the unpleasant aspects of the Provisionals' methods were overlooked or swept under the rug, their logic seemed sound enough to anyone prepared to overlook a little matter such as the likely Protestant reaction. There had been a particularly nasty civil war less than fifty years before, precisely over the question of accepting the Treaty which partitioned Ireland, and there were still plenty of Irishmen who regarded Partition as a piece of unfinished business. There had been various outbreaks of IRA violence before, during and after the Second World War, and on each occasion the Irish government of the day dealt ruthlessly with them. But now there was a new situation. Whereas previous IRA campaigns had been utterly pointless, there was now a new IRA, under new management, with a programme designed to help Northern Catholics and perhaps, ultimately, to reunite Ireland. You did not need to condone violence or be a member of the IRA, still less a gunman, to feel some chord being struck in the national memory and to have a sneaking or indeed subconscious sympathy for the breakaway IRA. And since Fianna Fáil was the party which had always opposed the Treaty, it was in Fianna Fáil that sympathy with the notion of active support for the Northern Catholics was mainly to be found. What was disclosed on 9 May 1970 was a prima facie case that this sympathy extended into the upper reaches of the government.

Now it is no business of an Ambassador, least of all a British Ambassador in the Republic, to interfere with domestic politics or the administration of justice, and I did not know then, and do not know now, the full details of the chain of events that led to the government crisis. However, there were certain basic facts in the situation. Jack Lynch was no less firm than any other Irishman in his belief that Ireland would one day be reunited. But—and these points are vital for an understanding of everything that has happened since—he believed these three things :

1. Reunification could never be brought by force, but only by consent.

2. There would never be any intention or attempt by any

government in Dublin to impose its will or interfere in any way with the social or religious structure of Northern Ireland. In speech after speech, beginning with a major declaration in Tralee in the previous September, he had called upon the Northern Irish to work together with the Southern Irish to create jointly a new form of Irish society. (This approach to Irish reunification was most inconvenient to those Northern politicians, demagogues and soapbox clerics, the so-called 'Provisional Protestants in para-clerical uniform', whose livelihood, and indeed raison d'être, depended upon whipping up fears of a 'takeover by Dublin', so they largely ignored it.)

3. On a partnership basis, he relied upon the sovereign government and parliament in Westminster to accept the justice and good sense of his peaceful approach, which had no time limit or programme attached to it; all he required was an understanding, tacit if need be, that it provided a way, perhaps the only way, of averting a tragedy in the North.

In the Embassy we swiftly reviewed the situation. Certain facts were obvious. The real conflict was inside Fianna Fáil, between a peaceful approach and the use of force. A dissolution and general election were unlikely since Fianna Fáil had a great capacity for closing ranks and patching differences in the face of any such threat. As to which faction in the party would win, we were convinced that it would be Jack Lynch's. While it was difficult for an Embassy in Dublin to assess shades of opinion in rural Ireland, nevertheless our general impression was that the people were overwhelmingly in favour of the peaceful approach. The English in the abstract were disliked and mistrusted, and all Irish instincts and memories fortified such doubts. But the Irish had no stomach for a bloodbath, and their nightmare was that the violence typical of Northern Ireland should spread to the South. In addition, there was evidently great respect for the Taoiseach's judgement and leadership.

With all the self-confidence of the new boy and confidence in the vision of my staff, I therefore had no doubts about advising the Foreign Office that there would be no general election; that Mr Lynch would win the power struggle inside Fianna Fáil; and that while it would be disastrous to say so publicly, it was very much in the British interest that he should; the implications of any other outcome could be, to say the least, awkward. From that day in May 1970, until the day in February 1973 when I left on the eve of the general election, crisis after crisis hit Jack Lynch. As each one built up, or struck out of an apparently clear sky, I never once made any other prophecy except that he would survive it, and all my predictions were the unanimously held opinions of the Embassy staff, reached after long and detailed discussion. I can therefore claim no particular virtue as a prophet, clairvoyant, or gambler favoured by fortune. Dispassionately and clinically we dissected the political scene and drew the logical conclusions. Admittedly there were some real cliff-hangers, and the last, in December 1972, was the worst, but a lot had to happen first.

Of course, with all the wisdom of hindsight, it is easy to see the weak point in Jack Lynch's reasoning. We suspected at the time that while the Irish government obviously had close connections with the Northern Catholics, they were not well informed about the views, and likely reactions, of the Northern Protestants, and it seemed a little naive to suppose that a British government was ready to contemplate getting rid of the Six Counties—particularly when the more discerning were only too thankful that such characters as Paisley and Craig were our responsibility and not theirs. But it must also be remembered that a Labour government was in power in West-minster, not bowed down, as the Irish saw it, by the Unionist millstone round their neck, and had committed the British Army, apparently to protecting the Catholic minority against a sectarian police force. Change and reform were in the air, and overall Jack Lynch's approach was more constructive than any visible alternative. Nevertheless, it was obvious at the time that he was offering himself as a hostage to fortune by committing himself to a programme of protecting the Northern Catholics and gradually approaching reunification through the co-operation and good will of the British government. The Irish electorate and his own backbenchers were going to expect results. The future course of Irish politics was going to be largely dictated by events in Northern Ireland and Westminster, and it was going to be Jack Lynch's task to convince the British government that, for better or for worse, events in the Republic would have an important bearing on politics in the North.

During my time as Ambassador in Dublin, I came to the conclusion that here more than in most places the dramatic was prone to trip over the ridiculous, as in the case of the donkeys on the night the Embassy was burnt. If the streets of London were paved with gold, the pavements of Dublin were littered with banana skins. The arrest of Messrs Haughey and Blaney launched the normal processes of the law, and the law, in the shape of the District Court, added its quota of drama by dismissing the case against Neil Blaney, which was, to put it mildly, an embarrassment for the Irish government, although his co-defendant, Mr Haughey, was committed for trial. Mr Blaney's release called for a celebration in his Donegal constituency. Now the road from Dublin to Donegal follows a roundabout route south of the Border, and the normal practice, which Mr Blaney always followed, was to take the short cut through the North. He saw no reason to change his habits now. But since not everyone in the North was wholly convinced of his innocence, while others might want to celebrate his discharge, security problems arose, with the result that Neil Blaney made his triumphal return to Donegal, over British territory, with an escort provided by the British Army.

Meanwhile in another context the absurd contrived a notable triumph. At the height of the summer season we had an interesting example of the Isle of Wight syndrome. One Saturday afternoon the captain of one of the English mailboats radioed from mid-Irish Sea to the harbour master at Dun Laoghaire to say that he had on board a British Army sergeant and twenty-one men, all in uniform, returning from leave to rejoin their unit in the North. They had missed the Belfast boat and had been sent (by some transport officer from a bygone age) to Dublin. The harbour master, foreseeing the likely consequences of allowing the British Army to effect a landing in Dublin Bay, wisely rang up to alert the British Embassy. The duty officer did not even need to consult me. There was a telephone discussion with Army headquarters in Lisburn, who, persuaded that this was not quite like a trip from Southampton to Ryde, sent the necessary orders. The sergeant and his men were to change instantly into civilian clothes. If they had none they could sit in their underpants. They were in no circumstances whatsoever to leave the ship, but to go straight back on the return voyage and begin again. They had made a mistake and got on the wrong boat, ha, ha, ha. It worked, thank God. The Dublin press had a field day with the navigational prowess of the Army, everybody laughed, and we slithered past what could have been an ugly and embarrassing incident.

4

ONE of the many complicating factors at this time was the constant interplay of forces between Dublin, Belfast and London. Senior Ministers in the Irish government had apparently been involved in the supply of arms to the Northern Catholics. This confirmed the worst fears of the Protestants about the intentions of the Republic and increased their hostility to the Catholic minority and to the Labour government reform programme. It also increased the vigilance of the police and Army in their search for illicit arms. And it heightened the controversy about the legality of the Protestant gun clubs and the large number of licensed firearms held especially by farmers. Then two things happened in quick succession which changed the course of Anglo-Irish history.

First, Mr Wilson called for a general election. It was confidently expected (except by Mariska who has second sight in these matters), and earnestly hoped by the Irish, that Labour would be returned. Their concern was traditional and understandable. After all, the Opposition was the Conservative *and Unionist* Party, which had been the constant opponent of any form of Home Rule and the architect of Partition; and in recent months it was a Labour government which had sent the Army to Ulster to protect the Catholics and was imposing reforms upon very reluctant Ministers.

Mariska and I gave our first formal dinner party in honour of the Minister for Foreign Affairs, Dr Hillery, on 18 June—not because it was the anniversary of Waterloo, but because it was election night. Either the early returns would show that Labour was likely to be returned and our Irish guests would be happy, or there would be a marked swing to the Conservatives, in which case I could get in quick with a reminder that

British policy towards the North was bi-partisan and the Conservative leadership supported the reform programme. The evening passed pleasantly enough and Dr Hillery was just showing signs of preparing to leave when I suggested that Peter Evans, who was among the party, should go to the television room and see if there was any news. He came back a few minutes later to say that on the evidence of the first seven returns there would be a Conservative majority of around sixty. The Irish guests courteously concealed most of their dismay while I spoke my consoling words, and they went their way. But the result, so far as they were concerned, was that instead of a Prime Minister with a large Irish element in his constituency, and a Minister called Callaghan and a Minister called Healey, they would be dealing with a tough Unionist from Kent, the 14th Earl of Home and the 6th Baron Carrington. But personalities counted far more than titles, and the deep malaise in Dublin had other origins.

The Irish government crisis had proved one thing: the Provisional IRA, or militant Republicans, or the spiritual and physical descendants of the old IRA, or at any rate some persons and organisations in the Republic, were trying, apparently successfully, to get arms to the Catholics in the North. Presumably, also, the Provisionals had been trying since their formation in the previous autumn to establish a power base and popular backing among the people they were aspiring to protect. But the negative evidence suggested that they were not able to do very much. The British Army was probably more unpopular with the Protestants than the Catholics, who felt no special need for protection by the Provisionals or any other IRA. But during May and June 1970 there was a growing uneasiness in Dublin and a mounting fear that disaster might be looming ahead. It was not only the arrest of two prominent and powerful Ministers that generated it. The season of Orange marches was beginning in the North, with the near certainty of ugly riots unless they were firmly and skilfully handled. But there was in effect no serious government in London—only an election campaign, which to the unconcealed and natural delight of the Northern Protestants returned a Conservative and Unionist administration—and the news which reached the weakened and badly shaken government in Dublin from

Catholic contacts in the North lost none of its alarming aspects in the telling of it.

The new Conservative government was scarcely formed when the Dublin government had to warn it of the virtual certainty of a dangerous riot in Belfast, where an Orange parade was to be held on 27 June and routed, as a deliberate provocation, through a Catholic area. London and Belfast took no notice and the inevitable riot, injuries, deaths and routine destruction occurred. On the twenty-eighth Mr Lynch issued a statement pointing out that violence was a predictable consequence of protest meetings and Orange marches, calling for restraint on all sides and ending, 'I ask our own people in the Republic not to worsen the position in any way by word or deed'. But then disturbances led to a second major event and all uncertainties were clearly and calamitously swept away by the events in Belfast in the first few days of July 1970.

By 5 July it had become clear in Dublin that all the parties immediately concerned—the Unionist government in Stormont, the Orange Order, the British Army, the RUC, the Catholics and the IRA—were set on a disaster course. Quite apart from the deaths and destruction, the main casualty was the precarious relationship between the British Army and the Catholics. I did not know, and I did not much want to know, who ordered the Army to invade the Catholic Falls Road area of Belfast and take it apart in a search for arms on the night of 3/4 July, before imposing a thirty-six hour curfew. But the Irish in Dublin saw at once, and did not fail to tell us, what had been achieved. The British Army was now The Enemy; the Provisional IRA could now appear as the Catholics' only protectors; they now had their power base, their infrastructure, their political rallying point, their propaganda themes, their justification for gun-running and the armed defence and protection of the Catholic areas. Jack Lynch's 'peaceful approach' hung by a very tenuous thread.

The primary concern of an Irish government had to be not the Northern Catholics but the internal affairs of the Republic. Over the next two years I had to convey to the Foreign Office a steady flow of unpleasant and highly unpopular information : a series of deadly accurate warnings given to me by Irish Ministers about the consequences of measures taken in the

North without consulting them, and a series of equally unpopular reminders that no Irish government was going to do
anything which we thought would be helpful in the North
merely in order to please us or because we asked them to.
Historically they had no grounds for liking us, nothing in our
handling of the Northern situation was making us more lov-
able, and they liked the Stormont régime least of all. Their
overriding anxiety was lest the violence and disturbed conditions in the North should spread to the Republic, and while
Jack Lynch himself could see clearly that the interests of the
British and Irish governments coincided, it was a political
necessity for him to be able to demonstrate that his policy of
working peacefully with and through the British government
was producing results, and that he was doing his duty by 'our
people in the North' by constant pressure upon Westminster.
In the reverse direction, I had to be able to convince the Taoiseach that the British government understood his predicament,
would guarantee the reforms that would satisfy the Northern
Catholics, and would rely on him to do all he could to curb
political terrorists and the supply of arms to the North.

My mention of unwelcome information and accurate warnings raises a most pertinent question: how does an Ambassador know? How does he find out? How can he be sure that
what he reports to his Foreign Secretary will not be proved
next week to be utter rubbish? The short answer is that the
information he needs comes from all over the place, and part
of his job is not only to know what to look for, but also to
make sure that all the members of his staff, no matter how
junior, know what to be curious about. Government Ministers,
politicians of all parties in and out of office, the Press (which
means not only what is printed but what editors and political
correspondents know or think they know and can discuss but
cannot print), civil servants, other Embassies—the list is endless. The higher the political sensitivity of the Embassy staff,
the more harmonious the internal relations, the more positive
the leadership and the interest of the Ambassador, the more
likely the Embassy is to report fully and accurately, in the
form that the Foreign Office require. Form, it must be stressed,
as distinct from substance, because an Ambassador who trims
his opinions to please his political masters is considerably

worse than useless. But there remains the question of how an Ambassador and his staff get to know this necessary multitude of informants. The answer is by getting out and about, being as sociable and hospitable as purse and liver permit, merging into the social landscape and winning acceptance and confidence. When you come home at six in the evening from a heavy day in the Embassy, the day's work may be less than half done, so it is rather irksome when envious Members of Parliament cavil at diplomats swilling champagne on their endless round of dinners and parties at the taxpayers' expense, or say that all the work could be done by Foreign Ministers ringing each other up.

In this case, certainly, the telephone would not have helped, since the Foreign Ministers concerned were still strangers. The Falls Road affair happened only two weeks after the Conservative government took office—timing which instantly bred the suspicion that the new government was anti-Catholic and anti-Irish. And enough had happened to arouse all the latent anti-British suspicions of the Irish nation, skilfully and assiduously stimulated by capable propagandists. In the more sophisticated and courteous circles of political and public life in Dublin it was expressed rhetorically and without rancour: 'Will the British ever learn?' In the reverse direction, the question very properly was asked: 'Can't the Irish government do something to help?'

The Irish were particularly exasperated by the fact that, whereas Catholic areas had been torn apart in arms searches, Protestant areas were left untouched although it was widely, and rightly, assumed that they concealed a large number of illegal arms. Mr Lynch called it 'unilateral disarming'. And it did not help matters that the Falls Road affair happened just before the principal tribal event of the year—the Orange parades to commemorate the defeat of King James II by Prince William of Orange at the Battle of the Boyne on 12 July 1690.

Everyone, north and south, was intensely nervous as the day of the Orange marches, 13 July (as the twelfth was a Sunday), approached. On the afternoon of the Saturday a messenger arrived with an envelope addressed to me in Jack Lynch's handwriting. It contained a note which read:

My Dear Ambassador

I am sending you herewith an advance text of what I shall say tonight.

Yours Sincerely,

John Lynch.

I studied this text with some care, particularly the last few sentences which read :

It is for political leaders to govern wisely and justly. I accept the guarantees of the British Government that they will do so.

My Government is the second guarantor.

Therefore, you who have suffered distress and indignity in the North are no longer unprotected victims.

It is not in your interest to interfere, in any way, with any Orange parade. I ask you not to do so.

Obviously the idea that the Irish government was the second guarantor that the political leaders (in the North, presumably) would govern wisely and justly was not going to endear him either to London or Stormont. But the whole purpose of the address was to calm the Catholics, and even if he had not already recorded it it was clearly too late to embark on probably unsuccessful and certainly acrimonious negotiations about amending it. After deep thought I decided to do nothing, apart from thanking Mr Lynch for his courtesy. The essential thing was that the parades passed off without serious incident.

After two months as Ambassador I began to realise that I was stepping on to politically delicate and dangerous ground, liable to be in trouble with the Stormont government and the Unionist MP's, which did not matter, and with both the British and Irish governments, which did. But I could only do it my way, and looking back I felt that in a sense my entire training and experience would prove to have been a preparation for what was coming.

5

I WAS born in Kuala Lumpur in 1913. My father was a civil engineer building roads and bridges. My mother's family were mostly connected with the law. Both from the south of England, they had gone to Malaya to marry, in 1912. None of my forebears on either side, so far as I can trace, went to a university. In 1915, in the First World War, my father and mother came back to England with me so that my father could volunteer for the Navy. It is odd to think that Winston Churchill was First Lord of the Admiralty; I doubt if it occurred to my parents that twenty-five years later I would become his Private Secretary.

I was lucky to leave Kuala Lumpur at all. Home was a thatched bungalow with the inevitable verandah, on which, during my first few weeks of life, I was dumped every afternoon for my siesta, there being more traces of a cool breeze there than anywhere else. It was the sacred hour, and while my father came home every day for his lunch and always asked to see his firstborn child, my mother insisted that in no circumstances should I, already a notably restless infant, be disturbed. One day he was more than usually insistent and my mother relented. Moments later she heard a volley of revolver shots and rushed to the verandah, upon which converged my Ayah and assorted Boys. Fortunately my father was a very good shot with a revolver, and happily he had had one handy. On tiptoeing on to the verandah to peep at his slumbering son, the first thing he noticed above the cradle was several feet of python emerging from a hole in the ceiling, about to collect its lunch. But the day's events, I am told, did not end there. Friends were coming to dinner, and my father, who had a slightly odd sense of fun, coiled up the dead python on the drive, its head supported on a golf club, to greet the guests. Punctually, at the invited hour, my parents heard another fusillade, shortly followed by the arrival of an exultant friend and an ashenfaced wife announcing the successful shooting of a large serpent. Apparently it took a lot of drink and bonhomie to establish that this was the python's second death that day. I still do not care much for snakes.

Coming home for the war was an anticlimax and the consequences were sad. My father was rejected for the Navy because he was colour-blind, and became a temporary civil servant. The end of the war left him unemployed, but by the spring of 1919 he had found a job—a fairly lowly one, I suspect—at Thorneycroft Motor Works at Basingstoke. He bought a house near the factory—a large house with an acre or more of grounds including a sizeable paddock—for £1,200. Here my mother went in for intensive poultry farming and together my parents created a highly successful vegetable garden. Here I discovered that an umbrella makes an inadequate parachute (my jump off the stable roof was painful); I invented a bomb made of sawdust and methylated spirit (discovered and confiscated before ignition); went temporarily blind during an acute bout of measles; puzzled over how baby chicks appeared in eggs, and while from careful listening to conversation about eggs being fertile I deduced that male birds had something to do with it, I could get no clear explanation of why the cockerels were always jumping on the hens' backs.

In 1922 my father lost his job. The British engineering industry was buried in the post-war slump and he was lucky to find another one in Shanghai. The house in Basingstoke was sold, my mother and I moved to Northamptonshire, and for the next five years 'home' was a farmhouse three miles from the nearest village, hamlet or shop. It had its charm. Lighting was by oil lamps and heating by open coal fires and primitive oil heaters, all of which tended to smoke and smell. Domestic water was pumped up daily by hand from the well to a large tank in the roof. Hot water was produced by the simple expedient of putting a kettle on the kitchen range. There was a bathroom and a bath, but actually to have a hot, warm, or more probably tepid bath it was necessary to carry cans of

C

hot water from the wash-house across the backyard. Later, a kindly uncle gave my mother a hot-water geyser driven by a gigantic paraffin stove, memories of which came flooding back when, twenty years later, I heard and smelt the first jet engine.

But meanwhile my parents were faced with a cruel dilemma, resolved by an unsatisfactory compromise. It was unthinkable that I should be educated anywhere but at an English boarding school. This meant that one parent divided her time between being a wife in China and a mother in England, and I saw the other once between the age of nine and eighteen, when he came home for a few months' leave.

My mother would spend eighteen months in each country, and for school holidays when she was in China I was farmed out among various uncles, aunts and cousins. There was, of course, no air mail or air travel. A letter took six weeks, unless it was marked via Canada, which reduced it to four; if marked via Siberia it could take as little as eighteen days, in the rather unlikely event of it arriving at all. The result was that I had very little family life, no regular 'home' to which I could be certain of returning in the school holidays, and few consistent friendships except at school. Unconsciously I was being trained for the life of a nomad.

Between eight and eighteen I had the most conventional education that can be imagined, at first at a preparatory school and later at Wellington College. The prospect of boarding school secretly terrified me, for up to the age of eight I had never stayed away from home, even with relatives. The reality was better in some ways and worse in others. My parents could not really afford to send me to a boarding school, and everything had to be done on the cheap, with the result that I was acutely self-conscious. I suffered agonies of humiliation over my night-bag improvised from an old brief-case; the shapeless jerseys knitted by my mother with more love than skill, and—the crowning indignity of my first summer term—my cricket bat. Every other boy seemed to have an Autograph, the fashionable make, suited to his size, but my father, a very tall man, had had his bat adapted to my needs by cutting off the blade and leaving the great handle as it was. Calamitously this deformed monster was called a Sugg, and it instantly became an object of amazement and mockery throughout the school. I loyally defended the oddity as a cunning device to increase the power of the bat, but failed to convince. On the other hand, among the forty-five or so school inmates, there was company, companionship and competition.

In the embarrassing final moments before leaving me at school for the first time, my father as he embraced me whispered the two words: 'Work hard'. This was a novel conception, as I had not hitherto regarded lessons as something that needed to be worked at. I soon discovered what he meant. The fierce competition, the rigid syllabus, the learning by heart, would horrify today's educational theorists, but aided by the liberal use of intelligent punishment and the insistence on re-doing sloppy work, the system was extremely effective. Whatever its shortcomings, it gave us a very thorough grounding in the rudiments of language; it was highly stimulating for the brighter boys, and the devil took the hindmost. Anyway, it worked in my case and at thirteen I got a scholarship to Wellington.

Wellington, or to give it its full title, the Royal and Religious Foundation of Wellington College, had the reputation of being a 'tough Army school'. I went there on a scholarship in 1927 as a semi-invalid, having strained my heart in the school sports the previous year. I took part in no football or especially strenuous sports until I was seventeen; I developed a deep dislike of everything to do with the Officers Training Corps; but the authorities were tolerant enough, and the education good enough, to enable me both to become Head of College and to win a classical scholarship to Corpus Christi College, Oxford. However, the tensions along the way were considerable.

One's first loyalty was to the dormitory, and not only games but intellectual achievements were based on a system of rivalry and competition, in which all participated with varying degrees of enthusiasm. I was very ambitious and I conformed. Authority was obsessed with the problem of 'undesirable friendships'. Friendships between older and younger boys were in effect forbidden, and friendships between contemporaries in different dormitories were actively discouraged except in the upper reaches. Thus in a school of some 630 boys the circle of suitable comrades was limited to a dozen or so.

The only activities that cut across the local divisions were intellectual—the art, debating and playreading societies, and the aesthetes or intellectuals who formed a critical, self-questioning and irreverent group, with a dawning realisation that there was plenty to be critical about. I became an editor of the school magazine. Then I became a prefect and finally Head of the School, and I was brought face to face with a series of difficult problems regarding honesty and loyalty.

As Head of the School I probably had more responsibility for, and authority over, the everyday lives of more people than at any time until my career in the public service was well advanced. But there was always plenty of delegation of authority at Wellington, and I thoroughly enjoyed this as soon as I wielded the power myself. Even if I had no innate doubts about the rightness of the system I was helping to uphold, they would have been thrust upon me. The Master of Wellington had been a great headmaster but he had stayed on too long; he was old and tired and was losing his grip. The staff were splitting into two factions, corresponding roughly to reactionaries and progressives, and had a vested interest in encouraging rivalries on an inter-dormitory basis at the expense of the larger body. In retrospect it was clear that I was given, or took upon myself, too much responsibility for upholding a system, or at least an administration, about which I was becoming dubious. I cannot pretend that I lost any sleep over it. The Head of the School was an ex-officio editor of the school magazine, and so I squared my conscience by writing articles lampooning or gently criticising the régime which I upheld.

Between my last two terms at school I had a strange interlude. I spent the whole of April in Poland, in a village near Warsaw, giving Latin and Greek lessons to the son of a wealthy banker who wanted a nomination to Winchester. Amazingly, he came back into my life ten years later as a fighter pilot in England, his sister driving a War Office car, his parents living in London. After this break, back for my last term, when I was awarded the King's Medal, a large and handsome gold medal originally presented by Queen Victoria and normally given to the Head of School. I was, and still am, very proud of this award, although even then, I am afraid, my irreverent instincts turned against the citation with its list of virtues which, if ever combined in one youthful Galahad, would produce the ultimate prig.

In October 1932 I went up to Oxford. My two scholarships were together worth £150 a year. My mother, by taking European girls as paying guests in the house she had bought in North Oxford, made enough money to give me an allowance of £120. Nobody in those days thought of supplementing their allowance by finding temporary work in the vacation and the college would have frowned upon such a practice, so without my mother's efforts, and the scholarships, there would have been no question of going to university.

My father, who had been unemployed since his return from China the previous year, looked vainly for work in the depressed conditions of 1931-2. At the end of 1932 he found a humble job in the Johannesburg water works, got a lift on a Norwegian whaling ship and departed, vowing he would never return until he could repay every penny of such debts as he had incurred. I never saw him again. When the war broke out he thought of returning, but even then the prospects of an elderly man doing anything useful or profitable seemed poor. We kept up a stilted correspondence during the intervening years, but the abyss of age, temperament and separation was too great. In January 1940 I received a telegram from a stranger in South Africa to say that my father and three companions had been killed in a motor accident. It was a tragic life of ineffectiveness and failure in human contact. I cannot say I loved him or condemned him, because I scarcely knew him and perhaps that is the saddest thing of all.

At Oxford I did not take kindly to Honour Moderations, which occupied my first five terms. The work involved was just a continuation of the sort of thing I had been doing for the last three years of school. I was not seriously worried. Had I not since the age of eight been the infallible passer of examinations, the winner of scholarships, the one who surpassed his academic rivals? Scholars of Corpus always got Firsts in Mods anyway. So when I got a Second, the college authorities were not over-pleased, the blow to my vanity was shattering, and I was in a state of fury with myself because I knew perfectly well that I did not really deserve a First. The primary reason was blonde, beautiful, and wasteful of time and energy. But it was not her alone. After my intense absorption in the rigorous life of Wellington, the freedom and the beauty and the talk of Oxford all combined to make the classical texts seem far drearier at the time than they really were.

There was also politics. I joined the Oxford Union in my first term, attended all the debates and spoke in some of them, usually on themes supporting the League of Nations. Naturally, therefore, I was present in February 1933 when the motion 'This House will not fight for King and Country' was debated and won. To his dying day Winston Churchill maintained that that debate was one of the contributory causes of the war but luckily I was able to say truthfully, that I had voted against the motion. At Oxford, too, I had my first brush with a Communist Front Organisation, interesting because this was the period when Burgess and Maclean and Philby were being caught and corrupted, and because it was my first experience of the propagandist exploitation of what was then called 'peace' and has now become 'détente'. Fortunately the operation was so crude that only an idiot could have been deceived by it. After that I gave up politics.

College authorities ceased to regard me as a serious character after my performance in Honour Mods. For my part, I felt I had let everyone down including myself, as the diagnosis and cure were obvious. Philosophy and history were new worlds. There were some brilliant types who could get their First or Second Class Honours without overmuch toil, but I was clearly not of their number and would have to set about it the hard way. Time lost could not be recovered, so for my last two years at Oxford I kept a fairly rigid discipline and timetable.

The upshot was that in June 1936, after an oral grilling of one and a quarter hours, I got a First in Greats (Literae Humaniores). As soon as the examination was over and term ended, I went to a training establishment in London for six weeks' coaching in French, précis writing and other compulsory subjects for the Civil Service examination which I had not studied since I was fifteen.

The examination yielded one of my most treasured possessions, my initiation into the Civil Service, usually referred to as our 'SIR or MADAM letter'.

Civil Service Commission
Burlington Gardens
London W.1.
17 Oct 1936

SIR, or MADAM,

I am directed by the Civil Service Commissioners to inform you that your Certificate of Qualification for employment in the Junior Grade of the Administrative Class of the Home Civil Service has been granted; and that it has been sent to the Secretary, Admiralty, Whitehall, S.W.1. You should at once communicate with the Authorities of that Department with a view to ascertaining the date when you should enter upon your duties.

I am, SIR, or MADAM,
Your obedient Servant,
G. G. Mennell,
Secretary.

This was followed by a letter telling me when to report for duty, so the Civil Service Commissioners seemed to have resolved their doubts about my sex and posted me to the all-male Admiralty as an Assistant Principal. When you took the examination you could express preferences for particular Departments, and if you were high enough on the list, and there was a vacancy, your wish was granted. I had opted for the Ministry of Health, because I was interested in town planning, and for the Board of Education, because I was interested in the Director of Establishment's daughter. I was not high enough on the list to be accepted for either Department, and that was the first of a strange series of strokes of luck that marked my passage through public life.

Then came an even greater stroke of luck. The post of Assistant Private Secretary to the First Lord of the Admiralty, the most sought-after job available for an Assistant Principal, fell vacant. This normally went to an Assistant Principal in his third or fourth year, as a prelude to promotion. By some quirk of availability or suitability, it was given to me after barely seven months in the Admiralty, and I found myself serving the newly-appointed First Lord, Mr Alfred Duff Cooper. Not only that, but a few weeks later we set off overland, luxuriously by train, to Venice where we spent a week in the Admiralty yacht *HMS Enchantress*, moored at the entrance to the Grand Canal, as guests of the Italian Navy; we then went on a leisurely voyage round the Eastern Mediterranean, a trip to Cairo and visits to Malta and Naples, with one memorable episode during a brief stay in Cyprus. The Governor had organised a big reception for Duff Cooper and his most beautiful and altogether magical wife Lady Diana to meet the local dignitaries, including Munir Bey, the Head of the Turkish Cypriots. During the party I came upon Lady Diana sitting alone upon a sofa, her head buried in her hands, great tears streaming down her lovely cheeks. Much concerned I approached her. She was helpless with laughter. 'Peckski,' she sobbed, 'Peckski, Munir Bey has just been telling me how much he and Lady Palmer do for the Red Cross, and, he said, you know, I work hand in blouse with her.'

On the seven-week cruise the sum total of my labours was to sign the Archbishop's book in Malta. We returned twelve months to the day after I joined the Civil Service. I thought it had rather a lot to commend it. The winter of 1937-8 was darkened by the growing menace of Hitler's Germany, culminating in the invasion and annexation of Austria, but I was settling down happily to learn something of my official duties after the long joy-ride. Then suddenly everything changed. I received an invitation from a complete stranger to a cocktail party which, as I later discovered, had been arranged to enable a young man to meet a Hungarian girl whom he had admired at a distance at some political lecture. I was asked along as a friend of a friend of the hostess.

The party took place on 21 March 1938, a week after Hitler's invasion and annexation of Austria, when we were filled with depression and exasperation over Chamberlain's appeasement policy. It was a good party, but it failed in its basic aim because I met the lovely girl with the Hungarian accent, and that was that. Her name was Mariska Somló, and she was studying at the Royal Academy of Dramatic Art in London, where she lived with her parents. It was not so much an accent as an intonation. She took great pride in her faultless English pronunciation, pride which almost, but not quite, equalled her performance. She did not know how to boil an egg. She loathed appeasement. We had a happy evening. Then this lovely creature vanished from my life. She said she would come to a party I was giving on Boat Race night and didn't. I phoned her home and either she was away and the message to ring me would be passed on, or she was not available. I had lost her and I sat brooding on my sad fate.

Then one day, when I was working as usual, the telephone rang. It was Mariska, who sounded a little disconcerted at having been put straight through to the First Lord of the Admiralty's private office. Her story was typical of our life. I had told her that I would organise a Boat Race night party and would let her know where and when. Hearing nothing more, because, as it transpired, her mother had sabotaged all communication, she had gone to another party and sent me an angry letter, but by mis-spelling Sydney Street, Chelsea, she sent the letter to Sidney Street in the East End of London, the scene of Winston Churchill's famous siege in 1912, whence it returned to her via the Dead Letter Office. John Peck, claiming to be the First Lord's Private Secretary, was an impostor, probably a dangerous spy who must be unmasked, and to prove it she rang the Admiralty to show I did not exist. And there I was. So by mid-April contact was re-established.

For the last thirty-eight years we have demonstrated the wisdom of the warning signal in the Prayer Book, before undertaking the final commitment, about marriage being for better or for worse. We are obviously incompatible, and each considers the other to be the more incompatible of the two. We fought before and during our engagement, and, when there was time and we felt like it, throughout our marriage. I expect we shall continue to do so.

Almost from the day we met, international and intimate tensions under which we were living found expression in a series of monumental rows, sometimes about abstruse metaphysical and philosophic questions and sometimes about nothing at all. She had an unnerving habit of flouncing out of my flat, thinking later of some blistering retort or debating point she had failed to score, and writing me a scorching letter which she then delivered by hand to the messenger at the main entrance to the Admiralty. I would dash off a withering reply which might get posted or might be kept in order to continue verbally where we had left off; but with luck we always ended laughing or love-making. During the summer of 1938 I gave her a dog, a mongrel in which Collie and English sheepdog predominated. It soon became a bone of contention with her parents, with the elderly lady with whom she now lodged, and on occasion with me. By October it had been thrown out of everywhere and was living in my flat.

On 26 October we had the ultimate, definitive row and we parted for the final time.

Two days silence.

'Is that Flaxman 2673?'
'I've got your dog.'
'I'll take it away this evening.'

'I've come for my dog.'
'Will you marry me?'
'Yes.'

We were married in April 1939, once again in an atmosphere of political crisis as Mussolini chose that moment to invade Albania, and we had the happiest summer of our lives. And life took on an even fiercer intensity because we knew that peace could not last much longer. We had, like everybody else, been conditioned by years of pacifist propaganda to believe that war would be unspeakably awful and our survival doubtful; and yet, as Albania and Czechoslovakia fell and Nazism and Fascism continued on their victorious way, we saw that the price of temporary peace would be perpetual shame, and so when the war finally came in September, with half our minds we found it was almost a relief.

Official life was less idyllic. Duff Cooper, after fighting a lone battle for the naval construction programme against the deadly trio of Chamberlain (Prime Minister), Simon (Chancellor) and Inskip (Coordination of Defence), could not stomach the humiliation of the deal with Hitler at Munich in October 1938 and resigned. His successor, Lord Stanhope, could not stand the sight of me nor I of him. The Admiralty's blue-eyed boy had become a problem child. What to do with me? Again fate stepped in. Sir Thomas Inskip was transferred and replaced in Defence Coordination by Lord Chatfield, the former Chief of the Naval Staff, who asked the Admiralty if he could have me as his Assistant Private Secretary. The Admiralty agreed with unflattering alacrity and I was delighted. I had a damaged reputation to restore, the new work was fascinating, I was newly married, and the sun shone as the clouds piled up.

War broke on 3 September 1939, leaving the Minister for the Coordination of Defence with very little to do. The reason for this oddity was very simple. The three Service Ministers, including Winston Churchill now returned from political exile to be First Lord of the Admiralty once again, were all members of the War Cabinet which coordinated all major policy matters. There was a Military Coordination Committee, known throughout Whitehall as the Crazy Gang, with Lord Chatfield in the chair; its principal role was to try to make Churchill, with his vast energy and cosmic outlook, stick to the affairs of the Navy. By April 1940 Chatfield resigned and was not replaced. This left me without any prospect of a job, and I returned home that evening to Mariska somewhat thoughtfully.

Mariska looked intently at something she saw in the middle distance over my left shoulder and said, 'You will go back to the Admiralty, to Winston. He will soon be Prime Minister and he will take you with him to Downing Street.'

On the same day an announcement was made from 10 Downing Street that it was not proposed to replace Lord Chatfield, but that arrangements were being made for the First Lord of the Admiralty, as the Senior Service Minister concerned, to preside over the Military Coordination Committee.

A few days later I was sent for by the First Lord's Principal Private Secretary, Eric Seal, to be told that in order to help handle these new responsibilities, I was being brought back as an additional Private Secretary to deal with general defence matters. The Germans inconveniently chose this moment to invade Norway, and Mr Churchill was too busy to see me at once. However, the next afternoon Seal said that the First Lord was working in bed and the best thing would be to take him some papers and act as if I had been working for him for months. I went to Admiralty House.

It was the first time I had seen Winston Churchill at close range. He was sitting up in bed with a large cigar in his mouth, studying some maps. He took no notice of me, but at intervals he reached forward to stroke a fine black cat sleeping at the foot of the bed. 'Poor Pussy,' he said, 'poor Pussy.' I stood in silence for what seemed an age, while he comforted the cat. He then said, 'Poor Pussy. He's just had a painful operation. His name is Nelson. So you've come to work for me.'

'Yes please, Sir.'

'Good, what have you got there?'

I told him. He looked through the papers. A gentle, almost paternal smile. 'Thank you very much.' I was in.

Four chaotic weeks later Winston Churchill was Prime Minister and forming his government. Of the four Private Secretaries working for him in the Admiralty, he decided to take two with him to 10 Downing Street—the most senior, Eric Seal, and the most junior, myself. On that morning, 10 May, the great German Offensive burst upon Holland and Belgium, and life was never to be the same again.

I took my news back to Mariska.

'Well of course, that's what I told you.'

6

I was twenty-seven years old when Winston Churchill became Prime Minister and took me with him to 10 Downing Street. Other Private Secretaries were older and senior to me and served him with greater distinction, but I was the only one who served him throughout his wartime premiership, from the day the King summoned him to form a government in May 1940 to the day he flew back from the Potsdam Conference on 25 July 1945 to learn, on 26 July, that the British electorate had dismissed him from office.

A third of a century later, at a literary party in Dublin, I was listening to some people discussing a forthcoming book on Hiroshima and the atomic bomb, and I inadvertently dropped a real conversation-stopper. I mentioned that I had happened to be present when President Truman and Winston Churchill told Stalin that the first experimental atomic bomb had been fired successfully in New Mexico. It suddenly brought home to me what an era I had lived through. I do not want to add to the already vast literature about Winston Churchill, but there are personal aspects that I have to touch on. Painters and sculptors have done him a disservice by persistently portraying him in the 'Bulldog at Bay' style. This was only one side of his complex yet single-minded character. Here I want to touch only on his personal relationships and some aspects of wartime life in Downing Street, and I write only of those things of which I had immediate first-hand knowledge. In those five years I learnt many things quite apart from watching an impossible war being won and an impossible alliance held together: that humanity and humour, and human failings and weaknesses as well, are all part of greatness; that a collaborator, whether he be a junior assistant or senior Ambassador, is useless unless he says what he believes to be true and does not trim his views to please his master; that a great man not only expects and wins absolute loyalty from his juniors but gives it in return. I also learnt a personal lesson which all my career has helped to emphasise: never be surprised by anything; always be ready to deal with the unexpected by unorthodox or improvised methods, and above all, notice and care.

From 10 May 1940 until 27 July 1945 there was never a day or night when at least one Private Secretary was not with Winston Churchill—that is to say capable of being physically present by his desk or at his bed-side within a couple of minutes, or in the same train, ship, aircraft or car, and able to comply with any request, reasonable or not, on the telephone or in person. Four of us shared this duty. It is difficult to describe or imagine the loneliness of someone in Winston Churchill's position with the burden of responsibility that he carried and the knowledge that however much he shared or delegated it, the ultimate decisions were his. He had the marvellous basic certainty of the total understanding, support and love of Mrs Churchill. But he had few friends, and they could not be with him for much of the time. He therefore depended greatly upon the sympathy, loyalty and total discretion of his personal staff—the 'Secret Circle' as he called us. He hated change and new faces around him, and any newcomer was deliberately given a fairly taxing time. But once you were in, you were in totally and unconditionally; you were part of the Churchill family, and he knew that any secrets or indiscretions confided to the Secret Circle were secret absolutely. It follows from the way our life was organised that each of us could only have a quarter of the story. What we all had in common was the environment, and the task of ensuring that Winston Churchill's highly idiosyncratic and, let us face it, selfish method of working, and his personal approach to the conduct of war, were geared with a minimum of friction to the very complex machinery of government and the very diverse temperaments of the men who composed it.

Churchill required certain things of his personal staff, and so long as we provided them he was not an exacting master. He was liable at any time to fire a question such as 'When does the convoy reach the Clyde?' or 'Where is the *Ark Royal?*'

to which there were one calamitous and two correct replies. If you knew the answer beyond any peradventure of doubt you gave it crisply and positively. More often you said 'I'll find out, sir,' and you went and rang up whoever could tell you straight away. He never expected us to know anything, and I believe that if he had asked the date he would not have minded if we replied 'I'll find out, sir.' But he was exasperated, and very rightly so, by 'I think that convoy arrives on the seventeenth' and he would rise in wrath and say he didn't care what I thought, but when would it arrive. But we were very definitely required to know how to get an answer immediately, which entailed knowing which Duty Officer in which Department to ring up at any hour of the day or night. We also needed to know, deduce, infer, divine or simply guess what he was thinking about, so that any query such as 'What convoy?' was unpopular. He was inclined to fire such questions in the middle of meetings, dinner parties and other gatherings, and I some-times wondered whether he was partly showing off his staff. I achieved my moment of fame at some such party towards the end of 1943, when I was suddenly told, 'Gimme the moon'. I left the table distinctly thoughtful. There had been nothing in the conversation to give me a clue. I was alone and there was nobody with whom to compare notes. I reasoned, on con-sidering the people present, that it must be something to do with planning the invasion of Normandy the following year. Then I remembered having seen somewhere a table that he had had prepared, giving the date of the full moon in each of the summer months of 1944. After some rummaging I dug it out and gave the PM his moon.

He probably did half his work in bed. He never got up in the morning until there was something to get up for. Every afternoon he would retire for a siesta, an hour or more of solid sleep, as he had the blessed gift of falling sound asleep within minutes of the lights being put out or the curtains being drawn. On waking he would work in bed again until something com-pelled him to get up.

On many days the two events which roused him from bed were lunch and dinner—evidence of a life so sedentary, if not supine, that it might appear physically disastrous. Yet he spent many week-ends watching troop training, anti-invasion preparations and trials of new weapons, and he displayed energy and endurance to outlast many young and apparently able-bodied mortals. One result of his working methods was that he could, and regularly did, work on after dinner until one, two or three in the morning, and bed by midnight was a bonus for the staff on duty with him that night.

Most week-ends, Friday afternoon to Monday morning, were spent at Chequers, the Prime Minister's official country residence. But he worked most of the time, and one of the four Private Secretaries would go with him. The only time Mr Churchill queried my presence was characteristic. When the heavy bombing of London began in 1940 he was faced with a difficult choice : whether to disrupt his routine and stay with the Londoners, or whether to ignore the bombing and do what he always did. Having reckoned that Hitler would be happy to inconvenience him, he decided to do the opposite and continued to go to Chequers. So one afternoon early in the bombardment :

'Who is coming with me?'

'I am, sir.'

'Where is your wife?'

'At her first aid post.'

'Has she shelter?'

'Yes, sir.'

'Are you worried about her?'

'No more than usual.'

'All right, you can come.'

This, of course, was good administration; a Private Secretary at Chequers who was worrying about what might be happening in London was unlikely to be much use. But he knew I was the only one whose wife was in London and that we had scarcely been married a year, and he was genuinely and kindly concerned.

But it was at his own home at Chartwell that he came nearest to laying aside the heavy burden of the war. There were the same direct telephone lines, the despatch riders, the personal staff, but there were the whole paraphernalia of family and home, the cottage he had built himself (he once gave me a lesson in brick-laying), the gardens, his golden carp in the lily pool and his geese on the lake. One goose he was particularly attached to, because if he stood on the terrace and bellowed across the valley a call approximately transliterated 'Ah-wah-wah', the goose would reply from the lake with a distant 'Honk honk' and Churchill believed that he was the only person whom his faithful goose would answer.

There was one dreadful summer's evening when the Prime Minister had taken me down to Chartwell accompanied by General Ismay, a man noted for his tact and skill in dealing with Churchill. The PM's first act was to demonstrate his exclusive dialogue with his pet goose. What imp urged the general to tempt fortune by following suit and calling 'Ah-wah-wah' across the valley will never be known. To my frozen horror—for the outcome was predictable—the goose replied, 'Honk honk'. The Prime Minister was not only put out: he was genuinely grieved by the perfidy of the goose.

The Blitz on London, through all the tragedies and heroism, had its lighter moments. Winston Churchill liked watching air raids, and expeditions up to the roof of the buildings over the Annexe became a feature of the Churchills' entertaining. A stock of tin hats was kept for dinner guests, as protection against anti-aircraft shrapnel, and if there was a raid in progress they were invited to accompany the Prime Minister to the roof. His detective and either the Flag Commander or the Private Secretary on duty would go as well. One bitterly cold night his guests began to murmur that they were freezing to death, but Mr Churchill insisted that it was really nice and warm and they should not be fussing. It grew colder and colder. The raid was clearly in the outer suburbs. Suddenly there was a diversion. A diminutive, tin-hatted figure appeared out of the night between the battlements and the roof tops. 'Oy,' he said, 'what's going on up 'ere?' The detective swooped and tried to shush him, explaining who his distinguished visitors were. Using a suitable vocabulary, the night watchman indicated that he was not impressed and something queer was going on.

The Flag Commander had a go, and was eliciting the news that all the fireplaces in the Air Ministry were smoking like hell and something funny was going on, when the night watchman suddenly saw the light. Pointing at the Prime Minister, he said, "Ere, what's 'e doing?' A good question: Mr Churchill had perched himself on a convenient chimney pot, giving himself a source of warmth denied to his guests but interposing an airtight seal upon this vital flue.

In the autumn of 1940, when the bombing had got really rough, I happened to be the only Private Secretary in Number Ten one night, when going out of my room into the hall I saw a light. It was in one of a number of rooms near the top of the house that faced inwards on to a narrow yard, was unused and had no blackout curtains. It was not the moment to go to the top of rickety old buildings out of preference, so I yelled up the stairs, 'Put that light out'. Still nothing happened, except that the light grew perceptibly brighter. I grabbed my belongings and shot up the stairs. An incendiary bomb had come in diagonally through the window, ignited and rolled under the bed, where the bedding was beginning to blaze. It was a fairly simple matter for me to put the fire out, but a few moments later it could have been a very different proposition. Anyway, I have always liked to regard myself as the air raid warden who saved Number Ten.

I spent the entire war as a civilian and was never once in uniform. Even so, there were interesting moments, quite apart from the Blitz of 1940, the flying bombs of 1944 and the rockets of 1944-5. After the final German defeat in North Africa, Winston Churchill was in Algiers for vital staff talks about the next stage in Anglo-American strategy. These ended in general harmony. The main party flew back from Algiers to Gibraltar in the new transport aircraft, the York. The rest, including General Ismay and myself, were to fly in General Montgomery's special DC3. I was clutching the vital box which contained the conclusions of the conference—in fact, the entire future strategy of the Second World War. Unfortunately the aircraft developed a fault and could not be flown, but eventually a DC3 from the American air transport service, the MATS, which provided most of the air communications in the African and Mediterranean theatres, came to our rescue. It was at the Algiers airfield on the 'milk run' from Cairo to Gibraltar and was apparently empty except for a large quantity of mail bags, so we duly embarked on a fantastically hot afternoon in this austere aircraft which was equipped only for transporting parachutists.

I am afraid I had an ungenerous qualm about our crew. The MATS included a certain number of bomber aircrews who, after long spells of dangerous missions, were being rested and kept flying at the same time; others had failed to meet the exacting standards of bombing missions and felt themselves to be second class airmen; others again enjoyed hair-raising exploits such as coaxing grossly overloaded DC3s off the ground and over the airport buildings at Cairo. Our particular crew had evidently not had time to shave that morning, but had managed to stock up with immense cigars. However they were reassuringly workmanlike on the job, and we settled down as comfortably as we could on the bare aluminium seats—all except the most experienced traveller, Major Cunningham, Military Assistant to the CIGS; he curled up on the pile of mail bags at the rear end of the aircraft which were slightly more yielding. It was a beautiful afternoon as we flew at fifteen hundred feet along the African shore and out across the Bay of Oran. We dozed. Suddenly the door from the cockpit flew open and dense clouds of smoke billowed out. Through it there emerged one of the crew in some haste, cigar in hand, shouting 'Fire!' He hastened to the rear of the aircraft and returned with a fire extinguisher to the cockpit.

We felt slightly at a loss. Both engines were running normally. The wings were intact and there were no signs of flame or smoke outside. We had no parachutes and were over the sea anyway. The only person to react positively was General Ismay: he sat up and carefully put on his tie. Sounds of pumping and squirting came from the cockpit. Finally the crewman emerged again, still with his cigar, and signified that the fire was out. Understandably curious we asked 'What fire?' He uttered the immortal words, 'Hank didn't know it was loaded.' 'It' was a Verey pistol, and the signal rocket had had a brief flight ricocheting around until it settled in the radio and set it on fire. So minus communications we flew on and settled down to sleep again.

But not for very long. Cunningham suddenly sat up on his mailbags and said 'Jesus Christ' very loud and clear. 'Look at that!' and he pointed out of the windows. Astern of us on either side was a series of anti-aircraft shell bursts. At this moment two Spitfires flew across our nose from south to north and made it very clear that we were to change course smartly, which we did. The great mass of Gibraltar loomed up through the afternoon haze. Our crew, navigating by the simple expedient of following the coast line, had overshot and taken us over the Spanish territory of Tangier where the anti-aircraft gunners had been delighted to relieve the tedium of having nothing to fire at.

By now we were keenly interested in the closing moments of our flight. Down we came to the Mediterranean end of the airstrip built out over the sea—perfect. But half way along the strip we noticed that we were still some ten or fifteen feet above it. Then with a roar the engines were opened up and we soared up over the Atlantic without actually touching Gibraltar at all. I admit that by now I was praying both for myself and my precious box of conference conclusions—prayers that were doubled in fervour when the pilot took us well over mainland Spain in order to turn and try his luck at landing the other way round. He made a perfect landing and we emerged into the teeth of a brisk near-gale, down which he had first tried to land. We thanked the crew for a most interesting flight and were transported to the residence of the Governor, whose offer of drinks we did not refuse.

But this was not My Longest Day. This arose out of the only occasion when Winston Churchill delivered a major speech without a prepared text. Towards the end of the war he and his Cabinet colleagues decided that a loyal address should be presented to His Majesty as a tribute to the steadfastness and the example set by the Royal Family during the war, and a motion to this effect was to be debated in the House of Commons. We gave the Prime Minister the usual reminder that he had to prepare a speech, but he brushed it aside saying that it was not necessary as he knew exactly what he was going to say.

I went down to the House with him and took my place in the Official Box. Churchill rose to propose the motion and launched forth into his speech. The style was flowery, bordering on the fulsome, and he went on and on and on. I could feel, rather than see, the attention of the Members beginning to wander, until at last he sat down. He stayed to hear the speeches of Attlee and Sinclair, the Labour and Liberal leaders, and then stumped out. This was my signal to follow, and we went straight to his car to return to Annexe. On the way . . .

'Well, John, what did you think of my speech?'

'It was very eloquent, sir. I thought it was too long.'

'WHAT?'

'I am sorry, sir. I thought your speech was too long.'

'You bloody ignorant fool. You don't know a thing about the House of Commons. It was a historic occasion. Saying my speech was too long.'

An overpowering silence for the rest of the way. The normal ritual followed. He went into his office and after a few moments rang to ask for the Private Secretary on duty to go in. That, of course, meant me.

'Oh, it's you, you bloody young fool, saying I spoke for too long.'

'I thought you did, sir.'

'I want to see Brendan.'

So I called for the Minister of Information. When I showed him in :

'Brendan, this fool John Peck said I spoke for too long in the House, didn't you?'

'I thought you did, sir.'

'Well,' said Brendan Bracken, 'it was a very moving tribute to the King.'

I left them to it. Shortly afterwards, the Prime Minister went off to his afternoon sleep. When he woke up, around 5.30 pm, he rang as usual and I went in. He immediately started up again and I woodenly repeated that his speech was too long. He worked in bed until 8.15, during which time he sent for Beaverbrook, Oliver Lyttelton and Bridges. Before each I was castigated for criticising his speech, and each time I repeated what I had said.

Unfortunately there was a dinner party that night. I was not altogether surprised when I was sent for in the middle of the dinner and pilloried as an impudent young puppy who had said his tribute to the King was too long. 'I am sorry, sir, I thought it was,' I maintained. Then he made his first slip. He had either forgotten his ostensible reason for summoning me, or omitted to devise one; but when, after a pause, he asked me for some irrelevant or useless information, he knew that I knew why I had been sent for. Peace reigned until he returned to work at 11.00 pm. From then until 2.00 am he had only two callers, of whom the second was James Stewart, the Chief Whip, to tell him how the day had gone in the House of Commons. Naturally I was given the full treatment, and I remained silently mulish. I do not know what the Chief Whip said, but even bed-time was different. Normally the Private Secretary stood in the PM's bedroom while he stripped, scratched himself between the shoulder blades with a long handled hairbrush, and put on his sleeping garment—a vest of approximately the length of the miniest of mini-dresses. An interval while he went to the bathroom, then into bed and lights out. This was often one of the chattiest times of the day, when tomorrow's programme was discussed, ideas would flow, points for the Cabinet were noted down, and so on. On this night the whole ritual was performed in morose silence. As always I waited for ten minutes at my desk, as there were often final late-night thoughts. Sure enough, the bell rang, and would I come in.

The light was on, which was unusual.

'What am I doing tomorrow?'

'There is a Cabinet at eleven, and you have guests for lunch. You promised the House a statement on the progress of the war in Italy.'

'Oh, yes. Remind me in the morning to prepare something for the statement. I find that if I don't have something on paper I am inclined to run on a bit. Goodnight, John.' A seraphic grin.

'Goodnight, sir.' Lights out and peace. It had been a long day.

This episode illustrates three points. After his first outburst of annoyance that I—that anyone—should have criticised his speech, the rest of the day was spent in a probing exercise. My criticism might have been a hasty judgement: would I stick to it? By now he was doubtful. If I insisted under heavy pressure that he had gone on too long, then he probably had. Secondly, if I caved in during the afternoon or evening he would never have known whether I had had genuine second thoughts or was yielding to superior force—in which case I would have been useless as a Private Secretary. Thirdly, having satisfied himself that I was right, he gave way gracefully, humorously and without any rancour at all. How could you help loving a man like that?

On other occasions I had to be almost a peacemaker or fellow-conspirator. On 16 February 1943 the Prime Minister fell ill with pneumonia. His doctor, Lord Moran, commented in his book, 'It was one of Winston's foibles to pretend that he never allowed any of his illnesses to interfere with his work, though he admits that on this occasion the flow of his minutes dried up for a week.'

The intercom bell. I was on duty. 'John, will you come in.' The Prime Minister was sitting up in bed, looking sulky. Lord Moran was up against the opposite wall, trying to look at ease and master of the situation, and giving the impression of trying to stop a very aggressive terrier from nipping his shins. A row of some magnitude was evidently in progress.

Lord Moran had told the PM that he would have to issue a bulletin, and Mr Churchill had instantly demanded to see it. As Moran had not yet drafted it he was at a disadvantage so he sat down with pencil and paper and wrote it out. The Prime Minister said that it was an alarmist statement which would cause confusion and despondency and was in any case untrue. He would write an accurate one himself. He thereupon sent for his shorthand typist and dictated his own bulletin. On seeing it in type he was hugely pleased with his first effort in a new genre, but Moran said it was inaccurate and misleading and he could not possibly sign it. Temper, obstinacy and deadlock.

All this was explained to me by the Prime Minister with muted interjections by his physician. Briefly, I was to write the bulletin. In theory there was no major problem. It was for the doctor to say what was the matter with his patient and for the Prime Minister to pronounce on the political implications of the way his doctor presented it. It is one of the oddities of the language that 'She was poor but she was honest' means one thing whereas 'She was honest but she was poor' means another. So I tried reversing the phrases in Lord Moran's bulletin, in the hope that the substance would remain the same but that the nuance could meet the Prime Minister's objection. It worked, and after some minor negotiations on drafting and medical niceties the next day's papers announced: 'The Prime Minister has had a comfortable day. There is a small area of inflammation in one lung, but the fever is lower, and his general condition is not unsatisfactory.' At any rate it was better than the original, which said in effect that while his fever was lower and his general condition was not unsatisfactory there was a small area of inflammation . . .

A few days later I was involved in a bizarre episode. I was the Private Secretary on duty one morning when the Prime Minister decided that he would only deal with the essentials in his box. I went through it with him and found that nearly everything could either be deferred or dealt with simply, without having to bother him over much. There was, however, the tiresome folder of things requiring his signature. At that time a number of citizens of the United States and the Dominions wished to make their personal contribution to the British war effort, which they did by cheques made out to Winston Churchill. This meant that he had to sign them on the back. There was also a steady flow of photographs of himself that he had to sign for deserving individuals or institutions. There must have been ten or a dozen cheques and photographs to sign. Churchill looked at them with some gloom and then said, 'Sign these for me.' I gulped.

'You mean, sir, that I am to forge your signature?'

'Yes, can you? Let me see.'

'May I borrow your pen? The one you always use?' He scrutinised the sample. 'Hm Hm Hm Hm. All right, do them.' So I forged the Prime Minister's signature on cheques and photographs. I was privately rather proud of my rendering of his signature, but I never thought I should have to use my hidden talent before his very eyes. Then there remained the biggest challenge of all. At the bottom of the folder, there was a letter for his signature to, of all people, the Archbishop of Canterbury. Churchill always did the 'My dear Archbishop' and the 'Yours very sincerely' in manuscript, so I did too. I never pretended to be able to forge more than his signature, so if His Grace was ever puzzled by the calligraphy of this particular letter I hope he attributed it to the Prime Minister's illness; in a sense, he would have been right. Mr Churchill found it inordinately funny.

Winston Churchill once gave me a great example of loyalty to his staff. In February 1941, not long after Herbert Morrison had become Home Secretary and Minister of Home Security, I detected the beginning of a trend in the correspondence addressed to the Prime Minister by members of the general public. A number of possible sympathisers with Germany and Italy had been detained without trial under Defence Regulation 18B, many of them individuals of foreign origin who had come to the United Kingdom before the war. After the stories of the Fifth Column and the role it played in Hitler's conquest of Europe, we were rightly taking no chances.

But early in 1941 letters began to appear from relatives and friends of internees suggesting that the Home Office was being needlessly restrictive, if not harsh, in its attitude to visits, correspondence, and so on, seeing that the detainees were not prisoners and nothing had been charged against them. As the volume of complaints grew, and the letters in themselves seemed to be reasonable and showed no sign of central direction or an organised campaign, I did what was normal in such cases. I wrote a short note to the PM giving the facts, attached a couple of specimen letters and ended, as was usual, to save time and trouble, 'I submit a draft minute which, if you agree, you might wish to send to Mr Morrison.' In substance this outlined the facts of the correspondence and said that since 18B was a contentious matter, the Home Secretary might like to reassure himself that officials somewhere down the line were not being needlessly strict. The PM studied my minute and approved the draft. He then initialled the fair copy which was despatched through the normal office machinery to the Home Secretary.

The next day two things happened. A furious handwritten note to the PM arrived from Mr Morrison, saying that he was very willing to serve as his Home Secretary but he was not going to be told by Junior Private Secretaries at Number Ten how to manage his Department. At the same time, by way of clarification, his Principal Private Secretary rang me up, sounding slightly smug, and said, 'I put the PM's minute about detainees in to the Home Secretary . . . [pause] . . . with your minute behind it.' I simply, if sourly, thanked him for his courtesy and went to investigate. It was quite simple. There was a 'flu epidemic; the infallible lady who was responsible for seeing that such things left Number Ten in proper form had been stricken and this one had slipped out. I waited for the bang. When it came, it was twofold, terse and typical. The substance (not textual) was : -

Mr Peck,
    When you advise me to address my Ministers on matters of public concern, you should at least take the trouble to ensure that the minutes are despatched in proper form and that documents which are internal to Private Office are not released for scrutiny by others.
    WSC

Home Secretary,
    I regret that through an error in my Private Office my minute to you concerning the treatment of detainees was despatched with my Private Secretary's recommendation to me still attached.
    This does not mean that I do not fully endorse the views expressed by my Private Secretary. Pray let a searching enquiry be made and let me have a full report on this subject which could have grave political consequences.
    WSC

I do not know what the Private Secretary in the Home Office was hoping to achieve, but he did himself no good. For my part, the receipt of a blast for something which, while technically my fault, was known to all as a lapse somewhere in the machine, was more than offset by the knowledge that we had a master who would never let his staff down.

The end of the war brought two telephone conversations, after which I ceased to be surprised at anything. During the week-end of 27-30 April 1945 I was on duty at Chequers. On the Sunday night we had finally got the PM off to bed at 3.00 am. I had just fallen into a deep sleep when my bedside telephone rang. An apologetic telephonist put through an even more apologetic Colonel Gault, the Military Assistant to General Eisenhower, speaking from his headquarters in Reims.

'John, is that you? Sorry to bother you at this hour, but the

General told me to ask you if the war is over.'

'I beg your pardon?'

'Seriously, we've got a press message here which says quite clearly that it's all over. If so, nobody has told the General and he thought you would be the most likely to know at your end.'

'Well if it has ended, nobody has told the Prime Minister either.'

'So you think we had better carry on?'

'Yes, I think so. I'll let you know if there are any developments here.'

'Many thanks. So I can tell the General to go on with the war?'

'Yes.'

'Goodnight. Sorry to bother you.'

'Not a bit. Goodnight.'

So I went back to sleep, and the war went on.

Not many days later the war in Europe was really over, but not before I was involved in yet another unusual telephone conversation. The instrument of total unconditional surrender of Germany was signed in the small hours of 7 May, and all hostilities were to cease the following midnight. The British and American Governments were accordingly all set to declare 8 May VE Day. But on the seventh the Russians demanded that it should be postponed until 9 May. The PM was all for declaring the end of the war in Europe as soon as possible, and was not inclined to postpone it for the sake of what had by now become a pretty threadbare allied solidarity with the Russians. An instant decision was required which entailed telephoning to President Truman. But because the line to Washington was usually bad and Churchill could not hear well on the telephone he told me to ring President Truman and talk to him myself. When the call came through, not unnaturally the President of the United States wished to delegate his end of the conversation so his aide, Admiral Leahy, took the call.

'The Prime Minister wants to announce the end of the war tomorrow. The Russians want to go on until the ninth. On balance he is inclined to go ahead and end it on the eighth.'

'We want to end it too.'

'Right, so we will both end it tomorrow.'

'Yes. Fine. OK.'
'Goodbye.'
'Goodbye.'

And that is how Britain and America came to celebrate VE Day on 8 May, and the USSR on the ninth.

Meanwhile unsettling things were happening in my life. The elderly press officer at Number Ten retired and was not replaced. I was appointed, still as a Private Secretary, to be the link man between the PM and the parliamentary press correspondents. Then Lord Beaverbrook began to take an interest in me, and I detected the first whiff of a carrot luring me towards Fleet Street; an interest also in Mariska, to whom he gave a length of most magnificent Damascus brocade which he had made up into an evening dress by a leading couturier. He invited us to a fabulous weekend at his country house, and until the end of the war kept us supplied with fresh vegetables from his garden. Then the war ended and we vanished from his life. Six weeks later Leslie Rowan (the Principal Private Secretary) and I flew with Winston Churchill to the Potsdam Conference (where I shook hands with Stalin—cold and clammy like a fish on a slab); flew back to England for the election results and the fall of the Churchill government; and back to Potsdam forty-eight hours later as Private Secretaries to the new Labour Prime Minister, Clement Attlee. Thus is our public service non-political.

I never settled down with Attlee. After some animated and at times farcical negotiations between the Treasury and the Foreign Office I was allowed to transfer to the Diplomatic Service. The contrast with Winston Churchill was too great. He had been a very loyal and devoted Deputy Prime Minister to Churchill, an efficient chairman of committees—including the Cabinet itself when the PM was away—and an astute politician who managed to hold the always centrifugal Labour Party together. Those who worked for him for a long time spoke of him with affection. But to me he was grey and drab and utterly self-effacing, with no concern for his own or other people's comfort and well-being. (One bitterly cold day down at Chequers I found him shivering in his study. I asked him if he didn't want a fire. Yes, he said, but he didn't know how to get it done. So I rang the bell and a servant came to lay and light a fire.) I think that history will rank him more highly than did many of his contemporaries.

But the Churchill family kept in touch with us. In the winter of 1946, when the old man was out of office, he lived in Hyde Park Gate. One day Mariska and I were invited to bring Michael, then almost five years old, to a children's tea party. It was a wonderful party, but after tea Michael had vanished. I started to search. Through the half-open door of Churchill's study I saw a bright fire burning in the hearth and two large armchairs flanking the hearthrug. Churchill sat leaning back in one, hands in pockets, legs stretched out before him, and in the other sat Michael, in the identical pose except that his little legs scarcely cleared the seat of the chair. The two were in earnest conversation, discussing sea warfare, or the use of artillery, or some other matter of mutual interest. Churchill's deafness, which was always selective, was not troubling him. I did not interrupt their heart-to-heart, man-to-man chat. Michael sauntered along later to rejoin the party. He remembers enough of the occasion to be able to tell his grandchildren when the time comes.

I joined the Foreign Service in March 1946, after nine-and-a-half years in the Civil Service, nine of them as an Assistant Private Secretary. I had served three First Lords of the Admiralty, a Minister for the Coordination of Defence, and two Prime Ministers. Now we could start all over again.

7

(i) Holland

I came into the Foreign Service as a First Secretary, three rungs up the diplomatic ladder, and after a year in the newly-formed United Nations Department was given my first overseas post. I was sent to Holland in July 1947 to be Head of Chancery at the Embassy in The Hague. Not until fifteen years later did I serve again in an orthodox Embassy accredited to a foreign state, and that was as Ambassador to Senegal and Mauritania, in the newly-independent ex-French West Africa. In between, I had a series of posts which by traditional standards were decidedly off-beat and landed me in some odd situations. In retrospect the only consistent strand of experience running through a multi-coloured tapestry was the relevance of so much of it as a preparation for Dublin.

The Head of Chancery holds the key post in an Embassy. He has direct access to the Ambassador, to whom he is responsible for coordinating the work of the various departments or sections—political, commercial, information, consular, passports. He is answerable for the administration, accounts, security, morale and welfare of the Embassy (morale and welfare, apart from their intrinsic importance, having important security implications). The wife of the Head of Chancery obviously has an important part to play, too. Mariska was as unknown a newcomer to the Service as I was; but it was soon obvious that she was made for it, and played her part with a joyous and dedicated zest that often exhausted her but never deserted her until the day we left Dublin. She spoke fluent German but had been warned never to use it; at best anyone addressed in German would simply not hear it and turn away.

So she went straight to the Berlitz school for lessons, and as often as possible to a cinema showing continuous newsreels, until she could follow the commentary and absorb the sound and rhythm of the language. In no time at all she was coping happily in the kitchen and in shops, and before long she was speaking Dutch at parties with anyone having problems with English. I was less industrious and less successful.

Holland, hard-working, solid traditional Holland, gave us our first eye-opener. It was my first experience of a country in which religious differences were profound and yet successfully overcome. The political parties, trade unions, press and broadcasting were all divided on a religious basis—Catholic, Protestant and Socialist (non-sectarian). Even the smallest village had its two churches, or three if the Lutherans and Calvinists each had one. The sects all seemed to tolerate each other and work happily together for the common good. The rigour with which religious principles were applied to everyday life varied with the individual.

If comparisons have to be made, it is simply not true to say that the Dutch were less sincere and more casual than others about their religion. An incident towards the end of the war illustrates this. The agricultural island of Walcheren had been flooded, during the allied advance, to a depth of three or four feet. Families had to retreat to the first floor of their farmhouses and be rescued by Marines in small boats splashing in through their front doors. One young officer engaged on this errand of mercy was met by a patriarchal figure at the top of the stairs clutching a bible and refusing to be evacuated because 'it is written : thou shalt love the land the Lord thy God giveth thee'. Without hesitation the rescue party retired to find the regimental padre and began again. This time the padre, through an interpreter, shouted up a counter-quotation. Texts were bandied up and down for some time until the padre found in a minor prophet what was evidently the clincher. The old man was silent for a while and then said quietly, 'Yes. It is the Lord's will. Let us go.'

The Dutch had their share of selective puritanism and of religious jokes as well. We lived in a suburb of the Hague called Wassenaar. A road led across the dunes to a point on the beach called Wassenaase Slag. This was no different from any other part of the sands that extended as far as the eye could see in either direction, except for two distinctive features for which we were indebted to our mayor, a charming man with thirteen children. The first was the ingenious adaption of a German gun position to serve as a police post. On this there perched throughout the summer days a lady in a white overall, universally known as Ogpu Annie. One of her tasks was to ensure that on Wassenaar beach, which extended for some hundred yards in either direction, no lady was seen wearing a two-piece bathing suit. (This was before the bikini was invented, and at worst a few inches of midriff were involved.) In vain the Embassy ladies asked Annie which of the two pieces they should discard, or suggested tattooing 'CD' on their tummies. With the aid of powerful binoculars, an amazing turn of speed, a robust voice and a strong belief in her own authority Annie ensured that never a navel was seen on her beach. Her other duty related to demarcation lines. The beach was divided into two parts by three rows of coloured posts running down to the water—a black row in the middle, a yellow row at one end and a red at the other. Two notices proclaimed their purpose:

BETWEEN THE BLACK AND YELLOW POLES IT IS FORBIDDEN FOR A MAN TO FIND HIMSELF IN A SWIMSUIT. BETWEEN THE BLACK AND RED POLES IT IS STRICTLY FORBIDDEN FOR A WOMAN TO FIND HERSELF IN A SWIMSUIT.

However, Annie or somebody made a dreadful discovery. Along the central row of posts it was possible and legal for a boy and a girl to sit and hold hands. So on either side of the black poles a strip a few yards wide was marked out by two rows of mauve poles and declared a cordon sanitaire by the one forbidding instruction:

DOORLOPEN—CROSS AT THE DOUBLE.

These regulations were probably more helpful to the conscience of the legislators than the morals of the public. It was only a few minutes' walk to the end of the corral. Beyond it lay the vast sweep of the unpatrolled and uninhibited dunes.

The tale was told of a little town further up the coast with a progressive council which passed a decree permitting mixed bathing. One hot day shortly afterwards the oldest member of the council walked over the dunes to see this great sight, and to his horror saw men and women bathing together. He rushed back and called an emergency meeting of the council to discuss the outrage. Gently they reminded him of their recent decree on mixed bathing. 'But I would never have agreed to this. I understood that we were allowing Catholics and Protestants to bathe together.'

Frivolous, admittedly, but a genuine aspect of Dutch life in 1947. It was not until many years later, when I became involved in Irish affairs, that I was able to appreciate fully the significance of the Dutch example. Catholics, Calvinists, Puritans, Prince William of Orange, all left their clearly marked imprint on the Netherlands and Northern Ireland. And yet these common elements have yielded such divergent results that anyone concerned with Northern Ireland can only regard the political and religious maturity of the Dutch with envy and with shame. The key must be sought among the other forces at work in Irish history. Loyalty, many-sided, is not a many-splendoured thing.

In the strenuous life we were leading nobody knew that in 1944 Mariska's suprarenal glands had almost entirely failed under the stresses and strains of the first five years of the war, and that she had been kept going ever since by a six-monthly implantation of adrenalin. In this condition her doctor had put a veto on any more children. But as she seemed to be thriving in the hurly-burly of diplomatic life the ban seemed silly, and in March 1950 she told me she was expecting a baby in August. We should by then have been in Holland for three years and thus due for a transfer.

The Foreign Office unfortunately got their timing all wrong and after valiant efforts on our behalf by the Ambassador we were posted back to London far too soon after Mariska had had a difficult confinement and produced our second son, Nicholas. Meanwhile a minor miracle, as it seemed to me, had happened. The medical tests showed that during Mariska's pregnancy the unborn baby was making enough adrenalin for

D

two. Her own suprarenal glands, thus stimulated, resumed their own responsibilities and from that day to this have depended on no outside aid. This may be a common phenomenon, but for myself I have never heard of any other example of filial piety finding practical expression in the prenatal state.

Young men and women join the Diplomatic Service knowing that they are liable to be posted anywhere in the world; but they cannot foresee all the painful decisions that they will have to take. The Foreign Office does all in its power to be humane, but the nomadic life is bound to be hard on the children. Michael was six years old when we were sent to Holland. We were young and enthusiastic about our new career, and there was a lively social and diplomatic life in The Hague. We explained that it was part of our job to meet new people, and Michael seemed to like the young Irish girl whom we had brought to look after him. But one evening, as we were kissing him good-night before going out to yet another dinner or reception, he said without any trace of irony but in all sad innocence, 'Mummy, when you have got to know everybody in Holland, will you be able to stay at home with me?'

Nine years later in New York, his brother made his own illuminating comment on the nomadic life. At the age of six he was exposed to television for the first time, and became addicted to a children's programme in the course of which a man dressed as a New York cop came round with a tin funnel on the end of a hosepipe and asked each child his or her name and a few other questions. We got Nicholas an invitation to the show, and while his governess took him to the studio his doting parents sat by the TV set to watch their little ewe lamb perform. The Cop came round.

'And what's your name?'

'Nicholas Peck.' The English accent could not be missed.

'Hi Nicholas, where are you from?' A long pause.

'I forget.'

'Oh, well.' The cop moved on. Later, at home, in my mortification :

'Nicholas, did you enjoy it?'

'Oh yes, Daddy.'

'Tell me, when that cop asked you where you were from,

why did you say you forgot?' It came in one breathless and revealing sentence.

'Well, Daddy, I didn't know whether to say from Holland because I was born there, or from London because that's where we lived, or Egypt where we went to, or Cyprus where we came from to here, or East End Avenue where we live now, so it was easier to say I forgot.'

'All right, you win.'

So home has to be where you happen to be at the time, and the pains and the problems of education and adolescence have to be coped with somehow. But for the time being, when we were transferred with our brand-new Nicholas from Holland to London, home was really to be our little house in Chelsea.

Back in the Foreign Office I was posted first as Assistant and then as Head of Information Research Department, and thus became, at thirty-eight, one of the youngest Counsellors in the Service.

This Department, having world-wide interests, gave me world-wide perspectives which later made me very receptive to a precept of that astute philosopher-politician Leopold Sedar Senghor, the President of Senegal: 'When a problem is insoluble, start by placing it in a broader context'—advice which is as valid for Ireland today as it was for West Africa fifteen years ago.

(ii) The Middle East

Early in 1954 I was given an extraordinary job with the compact title of 'Head of the Political Division of the British Middle East Office and Political Adviser to the Commanders in Chief Middle East'. The title just about describes the job. The accommodation scarcely matched this implied but illusory grandeur. My office was a corrugated hut in the Egyptian desert, whose dust spread in a not so fine film across my desk. Flies, with an expertise gained from long practice, flew in steady lines through the beaded screen intended to exclude them; finding all the parking space taken on the filthy fly paper hung from the ceiling, they settled on the back of my neck and my bare fore-arms like guilty motorists dodging the meterman. The mid-day shade temperature remained normal, 98.4 degrees, for six weeks on end. Then it got a bit feverish.

There was no air-conditioning. This was part of General Head-quarters, Middle East Land Forces, beside the village of Fayid on the Great Bitter Lake in the Suez Canal Zone of Egypt. Here Mariska and I lived as the guests of the Army, from whom we received all possible kindness and consideration.

Life was hard but it had its moments. My own status was odd enough anyway. As a civilian, I had to be integrated into GHQ and given a military rank, and in all matters of housing and administration I had to be treated as an Army Officer, Married. The military member of an inter-service committee under my chairmanship was a Brigadier, and I had to trump him. It was therefore decided that I was With but Below the Major-Generals, as distinct from With but Above the Brig-adiers. Where the committee was concerned the distinction was metaphysical, particularly after the Brigadier was replaced by a Colonel. But on the physical plane it was important. The furnishing and equipment of Quarters, Officers, Married, was carefully graded according to rank, and it meant that I quali-fied for bedside mats, or an extra lamp, or something. We made one interesting discovery, academic in our exalted posi-tion. It had been decreed by the War Office that for the quarters of an Officer, Married, up to and including the rank of Lieutenant Colonel, the bedroom furniture should include one double bed; for officers of the rank of Colonel and upwards, two single beds. I have always wanted to meet a member of the Army Council present at the meeting when it was decided where to draw the line.

During the summer of 1954 we were all preparing to evacuate the Suez Canal Zone and move to Cyprus. Mariska and I had already paid a house-hunting visit to Nicosia and had found an ultra-modern house, curiously attractive in its ugliness, on the outskirts of the town. We could scarcely have found anything less appropriate to the situation which devel-oped when we arrived, since it was made almost entirely of glass.

We had first to leave our army house in Fayid. This entailed a marching-out inspection. On a very hot afternoon three large sergeants came and did the inventory with Mariska and me. The kitchen and bathroom block was separate from the main bungalow, and because the alphabet is an inflexible instrument we trudged for miles hunting for Baskets, fish, frying, Baskets, paper waste, Baskets, linen, soiled, Mats, bath, Mats, table, etc. We finally emerged exhausted but triumphant, and I still treasure my copy of the 'Army Form to be Prepared in Triplicate', entitled

BARRACK DAMAGES

Requisition and Estimate of Repairs	£	s	d
Room 2 Replace 1 Standard Lamp Holder	1	10½	
Room 3 Replace 1 Broken Window		2	6

I acknowledge that the repairs detailed herein have become necessary in consequence of neglect or wilfulness by the unit under my command.
Sd. Officer Commanding . . . John Peck

I added a nominal roll of the unit under my command, viz.
Private Michael Peck, aged 13
Private Nicholas Peck, aged 4

Then we left for Cyprus. We arrived in the wake of fierce rioting by the Greek Cypriots against the British, who had blocked an attempt by the Greek Government to have Cyprus debated in the General Assembly of the United Nations on the grounds that, Cyprus being a colony, its affairs were a domestic matter outside the UN's jurisdiction. A few weeks later came the discovery of extensive arms smuggling by sea from Greece. On 31 March the first bombs went off and blew a large hole in the Nicosia barracks which housed GHQ.

The smuggling and storing of arms, and the manufacture of hand-grenades (the Cypriots' favourite weapon) was island-wide. Priests, school teachers, parents, all disseminated the hate-propaganda being poured out by Athens radio. The plumbers and garage mechanics made the bombs, young men on bicycles threw them into cafés and bars, barracks, and private homes. Because it was not intensive, the risk of any one person or family being killed or injured was at first not large—certainly not large enough to justify abnormal or alarmist security measures. The unrest and violence in Cyprus were tackled in the time-honoured way : more money to raise material standards, an offer of a more liberal constitution at a later date, more police to maintain law and order, and, in the words of the then Prime Minister, Mr Anthony Eden, 'We arranged to strengthen the security and intelligence departments of the Government of Cyprus. These were bearing a dangerous burden and needed the reinforcement of experienced officers from other colonies and from Britain.'

In August I watched the first contingent of paratroops landing in Famagusta to help maintain law and order. But to the newcomer to Cyprus it was quite obvious that whatever the situation there might be, it was not a colonial situation; it was one aspect of an age-old dispute between Greece and Turkey which by an accident of history was being fought out on British territory. In 1955 a new Governor was sent to Cyprus, Field-Marshal Sir John Harding. A realist with long experience and broad vision, he instantly placed Cyprus in its true Mediterranean context and was prepared to apply the first principle of political warfare and civil disturbance: the security situation can never be restored by security measures alone, and any attempt to do so without tackling the root causes, which are political, will probably make them worse.

That Christmas, Mariska and I were doing our shopping in Nicosia. Ledra Street was crowded. Suddenly there was a volley of shots. Everybody scattered except ourselves, two British soldiers lying at our feet, and two passers-by—a doctor and an old English lady. The soldier at my feet died instantly. Mariska helped carry the other, streaming blood, into a nearby shop and the police and ambulance were summoned. He had only minor flesh wounds. The gunmen had vanished. Later the police rounded up a number of leaders of the terrorist organisation EOKA and the witnesses were summoned to an identification parade, but recognised none of them. Afterwards I demanded to see the Commissioner of Police, who had come under contract to the Cyprus Government from, I think, the former Palestine Police.

'Well, we had a good look at your EOKA men, but none of them did it.'

'A pity.'

'I suppose you realise the EOKA had a good look at us, so they can now recognise the key witnesses.'

'Oh, mm, well, yes . . .'

'So what do you advise?'

'You had better keep clear of the middle of town.'

'That's all very well for us—we're leaving soon—but what about the others?'

'Oh, well, we shall have to think about that.'

The episode did not increase our confidence in the local police administration. But we had already been told we were on the move.

(iii) New York

Middle East to Midtown Manhattan, from being Political Adviser to the military to becoming Director General of the British Information Services in America is an abrupt but not abnormal transition in the Diplomatic Service. But the Suez Canal and Cyprus were still to haunt my working life. As Director General I was technically part of an orthodox Embassy, the British Embassy in Washington. However, Washington was a handy 220 miles away, and while we got our general policy direction from the Embassy and our information, trade promotion and reference material from London, I was in practice very much out on my own. The two burning issues during my time there were the Suez affair and Cyprus, both of which I probably knew more about than anyone in the Embassy, since I had just come from the Middle East. Conveniently, and, I hope, wisely, they gave me a pretty free hand.

We had a hard time settling in. Nicholas was five-and-a-half and we had brought a superb governess for him from London. We were installed in a suite in a midtown-hotel at Foreign Office expense. There was, however, the problem of finding a flat. We were given a rent limit, and Mariska looked at forty-four flats, all hopelessly unsuitable, until she found the ideal apartment—but it was above the rent ceiling. The Embassy Administration firmly said no, and were quite happy to keep us at vastly greater expense while the hopeless hunt went on. Finally I exploded, and requested the Embassy to book three single passages back to England and inform the Ambassador that since that was evidently what was wanted I should live in New York as a bachelor. It only took the Embassy two days to get permission from the Foreign Office for us to to have the flat. It proved ideal.

It was immediately obvious that there were going to be problems in British Information Services. We succeeded a brilliant and wealthy couple, perfectly equipped in every way to take on New York on its own terms, and very much at home in café society. Mariska and I had neither the private means nor the aptitude to play any such role, and the allowance given us by the Foreign Office to enable us to carry out our duties effectively guaranteed that we should need to play the hand very differently.

Then I discovered that there was an influential body of British press correspondents in New York who thought it wrong that BIS should be directed by a career diplomat, who could be assumed to know nothing of the business he was directing, instead of by a pressman. The *Daily Telegraph* wrote :

> British foreheads in the Middle East have been puckered over the appointment of the new head of British Information Services in New York. The individual singled out for this post is Mr John Peck, recently acting as chief of the British Middle East Office. He looks like being something of a misfit. He has only been to the US twice—for a week each time—and has little or no knowledge of the press. Yet there is no tougher assignment of its kind. Mr Peck will head an organisation which costs nearly a million dollars a year in hard currency. Several of his predecessors in New York have failed signally. I gather however that there is an idea in the Foreign Office that, as one of Sir Winston Churchill's assistant private secretaries during the war, he may get a flying start with the American press.

A gossip writer in *World's Press News* wrote : '[my predecessor], who is handsome, energetic and sophisticated, had just about mastered his job in this complex country of forty-eight states when he is transferred. He has been particularly successful in the society circuit among the publishers and such hostesses as Elsa Maxwell and Margaret Case. His successor is John Peck of whom I know little . . .'

There did not seem to be anything to do about my manifest shortcomings except get on with the job. And I had just received the following letter :

Aitken House,
Naussau,
Bahamas
26th December, 1955

Dear Peck,

I see that you have become head of British Information Services in New York.

I don't believe in these organisations that are scattered all over the world, and particularly in foreign countries. But, if I may say so without offence, I do believe in you.

So if there is anything I can do to help you, be sure that you will have my personal support.

And with good regards, and wishing you great success in your tasks,

I am,
Yours ever,
BEAVERBROOK

I showed this letter to one or two correspondents, and reminisced a little about my days with Winston Churchill and the lobby correspondents at 10 Downing Street. The *Daily Mail* correspondent soon felt able to write : 'The best export Britain has sent for a long time is Mr John Peck, new chief of the British Information Services, New York . . .' The *New Yorker* gave us a long and very friendly write up in 'Talk of the Town'. We persuaded people to accept us as they found us; and we settled in happily among them.

The Americans proved to be a nation of masochists with an incurable urge to listen to speeches, mine included. Thus it was that in the spring of 1956 I committed myself to the English Speaking Union to a lecture tour in the Middle West at the end of November, to talk about the Middle East, an easy and unprovocative subject that I knew intimately. Unfortunately at the beginning of November, after two days of public confrontation in the Security Council between Britain and France on one side and the United States on the other, we attacked Egypt.

BIS New York existed in order to present the British point of view to the American public and obtain American support for British policies. There were two obstacles to the smooth working of the machine at the moment when it was most needed. London presented a picture of a nation, a parliament, a Foreign Office and a Central Office of Information taken unawares and caught unprepared to present a united and convincing case to the world. Washington was worse. We had no Ambassador, as Sir Roger Makins had retired and his successor, Sir Harold Caccia, was out of contact in mid-Atlantic on his way to take up his new post. Foster Dulles, the State Department, and the US administration as a whole had risen in their wrath and more or less ostracised the Embassy staff. The response to my attempts to obtain instructions in Washington on how to handle the situation in New York was unusually precise: we are in a state of virtual siege; do nothing but keep your heads down until the storm has blown over; there is nothing that can be done.

I quietly disobeyed orders. The British and French governments were not insane, and had a rational basis for their action. There was a case to put, and American commentators and leader-writers ought to hear it. Sir Peirson Dixon and the British delegation at the United Nations were battling against fearful odds and had to be helped somehow. We did what we could. But the whole Suez affair poses a question that I have often been asked, and have more often had to ask myself, about personal integrity in information work. Could I honestly and decently propagate the British viewpoint about Suez if I did not myself believe that it was right? The answer is no, I could not. I did not, I did not have to, and if I had simply been a propagandist for Her Majesty's Government I would only have made matters worse. And with the Embassy in Washington apparently gone to ground and with BIS under orders to do the same, I could not have done so in any case.

Instead, I took an impersonal attitude as 'the man from the Middle East': 'The facts on the spot are such and such, British, French, American, NATO interests are so and so. I hope they are not seriously in dispute. From this evidence the British and French drew their conclusions, and acted accordingly. The American administration evidently thinks our action mistaken. But will you please tell me what you would have done in our shoes? The likely consequences of American policy are so and so. The responsibility is now yours. What do you propose to do about it?'

I do not think this is dishonest. And even if I had been an enthusiastic supporter of Anthony Eden's policy, I believe that in the prevailing climate this would still have been the right way to present the case.

But what about my lecture tour? I had committed myself to the English Speaking Union six months previously. Its subject matter which seemed so easy and innocent at the time had suddenly become topical and tense. I was due to set out on 25 November; to cancel would be discourteous and cowardly, and yet I was virtually under orders to do so. Luckily the Foreign Secretary, Mr Selwyn Lloyd, and the newly arrived Ambassador, Sir Harold Caccia, were in New York and together called upon me in BIS. I explained my problem.

'What do you want to do yourself?'

'I want to go and have a try.'

'All right, but don't get hurt.'

So with their joint blessing, I went to Pittsburg, Columbus, Louisville, Cincinnati, Indianapolis, Little Rock, St Louis, Kansas City, Omaha, Des Moines, Chicago and Milwaukee, returning to New York seventeen days later, on 13 December. By that time I had made seventeen public speeches, given thirteen informal talks to groups and seminars, sixteen radio or TV interviews, and sixteen press interviews, in twelve cities in eleven states, from Ohio to Nebraska and from Arkansas to Wisconsin.

I was amazed, and admittedly relieved, by the almost total absence of hostility. University audiences were naturally the most difficult, and the front rows in the auditorium always seemed solid with Arab students. But the prevailing attitude was curiosity: the British seem to have done something very wrong but we believe that they are neither wicked nor foolish and we just want to know why they did it. The moral hysterics of Washington were simply not reflected in the Middle West.

I had one brush with disaster. In St Louis, Missouri, the English Speaking Union organised a reception followed by a dinner with plenty to drink at both, after which I had to speak. There were about a hundred and fifty people seated round circular tables, and the usual high table on its dais. Having no script I could survey the audience as I spoke, and my eye lit on a man some two rows back who seemed eager for my talk to end. Almost before the chairman had invited questions he was on his feet and into the attack. It was immediately evident that he was very angry and very Irish. His question became more and more convoluted. His anger rose, waves of embarrassment surged round the room, and the chairman looked despairingly at me. I rose to my feet.

'Mr Chairman,' I said, 'I think our friend here wants to ask me this : Would it not be reasonable to suppose that the bloody British are treating the poor downtrodden Egyptians just like they have always treated the poor downtrodden Irish?' The audience held their breath. Up he jumped again.

'God bless you, my boy. I couldn't have phrased it better meself. That's just what I was asking you.' I rose.

'I thought so, Mr Chairman. The answer is no, sir.' It seemed to take an age for the laughter to subside. The Irishman sat beaming. We caught each other's eye at intervals as the questions wore on, but the evening had been made and no serious hostility would have been possible. At last the chairman called the final question, and a gloomy female somewhere at the back asked, 'Is not all this trouble caused by the shade of Queen Victoria still pacing about the corridors of the Foreign Office?' I was exhausted.

'Certainly not,' I snapped back, 'it's caused by the ghost of George the Third still haunting the State Department.' Oh God, I thought, that's torn it. But the audience were prepared to enjoy everything and we trooped happily out into the night, my new-found Irish friend with his arm around my waist wanting me to tour the night life of St Louis, and a cautious consul shepherding me gently home to bed. It was probably just as well that Ireland lost.

In three months' time the excitement over Suez, the last British attempt to impose law and order on the grand scale, had died down, and interest focused on Cyprus. Terrorism in Cyprus had reached such a pitch that the British sent Archbishop Makarios, the head of the Greek church in Cyprus and leader of the Greek Cypriots, into a year's exile to the Seychelles. Released then on condition that he did not return to Cyprus, he went first to Athens and then on a propaganda tour in Washington and New York. This was not wholly successful. He got massive publicity, but his interviewers asked him a series of very awkward questions, his answers to which were most unconvincing. American TV is essentially fair and always offered me equal time, which I declined on condition that it was offered to the Turkish Cypriots. But many of the journalists would come to me for background information, and I would suggest that they might ask the Archbishop about one or two aspects of his policy that were not entirely clear. It is interesting now to note the point on which the Archbishop got into difficulties. His slogan had always been 'self-determination for the Cypriots'. Under pressure he said that this meant the rights of the Greek Cypriot majority to be united with Greece. When pressed to say whether the Turkish Cypriots had a right of self-determination he never succeeded in giving a satisfactory answer.

The manager of the hotel where the Archbishop was going to stay in New York rang me up to say he had a very delicate problem. He did not want to create any difficulties for BIS to whom he was well disposed; but his hotel had two flagpoles and an invariable practice of flying the Stars and Stripes from one and the national flag of any visiting VIP on the other. Was I going to raise hell?

'On the contrary. I like the idea.'

'That's mighty generous. Sure you don't mind?'

'I'll go further: promise to do it?'

'Well, what do you know? Sure I'll promise.'

'Fine—but have a look at his passport: he's a British subject and the Cypriot flag is the Union Jack.'

He kept his promise.

And I believe the Greek faction were not over-pleased, which was silly, because there were propaganda points to be made either way.

We may conceivably have helped Makarios along the road from Greek nationalism to the discovery of a Cypriot national identity, precarious but real. It was not long before Britain, Greece and Turkey, not to mention the Cypriots themselves, had agreed to the establishment of the independent sovereign Republic of Cyprus within the Commonwealth, with Makarios as President. Three months later my own official concern with

Cyprus affairs ceased when I was transferred from New York to Strasbourg. But during the four-and-a-half years of my involvement I had seen and experienced ingredients of a political warfare situation that were later to become familiar : the initial attempt to treat an international situation as if it were a domestic one; politicians dressed as priests or vice versa; violence alienating its own supporters; apparently rejected initiatives producing unexpected consequences; no final solution but a compromise only made possible by regarding the immediate situation in its wider context; and the futility of supposing that the maintenance, or the establishment, or the restoration, of law and order is a task within the power of the security forces to achieve if it is treated as an end in itself. It would be foolish to look for too many parallels between Cyprus and Northern Ireland, especially when in neither case has the end of the road been reached. Nevertheless, those concerned with one can usefully ponder on the other.

In May 1959 Winston Churchill paid his last visit to the United States. He was in his eighty-fifth year. Lord Moran, in his diary covering the previous three weeks, has six references to Churchill's low mental and physical condition and to his depression. The painful history continues in the same melancholy vein after his return. And yet, amid the misgivings of his family and with the reluctant consent of Lord Moran he set off by air for Washington on 3 May, and manifestly enjoyed himself during his stay in America. It is a good illustration of the value to be attached to Lord Moran's chronicle.

I was invited to a dinner given in honour of President Eisenhower by the Ambassador, Sir Harold Caccia, on 7 May 1959. Besides the President and Vice-President and Winston Churchill himself, the guest list included many of the admirals, generals, politicians and diplomats who had been members of the great wartime team. Everyone knew that this was the last farewell, but it was a relaxed and happy evening. After dinner there was no formality or ceremonial, and everyone from the President downwards wandered around chatting and reminiscing. One by one the guests shook hands with the old man and went out into the spring night. It was time for bed. I stood in silence and waited. 'John, will you come up with me . . .' Fifteen years dissolved, and we were back in his bedroom in the

Downing Street Annexe. I stayed with him until he was ready to put out the light, half expecting to be asked what was on the agenda for tomorrow's Cabinet. He spoke slowly but lucidly. He knew who I was and what I had been doing, and talked of his visit to New York the following day.

'Good night, John, thank you very much.'

And up to New York he flew, to stay with his oldest American friend, Bernard Baruch. Two days later I was invited to lunch with these two old gentlemen, and the following evening Mariska and I were invited to take coffee with them and then go with Winston Churchill to the airport. It was the last time we saw him.

(iv) Europe

In June 1959, Mariska and I left New York to go to Strasbourg, to a post with another pithy title, 'United Kingdom Permanent Representative to the Council of Europe and Consul General'. My briefing in the Foreign Office was short and to the point. Western European Department said, 'We have missed the bus by not joining the Common Market. Do all you can to keep things happy between us and the EEC countries, while we prepare the way for an application to join later'. Personnel Department said, 'Three times a year a large number of MPs will be coming to Strasbourg. Do all you can to show them that the Foreign Service is composed of reasonable and helpful people. Some of them may take a bit of convincing.'

It was in Strasbourg, at the Council of Europe, that Mariska and I first consciously began to think of ourselves as English-speaking Europeans. The Council of Europe had first been conceived and its statutes outlined at a great European conference in The Hague when I was there in 1948, and I still have the draft of Winston Churchill's remarkable speech exactly as he dictated it.

In view of what happened later, the structure of the Council of Europe was significant. In essence, it was very simple. Decisions of substance, if any, were taken by the Committee of Foreign Ministers by unanimous vote. In other words, each one of the eighteen members had a veto. Since any political decision had to surmount the neutral postures of Austrians and

Swedes, topics of any major consequence for Europe were automatically excluded. The normal procedure was for the Ministers, who met once every six months, to agree unanimously to refer any item which was not of the most elementary or platitudinous nature to the Committee of Ministers' Deputies, otherwise known as the Permanent Representatives, of whom I was one. We met monthly, and our normal procedure was to study each of the items referred to us and agree unanimously to set up a committee of experts to study it and make recommendations to us. An expert for this purpose usually meant a home civil servant of the department mainly concerned, or simply somebody who had read the file. This procedure brought home to me once again the lesson I had learnt in the United Nations Department fourteen years earlier. For while the Foreign Office might be Europe-minded, and anxious to show willing, it was exceptional for any department of the Home Civil Service to raise its sights above the level of the parish pump; and the Foreign Office carried even less weight in domestic discussion of international affairs than it had done fourteen years earlier. A striking exception was the Department of Education. So, plucking at what straws I could, I tried to make bricks with which to join in building the edifice of Europe.

Many of the matters we discussed were recommendations to the Committee of Ministers from the Consultative Assembly. This parliamentary body met three times a year and provided me with our busiest and most stimulating periods. Many of the friendships we then formed with MPs of all parties, not only from Britain, have survived until today. But the British MPs made less impact than they should have done, for two main reasons.

Although the Consultative Assembly, as its name implies, had no powers of compulsion, the influence of individual members in their respective national parliaments, and the authority of a report from a Committee of the Assembly, were by no means negligible. Consequently the president and rapporteur of these committees were gentlemen of considerable authority and power in Europe, and election to one of these posts was the reward for many years' dedicated service to the Assembly. The leaders of all three political parties in Britain, reckoning that most MPs were remarkably insular and ignorant of European affairs, used to appoint members to the Strasbourg delegation for only a few years, in order to expose as many of them as possible to the atmosphere of Europe, but they thereby forfeited many chances of obtaining British chairmen and rapporteurs of committees. The MPs themselves felt that by spending too long in Strasbourg they were losing their chance of being appointed to parliamentary secretaryships which would set them on the ladder of political preferment in Westminster.

Secondly, British MPs were less than helpful in their approach to the language problem. The only official languages were English and French, and there was a simultaneous interpretation via headphones from one to the other. I tried to impress on our MPs that an impassioned harangue on the theme that we were batting on a very sticky wicket, and if we did not pull our socks up we were likely to get the dirty end of the stick, would perhaps be rendered into serviceable French by the intepreter, but that this was not much help to the Scandinavians, Germans, Dutch, Austrians, Greeks and Turks whose working international language was English. I did not see why, when bewildered Danes and baffled Dutch were asking 'Put the foot in what?', I should have to go round saying, 'Cowpat, cowpat,' but I do not think I made any impression.

It was easy to laugh or be cynical about the Council of Europe. Nevertheless, it had a number of solid and practical, if unspectacular, achievements to its credit in the fields of justice, health and education. More important was its intangible influence at a time when there was a severe risk of a dangerous polarisation in Europe. Its main value was that it was the only body on which Ministers, officials and parliamentarians of the EEC and EFTA could meet and all be Europeans together; edges could be blurred, and the anomalies in the British position could be brought into focus in the broader context. I believe it succeeded.

We had various ministerial visits to Strasbourg, our most traumatic experience being with Mr Edward Heath, who was then Lord Privy Seal and the Minister charged with European affairs. He was due to make an important speech to the Assembly at 3.30 pm after a lunch given by the Secretary

General of the Council of Europe, Signor Benvenuti, at his house. The lunch party dragged along laboriously and was over before 3.00, leaving the Lord Privy Seal with some twenty minutes with nothing to do and nowhere to go. As our house was near the Assembly Mariska and I asked Mr Heath whether he would like to come to us and have a chance to look at his speech or have a few minutes rest—an offer which he gladly accepted. As we walked from the car to the front door, loud noises of jazz could be heard within. Mariska took off like a rocket, through the door, across the hall, into the drawing-room. But it was too late, and Mr Heath saw the scene in all its horror—the gramophone going full blast, an empty wine-bottle on its side on the floor, an empty glass and a crumby plate beside it, and on the sofa, prostrate and snoring, coated in mud, in the midst of his debauch slept Michael, our first-born son.

It was all very simple. A kind neighbour had a shooting lodge up in the Vosges, and had invited Michael, who was an excellent shot, to join him the previous evening for a wild boar hunt. From 3.00 am until 9.00 am Michael had been trudging in the mountains and had then returned by train and on foot to the house; where, since he knew we were out for lunch, he had taken his snack on a tray to where the gramophone was, and sleep overcame him. Nobody could be cross with him, but Mr Heath, whenever I have met him in subsequent years, has not failed to tease me about my family. In fact, the last time I heard the story was at Chequers in 1971, when Mr Heath as Prime Minister had invited Mr Brian Faulkner and Mr Lynch to join him there for talks; during lunch he gave them a graphic description of his visit to the Peck household in Strasbourg.

I left Strasbourg in the summer of 1962, to be promoted and sent to Dakar as Ambassador to Senegal and Mauritania. It was hard to think of anything concrete that had been achieved during our three years with the Council of Europe. And yet those who worked, either intermittently or all the time, with the Council, were brought, if only subconsciously, to believe that a new force in the world, a new entity greater than the sum of its parts, was being born in Strasbourg. What can happen among eighteen nations can happen within a much smaller—even the smallest— international group. There will always be frightened little men, scared of the unknown and of losing their chance to croak in their own little pond. In the days of the Heptarchy, when the Seven Kingdoms were being forged into a single England there was surely a wall that has been excavated in Northumbria, and has daubed on it the graffito 'No to England Wogges begin at Lincoln'. The rest of us try to be our age.

(v) Senegal

As we sailed into the port of Dakar on the morning of 9 November 1962, we observed, on one side, a man floating through the sky under a scarlet kite towed by a speedboat, and on the other, a gaily painted pirogue, the traditional flimsy but amazingly seaworthy craft of the Senegalese fishermen. This contrast haunted us throughout our time in Dakar. It is what Senegal is about. It certainly gave us our share of un-usual human and diplomatic situations.

There was an English girl who was working as a teacher in a school in Dakar. She was good at her job, and lived happily in a little flat on the edge of the predominantly Lebanese quarter. One morning she arrived at the Embassy in an agitated condition and told the following story.

In the small hours of the night before she had been disturbed by a noise, switched on the light, and found a strapping Senegalese standing in her bedroom dressed in a singlet but no trousers. He said, in courteous French (but using the second person singular, in the Senegalese style), 'Mademoiselle, please excuse me for disturbing you; but I am a thief, and I must ask you to give me all your money. Otherwise I must rape you.'

Terrified, the girl said, 'If you will give me my handbag from the dressing-table you can take it all.' He got the bag and turned it out: she had about five thousand francs, worth some seven or eight pounds.

'It is all I've got.'

'But, mademoiselle, you have not got much money. I will only take half.' And he counted out half of what she had and returned the rest.

'Now, mademoiselle, I must ask you to listen attentively. I urge you to leave this apartment immediately. All of us thieves in Dakar will now know that I have penetrated your bedroom, and you will no longer be secure here. It is imperative that you find another apartment at once.

'I entered by your balcony. It is the custom of us thieves to discard our trousers in order to frighten young ladies into handing over their money. Would you now be good enough to fetch me my trousers.'

The young girl went and found his trousers. He put them on.

'Now, mademoiselle, I repeat that it is essential for you to leave this apartment and find another. Please show me where your front door is. Good night, and thank you, Mademoiselle.'

Angry, alarmed, but intact, she sought the Embassy's advice. Unfortunately she was most reluctant to leave the flat, but we fixed bolts and bars on the shutters and she had no more nocturnal visitors before she finally decided to move out and stay with friends.

Then there were the beggars. In Strasbourg, in the spring, we had seen tattered little children roaming in the restaurants selling little bunches of lily-of-the-valley. One evening a friend from the Council of Europe, leaving a fashionable restaurant, followed a particularly scruffy pair of urchins as they left with their takings. They walked to a neighbouring street corner, where, after a few moments, a large limousine drew up. They clambered in with a precision of timing and a manner that suggested some experience of the manoeuvre and were whisked away into the spring night. So I was not surprised to find in Senegal that begging is a recognised family business, particularly as it has the seal of Muslim approval. In its worst form parents mutilate their infant children to make them even more pitiable; in Dakar there are some elderly and unemployable cripples who had no other means of existing except to squat or sit or lie on the pavements and beg. There was a little group whose favourite pitches were outside a large department store and the principal post office. Mariska always gave them something—only a few centimes, but she always said a few words and smiled at them.

At one year's end Mariska, exceptionally, had been housebound for two or three weeks. Then one day she went to the post office, past the usual beggars. She came out, gave them her customary centimes, and got into the car. As Seck, the chauffeur, was starting to drive away the beggars called out to him to wait, and one of them dragged himself to his feet and limped painfully over the pavement to the car. Mariska lowered the window.

'Madame, we have not seen you in Dakar for a long time and we were very concerned lest you might be ill. We were very sorry that we were unable to give our New Year greetings, but we hope that you will now accept these from the beggars of Dakar,' and he gave her two neat and pleasant little New Year cards.

Mariska wept. Seck, an ex-boxing champion who besides being my chauffeur worked as a bouncer in a night club, watched in amazement. 'Madame,' he said, shaking his head, 'it is not possible. In all my life I have never seen anything like that.' Cynics would say that the beggars were making a shrewd investment; but if anyone was a hardened cynic and skilled fund-raiser it was Seck, and he was shaken not by any cunning of the wretched beggars but by the humanity of their gesture.

On the other hand, one day in Dakar we met an English couple who worked in Rhodesia. The wife actually said to me, 'Do tell me, what does it feel like to shake hands with a black?' I replied truthfully, 'Not half as nice as stroking their backs while you dance with them.' I doubt whether West Africa would produce many such English. I hope not.

The point is that in the ex-French colonies any colour bar is caused by practical and not obsessional considerations, and in a newly-independent country like Senegal many of the leaders and prominent people had served as MPs, civil servants, or even as Ministers in the central government in Paris. Both the Presidents to whom I was accredited, Senghor in Senegal and Mokhtar Oudh Daddah in Mauritania, had married French ladies.

Every aspiring diplomat should serve in a black African post. The problems and responsibilities are the same as anywhere else only more so. You must never cease to be anything but patently though unobtrusively British, being accepted as part of the landscape, but there is an art in applying the right touch and developing the right style (which usually means just being natural). You have to gain the confidence of the government to which you are accredited and satisfy your own that you are carrying out their instructions correctly. This was not always easy in Senegal and Mauritania, where some of the general instructions from the Foreign Office were almost impossible to apply to the French West African scene. In the old days an Ambassador or Governor, having acted somewhat individually, could always plead that 'the frigate carrying your Lordship's instructions was regrettably delayed by contrary winds'; today the unusual situations that can crop up in Africa at least give you ample scope for instant decisions on what to do and how to do it, but there are no convenient excuses for not having obeyed orders. Another problem is that democracy as we know it is an alien growth, the acceptance of an opposition being regarded by the mass of people as a sign of weakness unacceptable in a true leader. This meant we had to know who any potential alternative leaders might be, but to know them socially could be awkward. This was contrary to all our instincts.

In July 1966 we were transferred from Senegal to London where I was made an Assistant Under-Secretary of State and took charge of overseas information and cultural activities; not, however, before Africa had served up its final paradox to match the pirogue and the hang-glider that had greeted our arrival in Dakar four years earlier. On an Air France flight not long before we left Senegal, we found ourselves in a VIP lounge with the Finance Minister and a senior official of a black African republic on their way back from a meeting in Paris. They were deep in a very animated argument which we could not help overhearing, and in any case I thought I might learn something useful. No such luck. They were passionately debating the rival merits of the Channel Tunnel and a bridge to link England with France.

So I passed, after my three-and-a-half year stint in the Foreign Office, from Dakar to Dublin. I felt that I could look back on enough relevant incidents and experiences to help me along what was clearly going to be a path beset with pitfalls. At school I learned about conflicting loyalties; at Oxford I saw how cynically the concept of peace could be perverted by traitors for political ends, and in the famous debate in the Union on 'This house will not fight for King and country' the point was made that you can be a better patriot by being critical, if you have to, of the policies of the country for which you are prepared to die than by blindly serving 'my country right or wrong'. I had spent five wartime years as a servant of Winston Churchill. With all his faults he was magnanimous, tolerant and supple. When faced with an adversary his first inclination was to sit down with him and talk over their differences. He had no respect for the sham person, but he respected the honestly held and firmly maintained opinion of anyone, however unimportant in rank and however unwelcome that opinion might be. He allowed me to stand up to him when he saw that I was certain that I was right, and he never bore malice. I had spent three years in Holland, where different religious sects were living and working together for the common good, even though political, economic, industrial and social life was constituted and divided on a confessional basis. I had seen much evil and little good come from partition or threats of partition in Palestine, India, Cyprus, West Africa. In Cyprus I had seen the frauds perpetrated in the name of self-determination and democracy, an international dispute mishandled as a colonial affair, and was sampling the distinction between the rule of law as a basic ingredient of the democratic faith and 'law and order' as something which the whole panoply of security was committed to uphold no matter what the justice of the law or the causes of the disorder. And in Strasbourg I had served on a multinational body offering wider perspectives than narrow nationalism and parochial pride. For the immediate future, however, there seemed enough to think about in Dublin.

8

THE new role of the British Army in the North which resulted from the Falls Road episode at the beginning of July 1970, the growing involvement in Northern affairs of persons in the Republic, and the precarious situation in which the Irish government found itself, all interacted to create a situation which it was in the interest of all parties to defuse. The defusing process called for real cooperation between the governments in Dublin and Westminster. But no serious dialogue developed and the fuse continued to burn.

There was a basic difficulty of ministerial responsibility. According to the Irish Constitution the Six Counties of Northern Ireland were part of the sovereign territory of the Republic, and therefore not the concern of the Irish Minister for Foreign Affairs. In the British view the Six Counties were an integral part of the United Kingdom and therefore not the concern of the Foreign Secretary. The Irish did not consider that the Northern Ireland government, to which, for fifty years, the British had delegated most of its internal administration, had any standing in the matter. In the government of the Republic Northern Irish affairs were handled by the Taoiseach personally; in Westminster they were handled by the Home Secretary, although the Prime Minister and the Minister of Defence were increasingly involved. On the other hand Anglo-Irish relations were overall the responsibility of the two Foreign Ministers.

The delicacy, if not the absurdity, of the situation was nicely brought out by a strange little episode just after the Falls Road search and curfew in July 1970. I had gone to London to pay my first call on the new Foreign Secretary, and just before going to bed at my club I glanced at the ticker tape for any late news.

I was a little startled to see that Dr Hillery had apparently arrived in Belfast, unheralded but not unnoticed, and gone on a walkabout among the aggrieved Catholics in the Falls Road area in order to take the temperature and show an interest. Almost at once the Foreign Office telephoned me to ask what on earth was happening? Of course I knew nothing, and technically Dr Hillery could cross the Border whenever he liked. Shortly afterwards he paid a courtesy call upon the Foreign Secretary. I understand that the atmosphere was quite cordial, even friendly, but that in no sense could it be called constructive. Dr Hillery learned that Her Majesty's Government took exception to his uninvited and unannounced intrusion into our internal affairs, and later commented laughingly that he had been summoned to the headmaster's study and given six of the best. On a day-to-day level we solved the problem in Dublin, and as far as I know in London also, by informal and commonsense arrangements.

Two trends emerged over the next two years. As Mr Heath was drawn more and more into the Irish situation, I was sent more and more instructions to convey messages to or discuss matters with Mr Lynch. At the same time more and more technical matters relating, for instance, to the problems of the Border, would crop up, often at very short notice or at awkward hours, and I or a member of my staff would deal with these by telephone. If the resulting arrangements were not strictly according to the rule book, they worked without friction because of the excellent understanding that I and the staff had with Hugh McCann, the Secretary to the Department of Foreign Affairs, and his staff, notably Eamonn Gallagher, who now grapples, in Brussels, with the no less intricate problems of the EEC fisheries. Whenever any of us had to have any contact other than with the DFA we either cleared it in advance or told them directly afterwards, and I made all my appointments with the Taoiseach through Hugh McCann. We all gradually built up an atmosphere of confidence which meant that nobody would break the unwritten rules or pull a fast one. In my not infrequent talks with Jack Lynch he must have known that I would have to report the politically relevant bits to the Foreign Office; but equally that I would never circulate anything he said as gossip in Dublin, and I got the impression that it was sometimes a relief to him to be able to sound off to a discreet out-sider. Gradually we all forged links that proved strong enough to hold when we badly needed them.

Personal contact on the highest level should ideally be resorted to rarely and then only for a weighty and carefully prepared discussion whose conclusions have virtually been agreed upon beforehand. Its success or failure depends even more on the personal rapport which the two men can establish and their capacity to understand each other's problems and point of view. I can only say that the relationship between the Prime Minister and the Taoiseach was accident-prone, and as path-finder and interpreter I could soon see why.

Mr Heath has a penetrating mind and, having discovered what he considers to be the right objective, displays great tenacity and courage, without overmuch finesse or flexibility, in attaining it. The Conservative and Unionist Party of which he was the leader had been out of office since before the civil rights disturbances had broken out in Northern Ireland. By the time he became Prime Minister the Labour government had drawn up its reform programme to redress the grievances of the Northern Catholics, was pressing the Unionist govern-ment to carry them out, and had brought in several thousand British troops to restore law and order. Since law and order were receding rapidly, the source of much of the trouble had to be sought elsewhere, namely in the Irish Republic. There-fore the role of Mr Lynch was obvious : to help to restore law and order in the North by restraining the IRA in the South. Mr Heath would do all he could to persuade Mr Lynch to attempt just this.

Mr Lynch is a Cork man, a lawyer, soft-spoken and gentle in manner. He does not appear physically impressive or robust. He is an attentive and serious listener, who revealed a subtle sense of irony when he was discussing some aspect of British activities in the North that he found mysterious. His state-ments on television were grave and measured. His speeches in the Dáil would in no way be classed as great oratory. His widespread appeal to the electorate was through his image of 'Honest Jack'. I never doubted the sincerity of his desire for friendly relations with Britain, just as he genuinely believed that reunification offered the only hope for peace with justice in the North; where he differed from the British policy it was in sorrow rather than in anger, hoping to reveal to us the error of our ways.

An admirer of Jack Lynch (or was it a detractor?) is reputed to have said that you could not understand him until you saw him stripped. Then he was revealed as pure whipcord. In his youth he had been a member of the Cork all-Ireland hurling team (hurling having been banned by the British Crown in 1366 because of the injuries caused to young men who could be more usefully and indeed more safely employed in battle); and it was whispered that he had an uncanny knack of knowing exactly when the referee was not looking his way. Those who murmured these things were not in the least surprised when out of the murk surrounding the Arms Trial in May 1970 Mr Lynch emerged unbespattered by the mud that was flying about, his political opponents routed, his party miraculously surviving and his leadership undisputed. For the first half of my term of duty in Dublin I thought it very important that the Prime Minister and the Taoiseach should get together. For the second half I rather hoped that they could be kept apart. It was not quite a dialogue of the deaf, but caught in the middle as I was, I sometimes felt that a pair of powerful hearing aids would come in handy.

Both men really wanted the same thing—peace in the North. The differences lay in their diagnosis and cure of the Northern sickness.

The Unionist government of Major Chichester Clark was being subjected to so many internal and external pressures that it would be hard to trace a simple and consistent policy during this period. But roughly speaking it was this: Stormont would gradually introduce the reforms demanded by Westminster, attempting, at the same time, to restore law and order and stamp out violence. IRA violence depended upon arms and ammunition, bombs, detonators and explosives. Restoring law and order therefore entailed (i) catching, charging, convicting and imprisoning those responsible for organising and practising violence; (ii) capturing their weapons, explosives etc. and (iii) cutting their supply lines. If these aims could be achieved, the IRA would collapse, the Catholic minority, once rid of IRA intimidation, would be free to accept the reforms offered to them, and everyone would live happily at peace. But since the headquarters, supply bases and training areas of the IRA were in the Republic, the Border had to be strictly controlled and heavy pressure had to be maintained upon the Irish government to play their part in crushing the IRA and preventing the Republic from being used as a base for terrorism. This policy therefore had to be carried out by the RUC and the British Army in Northern Ireland, and by the Foreign Office in relation to the Republic.

The Irish government saw things in a different light. The IRA was an illegal organisation, and anything that weakened it was good, and anything that strengthened it was bad. But they maintained that ultimately the only method of destroying it, or at least paralysing it, was political and it had to happen in the North. The IRA lived on the support, militant, active, discreet or just passive, of the Catholic population, and without this infrastructure their organisation could not operate. The vast majority disliked being intimidated and manipulated by the IRA activists, but their dislike was submerged in their much greater dislike of Protestant discrimination against them and their growing anger against the British Army. The longer that the Army went on using military methods to suppress the IRA the more active recruits the IRA would get and the greater the assistance they would be given by the Catholic population as a whole. The Irish government considered that there were two prerequisites for Catholic support of moderate and non-violent methods : a share in the government of Northern Ireland, and even the slightest of hints that the British government would welcome reunification by consent. As long as the Unionist government refused the former and HMG refused the latter, the strength of the IRA and its popular backing would increase.

Neither attitude was wholly right or wholly wrong, and they could in certain circumstances have been complementary. In military terms neither the Army nor the IRA could win. If the political requirements were met, there would still be a security task to perform, but with the Catholic community and their moderate leaders given an alternative way ahead, the task would be that much easier.

In 1970 and 1971, no such elasticity was visible. Instead,

the situation underlined the old problem which had so far proved insoluble: the British Army is called in by the civil power to retrieve a bad security situation when that situation is already so bad that anything the Army does is liable to make it worse. And there is a corollary to this. By the mere fact of intervening the Army deflects some of the anger and passion in the situation against itself, and the necessity to protect the troops, or to allow them to protect themselves actively or vigorously against their civilian assailants, becomes an increasingly weighty factor in reaching policy decisions. None of this is in any way the fault of the soldiers themselves, and the British Army never fails to set an example of stoicism, courage, and tolerance in situations which are none of its making. The officers on the spot can often see more clearly than their political masters the political implications, as well as the security consequences, of the tasks they are required to perform, but they loyally carry out their orders just the same.

Such a situation produces great stresses on the British Ministers concerned. As the Army increasingly becomes the hate-object and hence the target, the greater becomes the pressure on the Minister of Defence to feel that the prime object of government policy is to protect the troops. But here, while the Army in the North was under the control of Westminster, the political situation that it was expected to cope with was the responsibility of Stormont, which meant that the Army was there to restore and maintain Protestant law and Orange order. And all the delays and dangers of a divided responsibility were clearly present.

If the British government accepted the premises of Chichester Clark's Unionist government in Stormont, and hence rejected the advice and warnings from the Irish government which I was regularly relaying to the Foreign Office, then the role and tactics of the Army were right and law and order would soon be restored. In 1970 nobody knew which was right; but it was the task of the Foreign Office to weigh the Irish argument and brief the Secretary of State so that the whole issue should be balanced in Cabinet. The divergent attitudes of Dublin and Westminster naturally posed problems for the staff of my Embassy. I had been told that every telegram I sent would be widely distributed in Whitehall, and 'every despatch I wrote would be printed [to get the widest circulation]' and 'go straight to the top'. This seemed to imply a recognition that what happened in Dublin was highly relevant to policy in the North. Whitehall was undoubtedly anxious to learn as much as possible about events in the Republic, and apparently very interested in our analyses, comments and predictions. But whether our efforts in Dublin made much difference to the ensuing policy decisions in London, or to the manner in which these decisions were implemented, was debated with considerable scepticism, as superficially the most frequent reaction seemed to be the deadly 'Oh really, how interesting'. There was nothing to be done about this except report and comment on things as they happened, and in any case events were gradually taking control over traditional habits of thought.

An apparently constructive though in fact unfortunate innovation was made. Since the merger of the Foreign Office and the Commonwealth Office the affairs of the Irish Republic had been handled by the Irish desk of Western European Department, and any material submitted went up to the top through the Head of Department and the Under-Secretaries responsible for Western European affairs. But the volume of work on Ireland now grew so substantially that a separate Republic of Ireland Department was formed to deal with it. So completely was it separated from the Western European Department that it did not report to the Under-Secretaries concerned with European affairs but to an entirely different Under-Secretary whose principal concern was defence and Foreign Office liaison with the Service Departments. This inevitably introduced the danger that departmental advice reaching the Foreign Secretary about policy towards the Republic would be related primarily to our military policy and interests in the domestic law-and-order situation in the North; and, human nature being what it is, this would in effect reduce the possibility that the Irish diagnosis might conceivably be considered correct, or at least merit serious discussion round a table. Sir Alec Douglas-Home would probably be the first to agree that in his global responsibility for foreign and Commonwealth affairs Anglo-Irish relations did not loom very large.

Around this time I also had to sample once again the pleasures of diplomatic and political unorthodoxy, with which

Downing Street, Dakar and elsewhere had trained me to be familiar. In the reshuffle of the Irish government in the wake of the Arms Scandal, the Taoiseach had appointed two able young men to difficult posts—Des O'Malley to be Minister for Justice, and Jerry Cronin to Defence. One day soon afterwards I was summoned to the Department of Foreign Affairs and was invited, in effect, to cooperate in a little political charade. There had been some alleged minor misdemeanour by the British Army on the Border. No, this was not a protest or even a formal representation, but the Irish government wanted to express their dissatisfaction. Now, to give the two new Ministers some experience and a closer sense of participation, they would like me to go, accompanied by a senior official of the Department of Foreign Affairs, to call upon the Minister for Justice. He, with the Minister for Defence at his side, would tell me all about it. This, being something new in my diplomatic experience, was very appealing, so Eamonn Gallagher and I walked the few yards up the street to the Department of Justice where, after a slight delay, we were received alone by Des O'Malley. He said his piece and I made the usual non-committal reply about reporting what he had said, and returned to the Embassy. Very soon Hugh McCann, the Secretary of the DFA, was on the line. It had been fully intended that the Minister for Defence should be present at the event, but he had got stuck in traffic and only arrived after I had left. In reporting to the Foreign Office would I very much mind indicating that both Ministers were present and making joint complaint. I replied that the light in the Minister's room had been very poor, and coming in out of the bright sunlight I could not be certain who was there and who wasn't. So no problem. However, during the evening I could not resist ringing McCann at his home : I had just drafted my telegram to the Foreign Office, but before I sent it off could he assure me that two was the final score, and that there were no other members of the government whom I had failed to notice in the twilight and who rated a mention in my report? We reckoned that this about squared the match and called it a day.

9

As death and destruction mounted in the North, the Republic during 1970 and '71 remained calm and peaceful. There were some Sinn Féin protests and agitations, some concerning social conditions—housing and fishing rights—and some specifically anti-British. Several of these were self-defeating.

I had only been Ambassador for a few weeks when I was told that Sinn Féin had occupied the British Rail office in Cork. We were just requesting the Department of Foreign Affairs to ask the Department of Justice to eject them when my secretary told me that the Assistant Manager of British Rail wanted to speak to me from the beleaguered office. He was in a state of great alarm, the staff were in a panic, they didn't know what was going to happen to them, couldn't I speak to the IRA, he was so worried. I made soothing noises, told him the police would soon have them out, this sort of thing was constantly happening all over the world, these sit-ins were not to be taken seriously, and not to worry. The Assistant Manager sounded a little crestfallen and slightly at a loss. It later transpired that the office had no Assistant Manager, and the Sinn Féin man impersonating him was trying to stampede the Embassy into some panic action; my reaction given in all good faith was about the last thing he wanted.

We also had the bomb hoax to end them all. Late one night the security guard on duty in Chancery heard a voice on the telephone.

'There's a bomb in your basement and you've five minutes to get out.'

'Oh, my kettle's just boiling for my tea—can't you make it fifteen?'

'Oh, all right then, fifteen.'

The Passport Office was occupied for the second time and the staff were barricaded in until the police rescued them and arrested the intruders. It was unpleasant, but in comparison with the North it all seemed fairly care-free. Dublin in late 1970 was more concerned with the trial of Mr Haughey and the enquiry into the use to which £100,000 of public money intended for relief work had actually been put and by whom. But the trial and the enquiry so muddied the waters that judicial and political visibility was approaching zero, and interest turned towards the traffic in arms and men in either direction across the Border. Then in the autumn of 1970 there was a diplomatic flurry about naval searches of Irish ships supposed to be running guns and explosives from England and Scotland into Ireland, North and South. The ship-owners took exception to the searches and the Fine Gael opposition front bench made great play of the proposition that since the Republic did not recognise Partition they could not recognise that Northern Ireland had any territorial waters anyway. And one day I had a cry from the heart of the Department of Foreign Affairs: 'For God's sake, John, life would be a lot easier if you ever found anything in these bloody ships.' Indeed, one of the crosses that all three of us—the Foreign Office, the Embassy and the Department of Foreign Affairs—had to bear together was the parliamentary question. While we were all trying to keep the temperature down, there were three parliaments—Westminster, the Dáil and Stormont, all with vigilant back-benchers apparently watching each other's answers like hawks and only too eager to put each other's temperature up. We used to long for the summer recess.

I soon became aware of differences in the political structure of the two countries which did not make mutual comprehension, or my role as interpreter, any easier. In any democracy, the ingredients which go into the decisions made by Ministers are threefold. First, there are the instinctive, tribal, ideological, personal convictions of the individuals who form the government. Then there are the opinions, needs, desires, wishes and hopes of the electorate, which may or may not be based on anything approximating to reality, but determine whether the government remains in office. Finally there is the Civil Service, the machinery of government, the voice of realism, hard fact

E

and harder economics. If a country has complicated financial and industrial difficulties, and is so penetrated by totalitarian ideology that its democratic machinery is badly strained and creaking, then the greater the power of the central coordinating body of officials. In Britain this body is called the Cabinet Offices, and the power it exercises over the policies of Ministers is very great. In the early 1970s the balance of these three ingredients in Britain and Ireland was very different.

Politics in Britain were, and probably still are, based largely upon class. A Conservative government was elected in June 1970. Their social and economic policies at home were designed to serve all the nation. Abroad, they were the progressive, European, party. But there was no escaping the fact that their political ancestors, if not their family forebears, had probably approved the Act to Prevent the Growth of Popery in 1704, and the Declaratory Act in 1719 ('. . . the said kingdom of Ireland hath been, is and of right ought to be, subordinate unto and dependent upon the imperial crown of Great Britain, as being inseparably united and annexed thereunto . . .'), approved the Act of Union of 1801, probably resisted the attempts in 1886, 1892 and 1914 to give very limited Home Rule to Ireland, and approved the efforts of those who, from 1886 onwards, tried to divide Ireland and ultimately produced Partition.

The two major political parties in Ireland are not based on class or on the possession or lack of land. They both spread across the whole social and economic spectrum. They are the political progeny of the opposing sides in one of the most tragic of civil wars, fought over the issue of the terms on which Ireland, or part of Ireland, gained her independence. But from the Norman Invasion to Independence, they share the same ancestral memories. While I was Ambassador the ruling party was Fianna Fáil, the party formed from those who had rejected the terms of the Treaty of 1921 and lost the Civil War that resulted. I have already remarked on its leader, the Taoiseach, Jack Lynch. His deputy, the Tanaiste, Erskine Childers (later to become President) was the elder statesman of the party and a very remarkable man. His father was half English, and won the DSO in the Royal Navy in 1915. He then became a passionate Republican and Secretary to the Irish delegation in the

Treaty negotiations in 1921. He later repudiated the Treaty, joined the Irregulars in the Civil War, and was captured and executed for possessing firearms in 1922. His son continued to follow de Valera, and when I knew him he was Minister of Health and a very steadfast supporter of Jack Lynch.

As I have said, the Minister for Foreign Affairs was Dr Patrick Hillery, from Co. Clare and very proud of it. After some initial sizing up we established a relationship of what I hope was mutual respect and understanding of certain unorthodoxies and informalities that the situation called for. George Colley, who succeeded Charles Haughey as Minister for Finance, was also always ready to discuss all manner of ideas about the North, informally and without any commitment for either of us. I often felt that members of the Irish government wanted, as my Embassy wanted, to confine Northern questions to their proper corner in the larger canvas of Anglo-Irish relations. But only too often the North would not let us. There was always a danger, among the major anxieties and minor annoyances about the North, of forgetting that the British and Irish governments were quietly working together preparing to apply to join the EEC. Men like Dr Hillery, George Colley, Brian Lenihan (Transport and Power) and James Gibbons (Agriculture), with their Departments, were working side by side with the British all through the worst of the Troubles. And Des O'Malley, as Minister for Justice, never allowed his fearful problems of security and politics linked to interfere with a working relationship which I personally valued very much indeed.

When Dr Hillery went as the Irish Commissioner to Brussels, Brian Lenihan took over as Minister for Foreign Affairs. It therefore fell to him to give us the farewell dinner, ritualistic but relaxed, when we retired. I always felt a bit guilty about this. The general election campaign was in full swing, yet the Minister sacrificed a day's electioneering and returned to Dublin through a snowstorm to host the dinner. I sometimes wonder if this courtesy cost him the handful of votes by which he lost his seat.

The Opposition Party, Fine Gael, was the party of those who supported the Treaty of 1921 and were ruthlessly victorious in the ensuing Civil War. Our Embassy contacts with them were of necessity social and informal, but none the less friendly for that; even though their leader, Liam Cosgrave, and the brilliant and eloquent economics expert Dr Garret FitzGerald were as vigilant as an Opposition should be in seeing that the government were not allowing the British to get away with anything; and where Border violations and infringements of territorial waters were concerned, Richie Ryan, then Opposition spokesman for Foreign Affairs, was like a terrier worrying a very special bone. In coalition with the much smaller Labour Party they were returned to power three weeks after I retired.

Liam Cosgrave is the son of W. T. Cosgrave, a former Sinn Féin MP who was imprisoned after the 1916 Easter Rising. He was Chairman of the Provisional Government in 1921-2, and President of the Free State from 1922 to 1932. This illustrates the tendency for Irish politics to run in families; moreover, when a TD (MP) retires or dies, it is not uncommon for his widow or next of kin to be nominated and adopted as a candidate in his place.

On the emotional, instinctive plane, therefore, there was a Conservative Party in power in Britain whose political ancestry was, to say the least, anti-Catholic, anti-Irish and anti-Home Rule, and even more anti-Independence and anti-Republicanism. Only two generations back it had become pro-Partition and become the Conservative and Unionist Party. Such sentiments were probably becoming less strong, however, and in any case Ministers had powerful civil servants to temper too atavistic an attitude. In Dublin there were leaders of both parties whose fathers had fought and died for Independence and on the issue of whether independent Ireland should be entire or divided. And government in Ireland was a simpler, less expensive affair, more closely attuned to the feelings of the constituencies. The Dáil met one day less a week than the House of Commons. The Taoiseach had no 10 Downing Street or Chequers, and no elaborate Cabinet Office machinery. The general effect was that if there were sudden orders from London to the Embassy to do something quickly, or a squall in the North, it was greatly to be preferred if it all happened at midday in mid-week. But it seldom did.

The trial of Mr Haughey dragged on through the autumn of 1970. At the end of that year (and indeed every year since)

Mariska and I went to the Wexford Opera Festival—a delightful event about which we had been told before we went to Ireland by a friend who said, 'In Bayreuth you go to wonderful opera and can have a drink in the intervals. In Wexford you can have a wonderful drinking party, and opera in the intervals.' (This is not fair, for although Wexford is en fête for a fortnight, and the fringe activities include a lot of singing, music and dancing in hotels and pubs, the operas themselves are first class, bringing devotees and critics in force from Britain, America and Europe.) We were in our hotel in Wexford changing to go to the opera when the radio announced the verdict in the Arms Trial : Mr C. J. Haughey had been acquitted. Mr Heath and Mr Lynch were in New York, attending the Assembly of the United Nations, where incidentally they met face to face for the first time. The Foreign Office was obviously going to need to know whether the acquittal precipitated another crisis in the Irish government, and equally obviously I should not show too much concern about a domestic matter. I telephoned to Peter Piper to lay on a staff meeting at 10.00 am the next morning, which was a Saturday. At 8.30 am I slipped out of Wexford in the police escort car, leaving Mariska to be seen around in the Embassy Daimler. A discussion, a few telephone calls, the drafting and approval of some telegrams, and so back to Wexford for lunch at 1.30 in the hotel restaurant. The acquittal was obviously a blow to the Lynch government, but again we prophesied confidently that the Taoiseach would survive. The government and the Fianna Fáil party gave Jack Lynch a huge welcome at the airport on his return, party solidarity was manifest and one more political hurdle was safely cleared.

But there was always the Border. People talk and act as if the Border were something as impenetrable and controllable as the Berlin Wall. I recently stayed in Leicestershire, where a cross-country equestrian event was due to take place, and a doctor friend was arranging with the county health services to have ambulances and Land-Rovers at some of the more hazardous jumps. When I arrived he was somewhat distraught, the organisers having just discovered that part of their course strayed unbeknownst into the neighbouring county of Nottingham, and a completely different ambulance service had to be added. When they asked me why I found it so comical I had to say that perhaps they would now begin to understand the Irish Border question. Towards the end of 1970 this question was indeed becoming important as guns and bombs played an increasingly large role in the Northern way of life.

As part of the policy of 'controlling' this Border, the British security forces in the North decided to block a large number of cross-Border roads by blowing craters in them and closing them with large spikes set in concrete. Thus cars and lorries carrying arms and explosives from South to North would have to use certain 'approved' crossing points where they could be more easily searched. The security advantage was obvious. North of the Border it was the responsibility of the Northern Ireland government, now headed by Mr Faulkner, to appreciate the context, the consequences and hence the value of this operation; and south of the Border it was my responsibility to learn and comment on the Irish assessment. I was told, clearly and concisely, what this was.

The land frontier between the two sovereign states of the Irish Republic and the United Kingdom of Great Britain and Northern Ireland is not actually visible. Nor does it fluctuate according to the price of crops and smuggled goods like that other undemarcated frontier I had had dealings with, between Senegal and Gambia. But its precise course is about as well known and as clearly marked as the boundary between Leicester and Nottingham, and this of course is precisely what it is— a county boundary. 1970-71 was the first time ever that it actually mattered whether the Border ran one side of a ditch or the other, or whether a culvert was British or Irish sovereign territory. As the Border followed its inconsequential and un-controllable course from the Atlantic to the Irish Sea it divided villages, parishes, farms, even cottage gardens. Blocking the roads across it therefore had several consequences. The village priest, the doctor, the farmer and the vet might have to make considerable detours to go about their normal business. The IRA swiftly exploited the exasperation of the local inhabitants and gained plenty of volunteers to unload arms, ammunition, detonators and explosives, from their cars south of the Border, carry them across the fields and load them into cars with northern registration numbers. The area south of the Border became one vast safe haven for gunmen on the run from the North, for IRA training camps and operational bases. These developments cannot be blamed wholly on the cratering policy, since they were inherent in the Border situation. But they were a bonus to the IRA and a source of alarm to the Irish government, who were naturally perturbed at this spread of IRA influence in the Republic.

When the archives of the period are opened to the public in AD 2001, researchers may be intrigued to discover, if such trivia are preserved, how the Irish Department of Foreign Affairs and the British Embassy spent much of their time in 1971. Week after week, it seems in retrospect—perhaps less often, but at any rate with tedious regularity—one of us would go down and trade a bundle of complaints, regrets, promises to investigate, requests for information. A British armoured car had invaded Irish sovereign territory. A helicopter had violated Irish air space. Irish villagers had filled in a crater in Northern Ireland. It isn't in Northern Ireland. It is. It isn't. Why didn't the Irish police catch those gunmen in the Cortina? (True answer—it goes quicker than one unarmed policeman on a bicycle). The Department of Justice has fully investigated your complaints of six weeks ago and finds them unfounded. The British Army has made a detailed enquiry and can find no evidence that any unit had come within five miles of the Border on the day in question. The regiment concerned is now in West Germany.

And so on. A more serious and much more delicate question was that of the administration of justice. There were several reasons for widespread and justifiable irritation in London and Belfast. The Provisional and Official IRAs were both—according to their own statements and propaganda—based in Dublin. Since they were illegal organisations, could their leaders not be arrested? Known members of the IRA were appearing before District Justices in some Border areas, charged with illegal possession of arms or some such offence, and the cases against them were being dismissed. More serious charges involving trial by jury invariably ended in acquittal. Requests for extradition of the wanted men were consistently refused on the grounds that the offences were political.

It was frustrating and also embarrassing, since I was under

constant pressure to twist the arm of the Irish government on the subject, and we all knew that it was as frustrated over much of this as we were. But the law is the law and sovereignty is sovereignty. At the end of some interminable conference of officials in London, I was asked rather aggressively when the Irish government was going to get the right verdict from an Irish court. I replied in some exasperation, 'As soon as the French President instructs Mr Heath what verdict an English jury is to return, and he fixes it.' But Mr Lynch was subtle and sensitive, and by conveying 'the sort of instructions that I should be required to carry out if we were prepared to interfere in the internal affairs of the Republic' I was able to make the point without formally doing so.

On 6 February 1971 the first British soldier was shot dead in Ulster since the emergency began in 1968, and four others were injured. The volume and viciousness of the violence began to mount. It was almost entirely organised by the IRA and the growing number of their supporters, because the potentially militant Protestants had nothing to be violent about. So long as they had Stormont with its built-in and permanent Unionist control, and the RUC and the British Army, since the Falls Road affair, supporting established order, they did not have to worry too much about the reforms that had been promised to the Catholics. They could probably force their own government to stall as long as possible and give away as little as they could. The death and destruction caused by the IRA were a strong enough safeguard : did not law and order first have to be restored? There was no flexibility anywhere. Major Chichester Clark's sovereign remedy was troops and yet more troops, and the British governments policy was to leave the Unionist government in Stormont to manage its own affairs, subject to London's overall control of the security forces.

Then everything seemed to go wrong at once. Major Chichester Clark resigned on 1 May 1971 and was replaced by Brian Faulkner, the first 'professional politician' to lead the Unionists after a succession of landowners and gentleman farmers. His planned remedy was internment without trial of suspected IRA members, with some important proposals to give the political leaders of the Catholic minority a share in the work of the Northern Ireland parliament. But a chapter of accidents involving security measures directed against Catholics led to their withdrawing entirely from political life, and they virtually retired behind barricades into 'no-go' areas in Belfast and Derry where the police scarcely ventured. From March to the end of July bomb explosions averaged two a day. Four soldiers were killed and twenty-nine injured between April and August. In confused and tentative fashion Faulkner and his government decided to introduce internment without trial. Published sources have said that the Ulster Cabinet agreed that if the internment were to be effective, it had to be introduced in the Republic at the same time. On 5 August Faulkner flew to London and persuaded the British Cabinet to agree to internment. About all this I was told nothing.

The most important social occasion of the Dublin year is Horse Show Week, during the first week in August. The Horse Show party always given by the British Ambassador on the Friday of Horse Show Week is one of the main events, since it is both a reception in honour of the British and other show-jumping teams and, in effect, the Queen's Birthday Party. On Friday 6 August 1971 I was sent instructions to ask Jack Lynch where he would be during the week-end as I might have to get in touch with him. It was only by the purest chance that I was able to carry out my instructions. Normally the Dáil rises on Thursday evening and Members disappear to their constituencies, but on this Friday the Taoiseach and Mrs Lynch were coming to our Horse Show party and I was able, in the most natural way in the world, to ask him whether he would be around over the week-end. The air was already thick with rumours of impending internment, so I did not need to say more. He has since disclosed in a radio interview that I called him on 9 August to enquire whether, if internment without trial were introduced in the North, the Irish government would introduce it in the South. (Since the round-up had begun in the middle of the night before, the 'if' was a trifle superfluous.) He not only stated most emphatically that there was not the remotest possibility of internment being introduced in the Republic, but he gave me the most serious and solemn warning that the consequences in the North would be catastrophic: for every man put behind the wire a hundred would volunteer. Of course I reported this urgently and earnestly, but without seriously expecting that it could affect decisions that had obviously already been taken.

If the published report that Faulkner's Cabinet had agreed on the necessity of internment being introduced in the Republic at the same time is true, and if by the time I was instructed to put the question to the Taoiseach the round-up had already begun, it seems to follow that nobody expected Mr Lynch to agree and that the Stormont administration did not expect internment to work. But since it had been introduced both North and South on two earlier occasions and worked successfully, it is perhaps worth pointing out here why those who thought it an appalling error in August 1971 were absolutely right. On previous occasions it had been introduced to deal with aimless IRA campaigns with no popular appeal or support anywhere. In 1971 it was introduced after two years of mounting unrest and violence caused by the general Catholic agitation for civil rights and Protestant reactions against it. The Provisional IRA did not cause the civil rights movement; the movement gave birth to the Provisional IRA. Internment therefore attacked the Catholic community as a whole. What was worse, it was directed solely against the Catholics, although there were many Protestants who provided just as strong grounds for internment, if internment there had to be. So their reaction, and Mr Lynch's warning, were entirely predictable.

In the few months before internment four soldiers and four civilians were killed in Northern Ireland. In the four months after internment thirty soldiers, eleven police and Ulster Defence Regiment men, and seventy-three civilians died—one hundred and fourteen against eight. The slope down which we were all slithering in the dust of the Northern Ireland government was getting steeper and bloodier every minute.

IO

WHILE all this was going on, plans were quietly being made for Mr Lynch to visit Mr Heath in London, and he announced in the Dáil on 6 August that their meeting would take place on 20 and 21 October. He added, 'The agenda has not yet been drawn up but I want to ensure that everything possible, everything useful and everything worthwhile will be on that agenda.' I was of course delighted, as it seemed self-evident that as things got worse in the North and in the Border area a comprehensive and objective review of the whole scene by the two heads of government was urgently needed.

It did not quite work out that way. On 12 August, when the force of the reaction against internment had become clear, Jack Lynch issued a statement appealing partly to the Northern Catholics and the Irish people as a whole, partly to the British government. His two themes were that his government would not condone any sort of armed activity and that resistance to internment should be political only; and that 'as an immediate objective of political action, the Stormont government should be replaced by an administration in which power and decision-making will be equally shared between Unionist and non-Unionist'. (20 August 1971)

I was having a quiet evening at Glencairn with Nicholas. Mariska was in France. The escort car had gone, as I was not going out, and my official chauffeur was back at his home. My own car was at the garage being serviced. To all intents and purposes I was peacefully marooned.

At around 9.00 pm the telephone rang: 10 Downing Street. The PM's Principal Private Secretary, Robert Armstrong, was on the line, at his most magisterial.

'Have you got a secretary?'

'No.'

'Got a pencil? Take this down.'

'Half a minute. What is it?'

'It's a message from the PM to the Taoiseach. It will be on the news at ten, and you've got to get it to him before then.'

I hadn't a clue what all this was about, but luckily Nicholas was standing by so he took it down and typed it out on Mariska's venerable and famously wayward typewriter. Meanwhile I asked Nicholas whether his almost as venerable Volkswagen was working that day (he thought it might go) and summoned the butler to do an urgent sweep of the grounds and see if there was any detective on duty who (*a*) could act as an escort (*b*) knew the way to Jack Lynch's house and (*c*) could radio to the Castle (Special Branch headquarters) to alert the Taoiseach's guard at the gate to ask Mr Lynch to stand by for an ambassadorial visit. Then, hoping for the best, I was able to ask what had been going on. Mr Heath's message to Mr Lynch was, in non-diplomatic terms, a fair stinker.

It appeared that Mr Heath had summoned Brian Faulkner to Chequers to talk about the mounting lawlessness and disorder in the North. Hearing of this, Mr Lynch had sent him the following telegram :

The events since the introduction of internment without trial on Monday, 9th August, clearly indicate the failure of internment and of current military operations as a solution to the problems of Northern Ireland. It must now be obvious to you that solutions require to be found through political means and should be based on the principal of immediate and full equality of treatment for everyone in Northern Ireland irrespective of political views or religion.

In the event of the continuation of existing policies of attempting military solutions I intend to support the policy of passive resistance now being pursued by the non-Unionist population.

In the event of agreement to a policy of finding solutions by political means I am prepared to come to a meeting of all the interested parties designed to find ways and means of promoting the economic, social and political wellbeing of all the Irish people, North and South, without prejudice to the aspiration of the great majority of the Irish people to the re-unification of Ireland.

Mr Heath's reaction to this was predictable, and in the circumstances perfectly reasonable. Mr Lynch, presumably for internal political reasons, and to show his concern for the Northern minority, had made the text of his message public. But for reasons we could not fathom his telegram was not sent through the Department of Foreign Affairs and the Irish Embassy in London but as an ordinary telegram through the Irish and English postal services. It therefore arrived some time after Mr Heath and Mr Faulkner had ended their meeting and dispersed. Understandably Mr Heath and Mr Maudling were not amused.

Improbably, our improvised communications worked rather better. Nicholas's Volkswagen started; a detective who knew the way was on duty and packed in the back of the car, and we thundered through the night (the silencer having gone missing) for the Taoiseach to receive the British Ambassador a few minutes before ten and be handed the following:

1. Your telegram of today is unjustifiable in its contents, unacceptable in its attempt to interfere in the affairs of the United Kingdom and can in no way contribute to the solution of the problems of Northern Ireland.

2. You should know that the principle of equality of treatment for everyone in Northern Ireland irrespective of political views or religion is the accepted policy of the governments of the United Kingdom and of Northern Ireland and is being fully implemented. By seeking to obscure this fact you do no service to any of the people of Northern Ireland.

3. The military operations to which you refer are designed solely for the defence of the people against armed terrorists whose activities, many of which originate in or are supported from the Republic, I hope you would deplore and join me in suppressing. These operations are thus a necessary prelude to the restoration of greater harmony between the communities in Northern Ireland.

4. While I naturally welcome contacts with you as the head of a friendly government, and while Mr Faulkner and

I have often made clear our desire to see greater co-operation between all governments concerned in promoting mutual prosperity and well-being of the peoples of Northern Ireland and the Republic, I cannot accept that anyone outside the United Kingdom can participate in meetings designed to promote the political development of any part of the United Kingdom.

5.   I find your reference to supporting the policy of passive resistance now being pursued by certain elements in Northern Ireland calculated to do maximum damage to the co-operation between the communities in Northern Ireland which it is our purpose, and I would hope would be your purpose, to achieve.

6.   I deeply regret the fact that, when a meeting has already been arranged between us to discuss the whole range of matters of common interest to our two countries, you should have publicly taken up a position so calculated not only to increase the tension in Northern Ireland but also to impair our effort to maintain good relations between the United Kingdom and the Irish Republic.

7.   Since the text of your telegram was given to the Irish press before it was received here, I am also releasing the text of this message to the press.

We read and listened in silence. I could not draw Mr Lynch out on this one. I doubt if the reply surprised him, and all he said was, 'We had better have a drink'. Nicholas was invited in and had a charming and relaxed chat with the Taoiseach.

The following day Mr Lynch issued the following statement:

It is regrettable that the British Prime Minister should have interpreted my message in the way he did. I had hoped that he would have accepted my offer to participate in discussions among all those concerned to find an amicable solution to the problems of Northern Ireland. My message was solely intended to try to bring the present unrest to an end and to begin again the promotion of economic, social and political progress for all the people of Ireland and the ensuring of peace and harmony among them.

No one who has examined the situation could accept that

the troubles in Northern Ireland originate in any measure from here. Of all the hundreds of people who have been arrested in the North in situations of public unrest in the past three years, charged and convicted under the ordinary law, and of the hundreds who have now been interned without trial no more than a handful came from outside Northern Ireland.

Mr Heath states that current military operations are a necessary prelude to the restoring of harmony between the communities in Northern Ireland. I believe on the contrary that these operations are driving them further apart. Evidence for this can be found in what is becoming the mass resignation of non-Unionist appointees from public offices in which they have given remarkable service in recent years.

Mr Heath also suggests that these military operations are designed solely for the defence of the people against armed terrorists. I would point out that we have received here in the past twelve days many thousands of refugee women and children, mainly from Catholic ghettos in Belfast, who have described the situation otherwise.

We should all be happy to believe that the principle of equality of treatment for everyone in Northern Ireland, irrespective of political views or religion, is the accepted policy of the Governments of the UK and of Northern Ireland and is being fully implemented. However, the fact that internment without trial is so patently directed at the non-Unionist community only does not encourage that belief.

So far as any question of impairing the good relations between Ireland and Britain is concerned I have spoken on this subject many times, in particular during the past 15 months, and have attempted to set these relations on a path which promised hope, progress and an ultimate final settlement, by agreement and through peaceful means only, of the age-old 'Irish Question'. The record speaks for itself.

Mr Heath's assertion that what is happening in Northern Ireland is no concern of mine is not acceptable. The division of Ireland has never been, and is not now, acceptable to the great majority of the Irish people who were not consulted in the matter when that division was made fifty years ago. No generation of Irishmen has ever willingly acquiesced in that division—nor can this problem remain for ever in its present situation.

Apart from this statement of principle, however, a situation where the destiny, the wellbeing and even the lives of Irish people are involved must affect us deeply. I remain convinced that the time has arrived for all those who can contribute to a peaceful solution of current problems in Northern Ireland to come together to discuss how this can be achieved.

It is hard to imagine the heads of government of any two other states brawling publicly in this fashion; but all the same, with great misgivings, Mr Lynch went to Chequers for talks on 6 and 7 September, and again on the twenty-seventh and twenty-eighth when Mr Faulkner was present. The positions adopted by Mr Heath and Mr Lynch are very clearly set out in the extracts I have quoted above, and it would be an abuse of the English language to describe the talks as negotiations. Nevertheless I found one glimmer of hope in a joint statement tacked on at the end of the communiqué issued after the tripartite talks :

Mr Heath and Mr Lynch agreed to keep in close communication with each other, personally, through their ministerial colleagues and at official level, as might be appropriate, on all subjects affecting the future of Anglo-Irish relations. In this respect the meeting between the two Prime Ministers scheduled for the autumn to discuss a range of subjects, including the Anglo-Irish Free Trade Area Agreement and the applications of both countries for membership of the European Communities, will be held on dates to be announced later.'

By the end of the year even this little glimmer had been extinguished.

The situation was by any standards confusing. The confusion had been pinpointed by the Home Secretary, Mr Maudling, as early as 22 September, when he said two things. The first was that he had been having talks with various political groups from Northern Ireland 'to find agreed ways whereby there can be assured to the minority and majority communities alike an active, permanent and guaranteed part in the life and public affairs of Northern Ireland'. He then said, 'One cannot create a cohesive government if people do not denounce violence or if people are not prepared to accept the will of the majority on the fundamental point about the Border which succeeding governments have always accepted in this country'. Yet six days later Mr Heath, Mr Lynch and Mr Faulkner issued a joint statement from Chequers stating, in effect, that without prejudice to the Border question (i.e. reunification) they were trying 'to find some agreed areas of enabling all the people of Northern Ireland to live in conditions of peace and stability which any democracy should ensure to its citizens without regard to their political conviction or their religion'. Mr Lynch was insisting that the only way to bring back the disaffected Northern Catholics into public life was to give them even the slightest ray of hope about the British attitude to reunification. Mr Harold Wilson, as leader of the Opposition, visited Dublin in November and on his return said in the Commons, 'I believe the situation has now gone so far that it is impossible to conceive of an effective longterm solution in which the agenda at least does not exclude consideration of, and which is not in some way directed to finding a means of achieving, the aspirations envisaged half a century ago of progress towards a United Ireland'. The Irish government was pressing Mr Heath to say that if a majority of the people of Northern Ireland wanted reunification the British would welcome it. But Mr Heath could not go beyond saying that if they ever did, 'I do not believe any British government would stand in the way'.

Of course all this is an elegant charade which fooled nobody. In the future that spread itself out before the politicians, there was not the remotest possibility of a majority in Northern Ireland voting for reunification, since the place had only been demarcated as it was in order to prevent a united Ireland and ensure a permanent Protestant and Unionist government. There was not then, and there has not been since, any suggestion that the British electorate as a whole should be consulted on whether they wanted to keep the Six Counties. Meanwhile, the 1969 Reforms imposed by Mr Callaghan on the North would be carried out at a pace and in a manner determined by Mr

Faulkner and the Northern Ireland government. Mr Maudling's offer of power-sharing depended on the Northern Catholics renouncing the claim to reunification of which Mr Heath, according to Mr Lynch, had 'recognised that it was legitimate for the non-Unionist population in the North to work for the reunification of Ireland by political means'. (Dáil, 20 October 1971). All the political leaders denounced violence, and the violence was still mounting.

Nor was the situation made any better by the stories which had started circulating after the internment round-up, alleging what was officially called 'physical brutality' against suspects in the custody of the security forces and has, inevitably, come to be called torture. The Home Secretary set up a committee (the Compton Committee) to investigate the charges on 31 August. On 20 October, during a long speech to the Dáil, Mr Lynch remarked that this enquiry had two serious defects : it was being held in private instead of in public, and the legal representatives of the complainants were not allowed to question witnesses other than their own clients. Nevertheless, the findings were damaging, and the resulting proceedings, which are still dragging on as the 'Torture Case' in Strasbourg, London and Dublin, have been like a chronic infection in the organs of the British security structure which even now, six years later, has not been wholly eradicated.

When I have been working under pressure for too long and something has to give, it is always my larynx; so in the middle of November I retired speechless to bed for three days and wrote a very pessimistic letter to Denis Greenhill, the Head of the Foreign Office, in which I blatantly exceeded my proper responsibilities by writing about Ireland as a whole. It was easy to follow the logic of the security policies being followed in the North, but I could not see any means of preventing them from leading us all deeper and deeper into the mire, unless the law-and-order obsession was accompanied by some sort of a fresh look at the political assumptions. Moreover the internal situation in the Republic was precarious. The Taoiseach had held his Fianna Fáil party together on a policy of denouncing both violence and violent intervention in the North, working with the British government for a just and peaceful settlement, and showing his electorate that he was keeping up all the pressure he could upon Westminster. After eighteen months he had precious little to show for it, and I knew that he and his government were depressed and frustrated. Any convulsion in Irish politics could only help the IRA, but any measures to avert it could only be the result of a British initiative.

I like to think that my commentary contributed something to the fundamental review that was to follow. At any rate it was better than sitting helplessly as a spectator watching a Greek tragedy unfolding to its predestined end. I could not think of anyone in Britain, Northern Ireland or the Republic, outside the IRA, to whom 1971 can have brought any satisfaction whatever.

But the year ended on a heart-warming note—an audience with Her Majesty the Queen. When an Ambassador is appointed, he and his wife are summoned to Buckingham Palace for the ceremony of 'kissing hands'. In the modern version of this ancient ritual, you do not actually kiss hands, but the Queen and the Ambassador as her representative, and his wife, have twenty minutes of private conversation. (This is of necessity strictly confidential, but I may say that when I 'kissed hands' before going to Senegal, the Queen was just back from a long tour in West Africa, and in a few minutes gave me a more perceptive commentary on Africa than I found anywhere in Whitehall.) The Queen was abroad when we first came to Dublin so I did not 'kiss hands'. Instead, Mariska and I were granted an audience on 10 December 1971. This, of course, had the great advantage that I had already been in the post eighteen months. Without adulation or sycophancy I can only say that it was the most encouraging experience of my diplomatic career. The Queen had not only read but had evidently studied with care all my despatches and telegrams, all the correspondence from Northern Ireland, and all the Whitehall papers about Ireland, and she appreciated all the nuances of Ireland *as a whole*. We left Buckingham Palace enchanted and comforted.

By the end of January 1972 I was tortured officially by doubts about the policy of the government I was serving as the Queen's representative; tortured, personally, by doubts about the impact of the reports, analyses, opinions that I and my Embassy were sending to the Foreign Office; tortured by doubts whether it might not now be too late for anyone involved in Northern Ireland, whether from London, Dublin, or Westminster, to make any dent at all in the monolith which had established itself in Stormont fifty years earlier. Was there to be no flexibility anywhere? Was there any point in carrying on? I had given my personal view that, unless some drastic initiative were taken, the situation in Ireland as a whole could only get worse.

Before the end of January every Head of Mission is required to send a despatch summing up and assessing the events of the previous year. My despatch of January 1972 was inevitably a pretty gloomy document. I had to describe the mounting tension and uncertainty, and the fear of an extension into the Republic of the steadily worsening security situation in the North. Above all there was a feeling of frustration, since the Irish government's liberty of action to curb the IRA was severely limited by the climate of Irish public opinion engendered by events in the North. Somebody had to make a move somewhere, and I had already expressed my views about this. In my annual review I ventured the opinion that to take no decision was itself a decision whose consequences could be more tragic with every day that passed (or words to that effect).

1971 had been a bad year for Jack Lynch's 'peaceful approach and working through the British' policy, and I said so. I knew this would not be welcome and it wasn't. But nearly thirty years earlier I had fought and won a twelve-hour battle with Winston Churchill over saying what he did not want to hear, and I wasn't going to change now and start the last year of my career by humiliating myself.

I was brooding over these things during the snowy weekend of 29-30 January 1972, and looking forward to the subscription concert to which we were taking friends on the Sunday evening—a pleasant prelude to my trip to London for the important ministerial meeting which I had been summoned to attend on Wednesday 2 February. But the roads were impassable, the party was off, and I prepared for my usual Cassandra act and for the usual Cassandra effect.

The telephone.

'Head of Chancery here. Have you heard the news?'

'No. What?'

'There was trouble at the civil rights march in Derry. The paratroops have killed thirteen Catholics.'

'Anything more come through? Well, thank you very much. Goodnight.'

II

So as we surveyed the ashes of our Embassy and the ruin of our hopes, we embarked upon our final year in Dublin and the Diplomatic Service. For Mariska it was one of her saddest moments. She had brought all her taste and talent to bear on the newly-finished redecoration of my room in Chancery, and now it all lay, a heap of ashes, charred ends and molten remnants under the rubble in the basement. In the Counsellor's room, next to mine, the chandelier still hung from the ceiling, the pictures were still on the wall, and the net curtains, tatty but untorn, still screened the unbroken window. It had been a straight up-and-down petrol fire, and it was weeks before the gutted roofless building could be made safe for the debris in the cellars to be sifted and sorted. But nothing from my room, where the first petrol bombs had been thrown, survived.

The team of experts from the Foreign Office arrived within a week and planned the conversion of Glencairn to its new role. Mariska, as a gesture of defiance and courtesy combined, provided a flawless lunch for ten in their honour, the dining-room being, with the library, the only part of the ground floor left available for private use. Over the next few weeks her laconic little diary is full of entries like 'Feb 15th carpenter, telephone people, telex people, TV people and just people here, electricians, gravel delivered, no telephone in my bedroom' or 'Friday 18th house swarming with people. We are functioning. Hosepipe burst, backstairs flood', and so on.

After the fire the flood of letters: Irish people expressing their shame and horror at the burning of the Embassy; Irish people rejoicing at the vengeance for the dead of Derry; English people damning the Irish; letters of sympathy and regret from English and Irish; personal friends happy that we were safe; totally unexpected letters from colleagues and acquaintances with whom we had had no contact for decades; moving letters from our own Irish friends, offering support and even sanctuary. Dual nationals sent back their British passports because they were ashamed of the paratroops, or their Irish passports because they were ashamed of their compatriots in Merrion Square. It was an emotional time for all of us.

Two patterns began to emerge, apparently contradictory but in fact part of a larger and, to us, more important scheme of things. People were striking attitudes which, however they tried to rationalise them, were simply tribal. The Rugby Football Unions of Scotland and Wales refused to send their teams for their international matches in Dublin, whereas the Irish team went to England four weeks after Bloody Sunday, three weeks after the fire, and were enthusiastically welcomed at Twickenham. Predictably, the Irish tourist season was calamitous. Not only were angry English people determined not to go among the Irish; many Americans did not know the difference between Dublin and Belfast, between Derry and Drogheda. I had letters addressed to me in Dublin, Northern Ireland, and (from the House of Commons) British Embassy, Belfast. But at the same time, I was getting letters and listening to comment on different lines. Things cannot go on like this. Cannot we make a fresh start? Have not the Irish and British governments enough common interests to enable them to rise above tribalism and the bloodshed and horror of the North? Is not this the great opportunity? It was a time for sanity. In fact, the two events of that bloody week had changed nothing basic. Everybody in close contact now knew that the security role and methods imposed upon the Army in Northern Ireland were self-defeating. Bloody Sunday and its aftermath merely proved the point. Burning the Embassy had discharged a lot of political pus that was poisoning Irish public life—indeed it put a stop to all anti-British rioting in the Republic and all but the most harmless of anti-British demonstrations. But the facts remained. The

British Army in Northern Ireland was performing a security role on behalf of the Northern Ireland government whose back-benchers would not tolerate any policy incompatible with 'the establishment of law and order'. But it was still to be Protestant law and Orange Order. I begged everybody, English and Irish, to make their political points without invoking this question-begging slogan, and to try using 'peace with justice' instead. I am happy to say that some of them listened.

My personal view of Mr Jack Lynch, the past and future Taoiseach was—and remains—that while his government made their share of miscalculations and mistakes during that turbulent period, all those concerned with, and committed to, peace with justice in the North owe a very great deal to his courage and tenacity in pursuing what he believed to be the right policy. He held his party together and maintained popular support for his 'peaceful approach' in the face of fearful pressures from all quarters and he never wavered in his outward confidence, whatever private qualms he may have felt, that he was right to put his trust in the British government. The ruling party, Fianna Fáil, was due shortly after the frightful week to hold its annual conference, and the stresses and strains and the pressure on its leaders were immense. The air was thick with rumours that the British government was contemplating an important new initiative, and I was able to convey confidentially to Jack Lynch a broad hint that these rumours were not totally unfounded, although I had no idea what was in the wind. Aided by this and perhaps by the emotional hangover from the night of the fire he scored an overwhelming personal triumph for his policy of peaceful cooperation which two weeks earlier had seemed, like the Embassy, to be a pile of ashes. I do not think that I ever succeeded in convincing British politicians of how much we owed him at that stage, or what the consequences would have been if he had lost his head.

Bloody Sunday had other consequences besides the burning of the Embassy. The IRA bombing campaign was stepped up and extended to England. Cross-Border activity increased, and there were more bank raids carried out in the Republic by men with strong Northern accents. The two governments pressed more heavily on each other to do something. I was summoned to London early in March, and when asked by Ministers what the Irish were doing I could only reply, laconically but accurately, 'Waiting'. Mariska and I did what we could personally to restore or maintain normality. Throughout the worst period she had insisted on being seen publicly going about her business, shopping in Dublin, attending all the functions to which she was invited, without any police protection or security precautions. She had intended to go to London for a few days at the beginning of February, but postponed her journey until she could not be suspected of running away from anything. We went every Sunday to the concerts at the Gaiety Theatre and sat in our usual box. None of this passed unnoticed, and I think it helped, but nothing could alter the underlying situation as I had described it to Ministers in London at the beginning of February.

In Dublin we had to face one more threat of trouble. The Provisional IRA announced a massive protest march on Glencairn. During the previous week every lamp-post in central Dublin had its poster calling the citizens to march on Glencairn, and the Provisionals were confidently predicting that 27,000 people would turn up. It was a lovely afternoon for a march, and the fact that barely five hundred appeared, many pushing prams, and scarcely outnumbering the massive police force guarding the grounds, well illustrates the change of mood caused by the destruction of the Embassy. Once again the donkeys introduced the inevitable note of farce. They resented the invasion of their privacy by the police; and when the loudspeakers on the lead car, to get the procession moving after handing in its petition, roared out some good revolutionary song, it was too much. They cleared a wall, a double hedge and a wire fence hitherto deemed impassable, and were only found two days later browsing peacefully on Leopardstown Racecourse. The Provisional IRA looked exceptionally silly.

During the confused weeks after Bloody Sunday and the fire, when nobody was quite sure whether they wanted to know us or not, a very pleasant thing happened. The Minister for Foreign Affairs, Dr Hillery, revived a custom that had been in abeyance for some years, and gave a St Patrick's Day dinner for Ambassadors, members of the Dáil parties, members of the legal profession, the armed forces—in fact a cross section of public life. Mariska and I were invited and of course we went.

There was nothing strange in any of this, except that both of us felt very strongly that we were being given something special, a cross between a hero's welcome and a greeting for a couple who had been too long out in the cold. Mariska noted in her diary that she was seated next to Dr Conor Cruise O'Brien, and we met his wife for the first time since we had been together at the Council of Europe in Strasbourg. Nobody can fail to enjoy listening to him discussing almost any topic, but I suppose that he will be regarded more as an analyst of the Irish than as a typical representative of them. The trouble about a gathering like that is that there is too little time, and we were startled to find that all the other diplomats had left long before, while we were still having a wonderful time with the Irish guests.

Mariska eventually left in the middle of March. On the evening of the twenty-second I gave a dinner at Glencairn to two of our closest friends in Dublin, and Nicholas and his girlfriend, and Lucy, one of the Embassy girls. Around ten I was summoned to the telephone. It was the Prime Minister's Private Secretary. How soon could I be in Downing Street? I said that I would be there at nine the next morning. I rang for the butler who called the chauffeur and rang Special Branch to send the escort. Lucy alerted the airport and fixed the ticket. Nicholas rang the Foreign Office and asked them to send a car to Heathrow. In ten minutes we resumed the party until well past one in the morning; then up at 6.30 and away to London.

I arrived on time for a hectic day in Downing Street. At some point I got a message to Mariska asking her to meet me around dinner time. By the time we met, the Northern Ireland government had resigned; the Stormont Parliament, after fifty years, had been suspended; direct rule had been imposed, and Mr William Whitelaw had been appointed Secretary of State for Northern Ireland. All this was to be announced next day. I arranged to see Jack Lynch early the next morning to give him the information in advance and hand him the text of the statement that was to be made in the House of Commons. The Foreign Office would telegraph the texts during the night.

I went straight from Downing Street to join Mariska and

we had dinner at the Carlton Towers. Then back to where she was staying in Eaton Place. Although the information was classified until the next day I told her the news, for she is famous for her discretion and she had in any case worked a lot of it out for herself. We celebrated privately until the car came to take me to Heathrow to catch the midnight plane. An hour or so to study the texts as they arrived in Glencairn and bed at 4.30.

Jack Lynch had of course been expecting 'an initiative' for weeks, but I think that he and most people in the Republic were amazed, as well as delighted, when it actually happened— and on such a scale. Having carried out all my instructions and said what I was told to say to the Taoiseach, I added a comment of my own. The battle of the British government to join the Common Market, which was in large measure a personal battle of Mr Heath's, had not yet been finally won, and crucial votes in the House of Commons were still to come. I believed then, and I believe now, that the decision of the Leader of the Conservative and Unionist Party to suspend Stormont, the fifty-year-old instrument of Unionist domination, before the battle of Europe was won was one of the most courageous and honest political acts of the century. And I said so.

Suspending Stormont could not bring peace to Northern Ireland or 'put an end to violence'. But it was the necessary prelude to true reforms. It broke the long jam, and the changes followed fast. For me personally, the end of the story came with the setting up of the Special Criminal Courts in the Republic; knocking down the barricades in the no-go areas in the North, and, above all, the recognition by Her Majesty's government of the so-called 'Irish dimension'. In October 1972 it appeared over Mr Whitelaw's signature :

> Whatever arrangements are made for the future adminis-
> tration of Northern Ireland must take account of the
> Province's relationship with the Republic of Ireland; and to
> the extent that this is done, there is an obligation upon the
> Republic to reciprocate. Both the economy and the security
> of the two areas are to some considerable extent inter-
> dependent, and the same is true of both in their relationship

with Great Britain. It is therefore clearly desirable that any new arrangements for Northern Ireland should, whilst meeting the wishes of Northern Ireland and Great Britain, be so far as possible acceptable to and accepted by the Republic of Ireland which, from 1 January 1973, will share the rights and obligations of membership of the European Communities. It remains the view of the United Kingdom Government that it is for the people of Northern Ireland to decide what should be their relationship to the United Kingdom and to the Republic of Ireland; and that it should not be impossible to devise measures which will meet the best interests of all three. Such measures would seek to secure the acceptance, in both Northern Ireland and in the Republic, of the present status of Northern Ireland, and of the possibility—which would have to be compatible with the principle of consent—of subsequent change in that status; to make possible effective consultation and co-operation in Ireland for the benefit of North and South alike; and to provide a firm basis for concerted governmental and community action against those terrorist organisations which represent a threat to free democratic institutions in Ireland as whole.

And that is what, more tersely perhaps, we had been saying all along.

But the suspension of Stormont and the introduction of direct rule did not bring an end to the problems North or South. Internment and the memories of Bloody Sunday lingered on, and resentment over the burning of the Embassy still smouldered. An outburst of tribal petulance meant that no British team took part in the international show-jumping competition in Dublin in August ('something might happen to the horses'), and brought much embarrassment to the British government, much sympathy for the British Embassy in Dublin and much annoyance to England's best friends in Ireland.

At this point we noticed an interesting phenomenon. The Scottish and Welsh Rugby teams, apparently fearing trouble, had refused to come to Dublin. The flower of English chivalry had felt obliged to stay away. But the music loving world, during the darkening weeks at the end of 1971, flocked to the Wexford Opera Festival. And that group of ladies' clubs called the Soroptimists, who had chosen Killarney for their annual convention, reviewed the situation after the burning of the Embassy and decided to hold their convention in Killarney. We formulated a Law of Inverse Heroics.

This contributed indirectly to a lunatic week-end at the end of July. The British show-jumping authorities had entered a team for the Junior European Championships in Cork on Saturday 29 July. I had been invited to attend the Robertstown Canal Festival at lunch-time on the thirtieth, and as Robertstown was some thirty miles from Dublin but 150 from Cork I might have declined the invitation to the show-jumping. I then heard that the British, having accepted, had withdrawn their team. Furious, I was determined to go to Cork as well. Kind friends invited me to stay near Cork on the Friday and Saturday nights.

But at 11.30 am on the Thursday I was summoned by telephone to be in 10 Downing Street at 4.30 pm. I went, sending Mariska down to Cork in the Embassy Jaguar and saying I would follow when I could. The meeting was to discuss 'Operation Motorman', the code name given to the massive operation by the British Army to knock down all the barricades surrounding the Catholic no-go areas in Belfast and Derry. I said I thought it was vitally important to give the Irish government all the details and arguments in advance. The operation was timed for early on the following Monday, and I was told to hand highly confidential documents personally to Mr Lynch on Sunday evening. This was fine, except that the papers could not reach Dublin before Saturday evening, and Jack Lynch was lost somewhere in a crucial and hectic by-election campaign in the wilds of West Cork. So was Dr Hillery. It was the worst possible time and place for the British Ambassador to be seen hob-nobbing with the Irish government.

However, it all went like clockwork. I flew back to Dublin on the Friday evening, reaching our friends in Cork at midnight. Saturday we spent at the horse show. Sunday morning we drove to Robertstown, where David Blatherwick arrived at the canal festival with the Motorman papers. David took Mariska to Dublin, and I took the papers to Cork. There, as the result of multifarious telephonings, I discreetly met Dr Hillery who had made an even more discreet rendezvous for me to meet the

Taoiseach at 12.45 am. We were both on time and spent an animated and ultimately constructive hour together. I then set off on the last lap back to Dublin. Mariska had said that she would leave me sandwiches and wine in the library, a welcome prospect around five in the morning after some five hundred miles of motoring and high politics after midnight. And behold—a few crumbs on a plate, two empty glasses, an empty bottle, and son Nicholas with a ravishing girl; and both sitting—demurely though somewhat surprised—on the sofa. I must say they were very nice about it, and so, remarkably, was I. Up at 8.30 to send the Foreign Office a colourless telegram saying, in effect, Mission Completed. It had been a good idea to code-name the army's operation Motorman. It is week-ends like this that bring alive the wording of the Queen's Commission when she granted me all power and authority to do and perform all proper acts, matters and things which may be desirable or necessary for the promotion of relations of friendship . . .

From the newspapers and the parliamentary reports from Westminster during 1972 we noticed a steady trickle of Conservative MPs going to Northern Ireland, spending a couple of days with Stormont Ministers, being shown around by the Army in helicopters and armoured cars, and returning to parliament as experts with a first-hand knowledge of the Irish problem. With the tactful aid of the Foreign Office we encouraged the thought that having been to the North it would not be too great a detour to return home via Dublin, and a number of them did. We arranged for them to meet a useful cross-section of influential opinion, and unless the mind was closed too tightly for a political locksmith to open it up in the period available I think we all believed it was time well spent. (By the same token, I should have thought that any Opposition spokesman on Irish affairs should spend as much time and study in and on the Republic as Northern Ireland.) However it was the Labour Opposition who gave us one of our more memorable experiences. A team of Labour MPs came to Dublin to compare notes with Irish Labour and trade union leaders, and we understood that the team, some six or seven strong, was to be led by Mr Wilson. We gave a drinks party for them out on the lawns at Glencairn, on a lovely July evening in 1972, so that they could meet a suitably representative body of Irish people. When they arrived there was no Mr Wilson, he having been detained by business in England, and the party was led by Mr Stanley Orme. When the party was in full swing I was called to the telephone to find Mr Wilson on the line, wanting to speak to Mr Orme. I detected a slight air of mystery about the proceedings, which was clarified when Mr Orme emerged to tell the assembled company that, actually, Mr Wilson was in England talking to the Provisional IRA. The effect was electrifying, the conversation animated, and the comments of the British MPs about their leader made me glad it was a stag party with no ladies present. (This is no breach of confidence—it all could not have been more public.) Anyway, it made the evening.

The end of Stormont and the beginning of direct rule by Britain were an immense encouragement to the Irish government, the vast majority of the Northern Catholics, and the small but growing number of Northern Protestants who had enough breadth of vision to see the utter sterility of Unionist politics in the North. But it was a political threat both to the Provisional IRA, Sinn Féin and to their opposite numbers, the illegal paramilitary armies and their paraclerical demagogues. The IRA responded with an indiscriminate bombing campaign in Northern Ireland and in Britain, specifically designed to kill and maim completely innocent civilian men, women and children and thus intimidate the government into yielding to their nebulous and impossible political demands. The arms and explosives trickled in from Britain, mainland Europe, the Irish Republic, the United States, and the money from bank raids, intimidated Northerners and Irish Americans.

Many of the bombs were made of ingredients which, as any schoolboy could explain, can be found in any farm or general store, and complete control of the international traffic was impossible. But inevitably there was heavy pressure on the Irish government to 'do more'. This led to an unfortunate incident, in the summer of 1972 at the Olympic Games in Munich of all places. Mr Heath and Mr Lynch were both present for the opening of the Games, and so had a chance for a chat which, on the Irish side, was clearly understood to be confidential. So they were not over-pleased to read, in the next day's papers, an 'official statement issued on the British side' which stressed that Mr Heath had called special attention to IRA cross-Border raids and added the threat: 'Unless it were felt both in Great Britain generally and in Northern Ireland in particular that the South is taking action against the IRA there is little hope of an acceptable solution.' The Irish also had views about bank robbers from the North crossing an obviously uncontrollable Border; the Opposition, and Mr Lynch's enemies in his own party, were watching like hawks to see if he was being pushed around by Mr Heath, so the breach of confidence, whether deliberate or a misunderstanding, did not add to the success of the meeting.

Nevertheless there was nothing to do but soldier on. Jack Lynch, with Stormont suspended in March and the interest of the Republic in Northern Ireland and the possibility of reunification formally recognised in October, felt strong enough to introduce the Criminal Justice Bill, which was to legislate for measures against the IRA even tougher than those in British law. He succeeded, but it destroyed him. In the debate in the Dáil, the fate of his government hung by a thread, and the last of my predictions that he would survive another cliff-hanger looked at one stage almost foolhardy—only to have the issue put beyond doubt by two incredibly timed bombs in Dublin, almost universally believed to have been planted by Northern Protestants, which swung the Opposition behind the government and saved the day. But the measure finally alienated the disaffected elements in Fianna Fáil; Jack Lynch could no longer rely on a parliamentary majority, and a general election was inevitable. Many thought, mistakenly, that he was acting confidently, from a position of strength, in calling an election. In my last official despatch, written on the day I left, I remarked that one advantage of retiring at that precise moment was that I did not have to forecast the result of the election. It is the only occasion in all my time in Dublin when I fled from a prophecy—which was in itself prophetic.

But for me, the formal recognition of the Irish dimension by the British government in October 1972 was the end of the Irish story. I would be sixty in four months' time, which meant that I would retire on 16 February. We had gradually reached the decision to stay in Ireland although we knew full well that it can be regarded as extremely bad taste for a retiring Ambassador to settle in his last post, because of the embarrassment it might cause to the new incumbent. Of course this would happen if the outgoing couple behaved as if they had never left the Embassy, and over the years there have been one or two spectacular examples of this kind, notably in Paris. Mariska and I made it clear that we wished to have no part in diplomacy or politics. We kept our friends and our interests, sought no publicity but did not refuse it if it came our way and were completely non-political. We never called at the British or any other Embassy unless we were invited. Most people seem to have understood perfectly.

At official level there was talk about the timing of my departure being wrong and the dangers of swapping horses in mid-stream —as there invariably is if an Ambassador has to retire at a time when politics and diplomatic relations are very lively. Certainly the Irish had grown accustomed to my face, but knew perfectly well that it would have the exact reverse effect if they said anything to the British government. But some British MPs and other visitors were evidently canvassed. All I could do was to say that we should be very happy to stay on if we were told to, but saw no reason to expect an exception to the very rigid rule that we had to be out by sixty. And that naturally was how it happened.

I had wanted, and virtually been promised, a minor extension until mid-April. It was not until 13 December that I was given the firm news that we had to be out on 15 February. With the approach of Christmas and New Year—celebrations which in working Dublin tend to merge—and nowhere else to go, there was nothing for it but to plan to move straight to the house we had found in Dun Laoghaire. Almost overnight it became our immediate future home. And here, five years later, we remain.

The letter with the news of our imminent departure happened to arrive on the day that we were giving a dinner party to welcome the new Canadian Ambassador and his wife. We had assembled a high-powered list of guests, chief among them being Erksine Childers, then still Tanaiste (Deputy Prime Minister), a very wise and experienced man, who had always been friendly and helpful. In my brief after-dinner speech I said how sorry I was that the Canadians and ourselves would

F

have so short a time together in Dublin, as we now knew for certain that we should be retiring in February; and everybody said nice words of welcome and the Canadian Ambassador replied. Then without warning Erskine Childers rose and made a speech, very warm and simple and obviously straight from the heart, not about our guests of honour but about Mariska and me and our time in Dublin. There is, of course, no text or record of it, but one of the points that he stressed went something like this : 'We in the Irish government soon discovered that the British Ambassador interpreted our position and our problems faithfully and fairly to his government. But we also learnt that he was a lucid and outspoken Ambassador, and I would like people on both sides of the water to know that when, as often happened, there were differences between us, we were never left in any doubt what the British felt, and why.'

After our retirement, when Erskine Childers had been elected President of the Republic to succeed Eamon de Valera, we occasionally met him at social gatherings, and at one of them in the autumn of 1974 he said how much he and his wife would like to come to dine privately with us. I asked his Private Secretary to let me know what date would be convenient. On 17 November 1974, in London, we heard on the radio that he had died. When I returned to Dublin the following day, I found on the doormat the letter from the secretary saying that the President and Mrs Childers would be glad to dine with us on 28 December. Mariska and I shared with the Irish people a profound sense of personal loss.

12

I REMEMBER very little about our last two weeks in Glencairn. Mariska's diary records an unending round of lunches, receptions, dinners, speeches, press interviews; giving a dance at Glencairn for some two hundred people, and a cocktail party for one hundred and fifty, and another for the entire Embassy staff. Our last concert at the Gaiety Theatre, during which at one moment I was listening to Prokofiev and at the next found myself in the manager's office surrounded by doctors and festooned with wires attached to an electro-cardiograph—while Mariska had to remain in her seat in the box as if nothing had happened, to avoid triggering off the alarm that would have undoubtedly ensued from the assumption that there had been an assassination attempt. An altercation next morning with my doctor who wanted to keep me prostrate for forty-eight hours, whereas I insisted that I had to pay my farewell call on Jack Lynch and then attend the formal dinner given in our honour by the Minister for Foreign Affairs—an argument which I won as the ECGs were all clear and my heart sound. Going to the England-Ireland rugby match at Lansdowne Road at which 45,000 Irishmen stood up and gave the English team an ovation when they ran onto the field such as has never been heard before or since. Mariska was having to spend every spare moment getting the new house in Dun Laoghaire in order, surrounded by painters, decorators, carpenters, plumbers, electricians; and we had to have everything we possessed out of Glencairn and into a completely unready house before we ourselves left on the fifteenth of February, to be replaced by Sir Arthur Galsworthy on the twenty-first. What reserves of energy and courage Mariska drew upon to sustain her, I shall never know, but she had not wholly recovered a year later.

Since we had had a fairly colourful three years, and our decision to settle in Ireland had aroused a lot of interest, some publicity at the time of our retirement was inevitable. But I was surprised to earn an editorial in the *Irish Independent*:

ENVOY'S SUCCESS

IN A SPEECH addressed to the Rotary Club yesterday Sir John Peck, Britain's Ambassador in Ireland, sounded a note of quiet trust that the broadening of the British and Irish horizons brought about by the enlargement of the Common Market would bring nearer the day when increasing mutual co-operation between the two parts of this country will be matched by peace throughout the island.

Sir John Peck, who is retiring and settling down here shortly, has undoubtedly had a difficult and onerous three years in his present office. In that relatively short time, however, he has managed to establish for himself a reputation as a level-headed man with a calm approach to all situations. This is impressive considering the political background against which he has had to operate.

He is the only British Ambassador to this country who has had his embassy burnt down. The outcry in Britain and the ensuing decline in the British tourist trade with this country must have been a burden to diplomatic relations between Dublin and London, adding to the effect of the low periods through which the North has travailed, including the past two weeks.

Sir John Peck could not have maintained Dublin-London relations at their present level of overall goodwill unless there was a significant and representative interest in fostering good relations between the countries. Nevertheless, it is a great credit to him that Dublin-London relations at the end of three difficult years are as good as they are now.

Two or three weeks later the *Irish Times* had another angle on my departure. In the middle of a political commentary from London the following passage occurred:

Ted Heath doesn't like (or so they say):

1. John Peck. It sounds odd, because many nice things are said about Peck both in the Foreign Office and in Dublin, where he had an excellent relationship (personal relations again!) with Lynch. But Heath is said to have refused to allow his term of service in Dublin to be extended. Why the story goes that Heath feels he should have gone down, as it were, with his ship when the British Embassy in Dublin was burned. One knows dedication is required of those who represent Her Majesty abroad, but that seems a little excessive.

2. Terence O'Neill. To put it mildly, there aren't many unionists that the Prime Minister likes, but O'Neill appears to irritate him more than almost any of the others.

This could have been awkward if, for example, I had been looking for a job in England, and a legal friend of mine suggested it might be actionable. This thought opened up mind-boggling vistas. The *Irish Times* hastened to assure me that they were not taking a swipe at me, and for all I know the story was true. I didn't intend to live and work in England anyway, and so this piece of Westminster gossip was left floating in the air.

My formal swansong was the short speech I made at the Minister's farewell dinner, which I wanted to be the link between the old life and the new. Somewhere in it I said:

We are looking forward to a lively and colourful retirement, the prospects for which are greatly enhanced by our decision to make our home in the Republic. I will not deny that some of our English friends think us slightly mad and say, 'Why Ireland?' To which we reply either, 'Why not?' or, 'Because of the Irish'. Why are we really staying here? I will give just one *public* reason. For many years we have regarded ourselves as English-speaking Europeans. Our joint entry into the Common Market is a landmark in the history of both our countries and is bound greatly to strengthen the forces that have always united us and discomfit those that have sought to divide us. Moreover, I earnestly believe and hope that our joint membership will strengthen the forces of reconciliation, harmony and justice between North and South and enlarge those already extensive, if too little publicised, areas in which this island never has been divided and, God willing, never will be. I like to think that by choosing to remain here we are making our own modest affirmation of our faith that these things are possible, and that we may be able to make some small contribution ourselves. . . . Happily I can spare you any politics tonight. Ambassadors don't talk about domestic politics, least of all during elections. And if you think there are major issues between Ireland and Britain to which HM Ambassador ought to make passing reference, I will do so. I will quote Richard Brinsley Sheridan, when he said, 'It is a very pretty little quarrel as it stands. Let us not spoil it by trying to explain it.'

Lastly, may I say thank-you on behalf of both of us to everyone who by their help, their understanding, their warmth and their tolerance has given us an insight into the meaning of true friendship and love.

On the afternoon of 15 February Mariska and I had a last sentimental walk through the grounds we loved so much and said our farewells to the household staff. Then off to the airport, where after a final goodbye to our Embassy staff we were away.

Mariska wept tears of parting and complete exhaustion. I began to brood. When you are young the idea of death is romantic and remote. The close of a diplomatic career is a sort of dying, and although the end of the line had been long in sight, the arrival at the terminus happens all too suddenly. All change. But I was free. No more eyeing the driving mirror to be sure the detectives' car was close behind. No more permission to go on leave, no telephone numbers where I could be traced at all times. No more authority or importance, no official or social obligations, no more sacrifices for diplomatic duty's sake. Never since I had joined Duff Cooper thirty-six years earlier had I enjoyed such a prospect of freedom. I had only brooded that far when we landed at London airport. For the last time we were given VIP treatment. We then spent two busy weeks in London putting off the old life, before returning unobtrusively to Ireland to put on the new.

Leaving the public service is a magnificently impersonal non-event. Nobody asks you to call to say goodbye. I gave the

Department a list of the Ministers and senior officials with whom I had had the most to do while in Dublin and the Department sought appointments. The Foreign Secretary, Mr Whitelaw and Lord Carrington were all kind enough to see me and be complimentary about the work of the Embassy; and of course I did the round of my colleagues in the Office. I was only sorry that the Prime Minister was too busy. It is an interesting commentary on Whitehall that Mariska, who had done so much, might not have existed. But the Queen acknowledges the role of her Ambassadresses, and we were both honoured by a farewell invitation to Buckingham Palace. And so back home to Dun Laoghaire in Co. Dublin.

This was, however, not quite the end. Early in June I received the following letter from Denis Greenhill, the Head of the Diplomatic Service. It meant and still means a good deal to Mariska and me.

Dear John,

Now that you have left us on retirement I should like to thank you formally and in writing for your long and distinguished service under the Crown.

You have filled with originality an unusual variety of posts in some very different places. Your wartime service in the Prime Minister's Private Office was a period of notable distinction and excitement of which you must have many fascinating memories. Much of what followed must have suffered in comparison.

We in the Diplomatic Service have found you a most congenial and stimulating colleague, and shall remember with gratitude your distinctly held views and your flair for the whole range of information work and your success at the Council of Europe and in French West Africa.

In Ireland both you and Mariska have had the opportunity to play a decisive role at a difficult and even crucial time. You established exceptionally close links with the Irish Government of the day, and I know how these helped our own Ministers. We all greatly admired the way in which you both endured the dangers and discomfort and maintained the morale of your staff. And we are deeply grateful to you both for this.

It is good still to be able to associate you with Ireland. I hope you and Mariska will have a long and happy retirement in your new home in Dun Laoghaire.

Yours ever

Denis

(Denis Greenhill)

But the Service still had its last word to say, inevitably about my diplomatic allowances—frais for short—and on 22 August said it:

Dear Sir John,

The auditors have recently been examining the payment of frais to Heads of Mission on departure from post, and in particular those departing on retirement leave. Diplomatic Service Regulation No. 24, para 15, states that Heads of Mission will not receive frais during retirement leave, and that frais will cease on the day immediately preceding departure from post.

You left Dublin on 15 February 1973, and frais should have stopped on 14 February. Unfortunately it was paid until 21 February (date of arrival of your successor), resulting in an overpayment of £13.83, calculated as follows:

$$15\text{-}21 \text{ Feb } \frac{7}{28} \times \frac{£664}{12} = £13.83$$

I am sorry that the discovery of this overpayment was so long delayed, but I now have to ask you to refund this sum to the Finance Officer of the Diplomatic Service at your earliest convenience.

Yours sincerely,

Finance Department.

This is the perfect conclusion to a career. It exactly matches the SIR or MADAM letter which admitted J. H. Peck Esquire to the public service thirty-seven years earlier. Together they form the two ends of a lovely rainbow curve of absurdity, a consoling reminder that the perils and pomposities of public life will always gain an added splendour from the laughing light of the ludicrous. I loved it all.

13

WHEN I retired to Dun Laoghaire I could look back on three tempestuous years in which the battle for sanity and justice in Ireland, even for Christian society itself, had swayed back and forth, and the pendulum of time swung inexorably between the poles of hope and despair.

Bloody Sunday and the burning of the Embassy marked its wildest oscillation towards hopelessness; but the swing back was spectacular. Within weeks Stormont and fifty years of automatic Protestant rule were swept away. The British government resumed its responsibilities, and also formally recognised the interest of the Republic in the affairs of Northern Ireland. The Irish government had introduced the toughest measures yet against the IRA. And all through the tensions and the traumas the two governments were willing and able to work together, and, moreover, were beginning to recognise a common cause. There was a dawning of understanding that we were not involved in a battle for the body and soul of the Six Counties between Catholic and Protestant, between Nationalist and Unionist, between 'traitor' and 'loyalist', the Irish Republic and Britain. Gradually there was taking shape, behind the tawdry trappings of tradition, a battle of the future against the past. By the end I had begun to realise that within Northern Ireland the problem of Northern Ireland was insoluble. Five years later it might appear that nothing has changed. But it has.

I felt I had made a start. Back in the autumn of 1970 I had been interviewed by the Dublin *Sunday Independent* and was quoted as saying :

Assuming that we both get into the Common Market, I think it is inevitable that both communities will be united.

The things that keep them apart are to an extent economic and social. After Common Market entry it's inevitable that there will be a much greater degree of harmonisation, which in the fulness of time will result in the Border withering away. . . . I think they (i.e. Northern Protestants) ought to know more about the life and cultural existence of Dublin. . . . If there is one thing I would like to see happening it is an increase in non-governmental contact between people of the North and people of the South. I can see a great deal of good in furthering social activity, travel and more cultural exchanges between the two. . . .

> (*Sunday Independent*, 8 Nov. 1970)

The interview provided me with one of my most treasured possessions. To my delight Mr Paisley, after some weeks of cogitation, honoured me with a special mention on the front page of his erudite and uplifting journal, the *Protestant Telegraph*. He, or somebody, wrote in the issue of 19 December 1970:

It is patently obvious that Peck has not a clue about the political-religious borders between North and South, nor indeed is he cognisant of the implications of his own statements. Such remarks of his, which are based on ignorance, serve no useful purpose other than to appease and flatter the Southern Government.

> (*Protestant Telegraph*, 19 Dec. 1970)

This was a great relief as I knew then that I was thinking on the right lines.

After Stormont was suspended and the British formally recognised the Irish dimension, I had floated the idea in London that it might be worth taking a look at the Statute of the Council of Europe, to see whether its multinational structure could be adapted to the bilateral situation in Ireland.

There was nothing novel in the notion of a Council of Ireland—or at least in the title. In 1920, when the Anglo-Irish conflict was at its height, the British government had introduced its Government of Ireland Act granting very limited Home Rule to two parliaments, one in the North and one in the South, with a Council of Ireland to serve as a sort of bridge or harmonising body until a single parliament could be agreed on for the whole of Ireland. But it was never set up as the degree of independence offered to the two parliaments was too small to satisfy the Irish in what is today the Republic, and the idea of the two parallel and equal parliaments passed away. But it is clear from the wording of the Government of Ireland Act that at that time, 1920, the British government regarded the existence of the two parliaments, i.e. Partition, as a temporary thing. When King George V formally opened the Northern parliament at Stormont in 1921 he concluded an emotional speech by saying, 'May this historic gathering be the prelude of a day in which the Irish people, North and South, under one parliament or two, as those parliaments may themselves decide, shall work together in common love for Ireland upon the sure foundation of mutual justice and respect.' But it was another three weeks before even a truce could be reached between the British forces and the Irish in Dublin, and another three months before the beginning of the conference which ended with the attainment of independence for the twenty-six counties of the Irish Republic. The Northern parliament lasted for fifty years and nine months, until it was terminated in March 1972. The Council of Ireland that I was tentatively proposing after those same fifty years was a very different affair. Taking the Statute of the Council of Europe as a model, I was thinking about (i) a consultative parliamentary assembly, with representatives of the Dáil and Stormont meeting to debate Irish affairs two or three times a year, and making recommendations but not empowered to take binding decisions; (ii) a committee of Ministers meeting regularly either in person or through permanent deputies, empowered either to take decisions, or refer them to their own governments; (iii) a strong permanent secretariat divided into sections dealing with, for example, agriculture, transport, tourism, culture, education, development, etc.; (iv) a permanent base, in some such historic place as Armagh.

At this point I retired into private life and shut myself off totally from all political and diplomatic activities and interests either in Ireland or Britain. I had not then realised the fundamental and fatal flaw in the concept, to which I will revert later; and I was therefore fascinated to read, on 10 December

1973, the text of the communiqué issued at the end of 'the conference between the British and Irish governments and the parties involved in the Northern Ireland Executive-designate' which met at Sunningdale on the previous four days.

The text of this document, which marks the highest point reached so far in formal Anglo-Irish relations, is to be found in Appendix II. I found it riveting, since enshrined in it was virtually a carbon copy of the blueprint I had been hawking around at the beginning of the year. I felt that the forward-looking Europeans among us could enter upon 1974 with high hopes.

At first things seemed to be going reasonably well. A Northern Ireland Assembly was elected by a proportional representation system, and a Northern Ireland Executive set up with moderate Protestants and the Catholic SDLP represented. This is always referred to as the 'power-sharing' Executive, but that term has, in more rigid circles, become a dirty word, and it seems more in keeping with other governmental systems to call it a coalition. The Executive and the Assembly struggled along in the face of very undemocratic and frankly disloyal obstruction from men calling themselves loyalists who invoked democratic principles at every turn—which demonstrates a second fatal flaw in the Sunningdale edifice, to which also I shall revert later. Setting up the Council of Ireland had to wait until the new constitutional arrangements in Northern Ireland had settled down. But at least something was happening.

Then disaster struck, from a different quarter altogether, and not for the first time in Anglo-Irish history it was caused by events that were nothing whatever to do with Ireland. During the winter of 1973-74 Mr Heath and his Conservative government became involved in a major confrontation with the British coalminers and hence with the trade union movement. The situation became so acute that he felt obliged to resign and face a general election which, in April 1974, he lost. This was a massive misfortune for the future of Ireland.

The industrial confrontation had already impelled Mr Heath to withdraw Mr Whitelaw, the first Conservative minister in decades to comprehend and be concerned about the Irish, from his post as Secretary of State for Northern Ireland. The election campaign, as always, left the country effectively without a government, and thus provided an opportunity, which the Northern Irish dissidents could not resist, to sabotage the Sunningdale Agreements. Although the Conservative and Unionist Party had discarded its disaffected Unionists, its precarious electoral prospects inevitably heightened the temptation of the Conservatives and the hopes of the Unionists to break the bipartisan policy of the Westminster parliament. In the election itself the massive Northern Protestant vote for the traditional Stormont Unionists was regarded, and treated, as superseding and annulling the votes for the PR-elected Assembly. The defeat of Mr Heath's government meant a further period of uncertainty while the new government established itself and took a fresh look at Northern Ireland and in particular at the security situation.

Mr Merlyn Rees, a gentle Celt from Wales of whom nobody knew for sure whether his velvet glove concealed a mailed fist, had to restart the sensitive task of establishing good working relations with the chiefs of the police and Army; and of sizing up, as a politician, what the security forces could and could not be expected to do. The timing of this April general election could only be disastrous for Ireland, and it was. The Northern 'loyalists', who since the suspension of their government in Belfast a year back had never swerved in their disloyalty to the will of their sovereign parliament, seized this opportunity and in May 1974 called a general strike which effectively paralysed the Six Counties, brought an end to coalition government and caused direct rule to be restored and the Council of Ireland to be indefinitely postponed.

Meanwhile politics in the Republic were following a fairly tranquil and, from the British viewpoint, encouraging course. In the general election whose outcome I had declined to predict on the day I retired, Jack Lynch's Fianna Fáil emerged as the largest single party, but were outnumbered by Fine Gael and Labour who fought and won the election as a coalition. Historically, Fine Gael was better placed than Fianna Fáil to co-operate with the British on matters north of the Border, and the groundwork had already been done by Mr Heath and Mr Lynch. After the signing of the Sunningdale Agreements in December 1973 there was in effect a Northern Ireland policy agreed by all parties in the House of Commons, all parties in the

Dáil, and by the Catholic political leaders and moderate progressive Protestants in Northern Ireland. That left the IRA
and the Protestant thugs and political irreconcilables blocking
the paths to peace, and as I have just described, they did
precisely that.

There was one unfortunate casualty of the change of government and the Strike. Just as the performance of the Dublin police
on the evening the British Embassy was burnt was unintention-
ally portrayed very unfairly on television, so the British Army
was portrayed in May 1974 as standing around watching a
general revolt against their own sovereign power without lifting
a finger to stop it. These scenes on British and European television screens, which caused so much bewilderment and dismay,
were certainly not the fault of the officers and men, who were
only obeying orders, or lack of orders, from on high. It was just
the end result of a chain reaction started by the British general
election. And here was another unhappy coincidence. Two
crucial decisions affecting the Army were both taken directly
after general elections brought a change of government: their
violent intervention in the Falls Road in July 1970 and their
passive non-intervention in the strike of 1974.

Two years later there occurred one of those sickening events
that in many hearts arouse despair over Ireland. Mr Christopher
Ewart-Biggs, who had been appointed Ambassador to Dublin
after the retirement of my successor, was assassinated, together
with a young secretary from London, Miss Judith Cooke, a few
days after presenting his credentials in July 1976. I have nothing
to add to what I said in the preface to this book, except to
restate my faith in the modern and true Ireland.

Three years later, in 1977, the Six Counties are still being
ruled directly from London. The Labour government survives,
and has sent a robust character, Mr Roy Mason, the former
Minister of Defence, to manage the North. He has his work
cut out.

During those three years, the campaign of murder by IRA
and Protestant thugs against the Army, the police and each
other, continued. Inevitably, the cry for stronger security
measures was heard again in Northern Ireland, and was echoed
by Conservative spokesmen in the House of Commons. Again
Messrs Ian Paisley and Ernest Baird tried to paralyse Northern

Ireland by a general strike, in the spring of 1977. But this time they were rejected by the vast majority of Protestants and Catholics alike; the people as a whole resisted and defied their bullying and intimidation; the strike was a failure and Paisley was left looking ridiculous. There have been fresh signs, too, of disunity and disintegration among the Protestant leadership, even though many still hanker after the old system of government by Protestants for Protestants for ever. Another glimmer of hope has come from the Peace People who suddenly and spontaneously appeared, sickened by the brutal stupidity of life in Northern Ireland.

In politics in the Republic, June 1977 brought another surprise. A general election returned Jack Lynch and the Fianna Fáil Party to power with an overwhelming majority; and it is in the interregnum between the old government and the new that this narrative ends and the discussion begins.

'Laudably and profitably,' wrote the English Pope Adrian IV to the Norman King Henry II in 1154, 'Laudably and profitably does your majesty contemplate spreading the glory of your name on earth . . . since you intend . . . to enlarge the boundaries of the church, to proclaim the truths of the Christian religion to a rude and ignorant people, and to root out the growths of vice from the field of the Lord . . . Whereas, then, you have expressed to us your desire to enter the island of Ireland in order to subject its people to law and to root out from them the weeds of vice . . . we therefore do hereby declare our will and pleasure that . . . you shall enter that island . . .'

For more than eight hundred years the English in Ireland have pursued this spiritual horticulture, although the garden where the weeds of vice still burgeon has dwindled to the north-east corner of the island. The weed-killers do not work. The task of 'subjecting its people to law' still baffles us. Something must be wrong with the English, or the Irish, or with new resistant strains of weed, or with the law. There must be some reason why, more than fifty years after the Partition of Ireland and the solemn retention of the Six Counties in the United Kingdom in accordance with the wishes of the majority of the local inhabitants, Northern Ireland has become the shame and bewilderment of the free world, and the propagandists' treasure trove for the free world's enemies. Why?

14

NOTHING about Ireland, especially Northern Ireland, is simple.
But the pieces of a jigsaw puzzle emptied out of their box into
a jumbled heap on the table are a meaningless mess until the
task of piecing them together has begun and a pattern begins
to emerge. There is no facile solution to the problem of Northern Ireland, partly because those involved, inside and outside the
Six Counties, not only are unable to agree on what solution
there can be but also differ fundamentally on what the problem
is. As a general proposition, what the rest of the world wants,
or at least what anyone who is interested or concerned wants, is
an internal political arrangement in Northern Ireland, and a
settlement of its relations with Britain and the Irish Republic,
which goes far enough towards satisfying conflicting claims to
make violent and undemocratic methods seem to be not worth
while. Clearly this would entail compromise all round.

Sovereign power and responsibility in Northern Ireland lie
where they have lain since Pope Adrian IV made King Henry II
of England Lord of Ireland, namely with the British sovereign
power in England. The full and correct title is 'the Sovereign
in Parliament', and it is to this person, or concept, that the
loyalty of the British subject is due. Until the year 1800 Ireland
had its own parliaments of a sort, but the extent to which they
were independent of interference from the English parliament
and executive had been a subject of controversy for many centuries. Then in 1801 the two kingdoms were combined and no
separate Irish parliament existed or was contemplated except
under a series of very limiting Home Rule Bills, all of which,
for various reasons, proved abortive. In 1922 Ireland was
divided into two. The principal part, the Twenty-Six Counties,

became an independent sovereign state. The Six Counties were given limited powers of self-government under the British Crown from 1920 to 1972, but the Irish Republic has never recognised Partition and claims sovereignty over the whole island of Ireland.

The responsible authority, the de facto authority as the Irish Republic sees it, in this Northern situation, namely the British parliament and people, has a multiple choice before it. There are no fewer than seven possible policies open to a British government in mid-1977, and on these I will elaborate later. They are mostly long-term in their effect and they are not clear-cut, in the sense that certain short-term activities or inactivities would be compatible with more than one possible outcome. But two things are as clear as crystal about the problems of Northern Ireland. First, the British government cannot solve them by contemplating only Northern Ireland. Secondly, a fundamental question of British political philosophy has to be faced, and it is this. Confronted by an intractable problem, such as Ireland has been for eight hundred years, do we (*a*) treat it in the normal parliamentary way, which in practice amounts to playing it by ear, taking ad hoc decisions as we go along, subordinating the real issues to our other national interests, party interests and electoral advantage, and dealing with each aspect of a very complex question piecemeal? Or do we (*b*) say : This is a very old problem, very deep and wide; we shall study it in all its aspects, consult all those whom we believe to be concerned; we shall formulate a long-term aim which we believe to be right, however unrealistic it may appear in the short term and however many antagonisms it may arouse; we shall seek to interest and involve those whom we have consulted; having made up our minds we shall not be scared off our aim by noise and threats or distracted by local and superficial considerations. And we shall approach the Irish question directly, as a thing in itself, and judge it accordingly, and not treat it as an issue subordinate to questions of economic policy, defence, European integration, devolution, or electoral advantage.

Now this second approach is thoroughly non-British. It suggests Planning; it has a strong whiff of authoritarianism and 'Daddy knows best', such as fascists and Communists offer; it is colonialism and trampling on the just rights of minorities; it is undemocratic; it is an international plot. But worst of all it runs counter to one of the most deeply-rooted beliefs and instincts of British democracy, based upon the metaphysical philosophy of subjective idealism : a problem overseas and therefore out of sight, such as the rise of Nazism and German rearmament, world food and energy crises, or Ireland, if it is not thought about does not exist, and if it is ignored will go away. To accept this philosophy entails regarding murder, mutilation and destruction and the heavy commitment of the Army as normal and conforming to Mr Maudling's 'acceptable level of violence' on British soil, though the level of acceptability depends on whether the violence happens in Northern Ireland on the one hand or Birmingham and London on the other. Fortunately the British system tends to throw up a Gladstone or a Winston Churchill or an Edward Heath when most needed, even if Mr Heath only had time to take a first but essential preliminary step. So the second approach is not ruled out.

But, whether or not the voting and ruling classes in Britain are concerned about Northern Ireland, there are others elsewhere who are : in the Irish Republic, in the United States, and in Europe, as well as collectors of material for the troublemakers in the Communist world. In any case, even for the 'out of sight, out of mind' school of political thought, there may be some advantage in trying to work out how the problem has reached its present stage; and the mere fact of tracing its history may give some pointers to which of the seven possible policies is the right one to pursue.

The seven possibilities are :

1. The restoration of the government of Northern Ireland as it was from 1920 to 1972.

2. Permanent direct rule from Westminster, perhaps leading to whatever degree of devolution is devised for Scotland and Wales.

3. The reunification of Ireland.

4. To wait for, or work for, the emergence of a supranational Europe into which Northern Ireland and the Irish Republic can be integrated and in which the meaning of national sovereignties becomes academic.

5. Total independence for Northern Ireland.

6. To do nothing, and allow the present situation to continue indefinitely.

7. To accept none of these possibilities, but to work for unilateral planning by the British government of an objectively just solution of the future of Northern Ireland, and a campaign on a national and international level to have it accepted and adopted.

(ii)

For better or for worse the relationship between England and Ireland has continued for a very long time. The Cynic of Downing Street may have said that a week is a long time in politics. A Stoic of Dun Laoghaire may reply that eight centuries can be a short time in history, and the story began a long time before that. The Irish are sometimes regarded as a people obsessed with the past—like the famous mythical bird that flies backwards; it can't see where it's going but it loves to see where it's been. It may be true, but the past is a great deal closer than it sometimes seems to be.

Students of folklore and nursery rhymes often stress the great accuracy of the oral tradition. What the child learns at mother's knee is imprinted on the memory, and handed on unchanged a generation later. This amazing accuracy was established when the first printed collections of nursery rhymes were assembled in the nineteenth century and texts could be compared. The fascinating discovery was made then that in many cases a rhyme which had been taken to America in the eighteenth century could survive unchanged and recross the Atlantic in the twentieth century in a purer form than the version handed down in families in England. The significance of this will not be lost to anyone who has studied the folk-lore and consequences of Irish emigration to America in the eighteenth and nineteenth centuries. A second significant point emerges from genealogy. With a surprising consistency of averages, family trees show that the eldest surviving son is born when the father is thirty-three years old; or, in other words, that three generations make a century. Thus in regions and in families where passions are or have been strong, the story of a great event three centuries or more ago, such as the English Civil War or the advent of Cromwell in Ireland need have been handed down only nine or ten times. To say that the American Revolution happened six generations ago brings it closer than two hundred years. It is true that television has blurred the tradition but it does not diminish the power of the child to absorb lasting impressions in infancy. On a recent evening around seven o'clock—peak viewing time for children—I turned on my television and idly switched to each channel in turn. There was a gun battle in what looked like Denver but could have been Derry; a very gory punch-up in Arizona—or the Ardoyne; and a riot in a bar which could be almost anywhere.

Today, children who were nine or ten years old when the present wave of bloodshed and brutality first swept Northern Ireland are being imprisoned for twenty years or more for their part in bombing, kidnapping, mutilation and murder. We are told that killing is in the blood; that these God-fearing people and their clergy practise and preach the doctrine 'Thou shalt hate thy neighbour as thyself' and that there can never be a Christian peace in Northern Ireland. But do we have to accept this judgement as final?

The long relationship between the two islands, Britain and Ireland, is confused and stained with much remembered blood, and what we are witnessing today in the North is the last, local, survival of what was formerly general and at times seemed almost normal. Moreover, Britain and Ireland do not exist in isolation. Britain is twenty-two miles from mainland Europe; Ireland is sixty miles from Wales and twelve from Scotland. From the day that the Roman conquest of Britain began in 43 AD any king, conqueror, country or church interested in the affairs of Britain could not avoid being interested in Ireland. When, today, a British soldier is shot in Belfast, or a cargo of machine guns destined for terrorists in the North is intercepted in America, there is a long back-history. So if peace is finally to cover the whole of Ireland, it is not to the North, nor to modern times, that the search for it must be confined.

But however broad or narrow the front on which we approach the problem may be, there are certain universal features of geography and politics which have to be taken into account. There are only three geopolitical entities : an island, a land with clearly marked natural frontiers, and a river valley. Put another way, the only natural frontiers are sea, and mountain ranges and deserts, (and not, apart from exceptional circumstances, rivers). The corollary is that any other frontier drawn for political or other reasons is artificial, probably unstable, and if it involves the partition of a natural entity, likely to be disastrous. Of course such a dogmatic simplification can be attacked by quoting plenty of exceptions. One of the longest frontiers in the world, between Canada and the United States, is unnatural yet stable, because there is nobody with an interest in changing it. But the examples of Palestine, India, Pakistan, Bangla Desh, Vietnam, Cyprus, suggest that the division of a natural geographical unit, even if it is politically expedient in the short term, is liable to bring tragedy in the end. This is not in itself an overriding argument in favour of the reunification of Ireland. It is an argument in favour of re-examining what is, as events during my mission to Dublin showed, a very peculiar national frontier.

Moreover, these two political entities, the islands of Britain and Ireland, are inconveniently situated in relation to each other and to Europe. The larger, potentially richer island lies between the smaller and mainland Europe. Britain always had a commercial and strategic importance for any tribe or nation, small or great, in north-west Europe. The Romans at the time of the birth of Christ had an uneasy hold over the loyalty of the tribes in conquered Gaul, and the strength and attitude of the inhabitants of Britain (who were all Celtic except for some Belgians in the south-east) were something to worry about. Ireland with its back to the Atlantic was of strategic or commercial interest only to a great power which had conquered Britain and feared a threat from the west, or to a seafaring nation in south-west Europe or the Mediterranean prepared to hazard the open sea route; and the Romans never cared much for the sea nor liked to sail out of sight of land. And the width and hostility of the Irish Sea shut off the pre-Christian Celts in Ireland from any need to worry about the outside world, except for a few traders, or to combine against any outside threat. In other words there was nothing to create a sense of unity or nationhood. The Celts in Britain were in the same situation when the Romans came. It was succinctly and prophetically summed up by the Roman historian Tacitus writing in the late first century AD about the Great Roman governor of Britain, Julius Agricola. He is explicit about the Celts :

> Their strength is in their infantry. Some tribes also fight from chariots. The nobleman drives, his dependants fight in his defence. Once they owed obedience to kings, now they are distracted between the jarring factions of rival chiefs. Indeed, nothing has helped us more in the war than their inability to cooperate. It is seldom that two or three states unite to repel a common danger; fighting in detail they are conquered wholesale. The climate is objectionable, with its frequent rains and mists.

And while his geography is vague, he introduces a character who was to reappear all too often in Irish history.

> In the fifth year of campaigning [AD 81] Agricola [Governor of Britain AD 77-83] began with a sea passage, and in a series of successful actions subdued nations hitherto unknown. The whole side of Britain that faces Ireland was lined with his forces. But his motive was rather hope than fear. Ireland, lying between Britain and Spain, and easily accessible also from the Gallic sea, might, to great general advantage, bind in closer union that powerful section of the empire. Ireland is small in extent as compared to Britain, but larger than the islands of the Mediterranean. In soil, in climate and in the character and civilisation of its inhabitants it is much like Britain. Its approaches and harbours are tolerably well known from merchants who trade there. Agricola had given a welcome to an Irish prince, who had been driven from home by a rebellion; nominally a friend, he might be used as a pawn in the game.

But even this first appearance of a refugee prince, the predecessor by a thousand years of Dermot Mac Murrough, is not the beginning; nor is Tacitus's description of that fissile tendency, which is familiar in Roman times; familiar in the fate of Irish rebels and nationalist movements, Redmond's Irish Parliamentary Party, the Civil War, the Official and Provisional IRAs; (familiar also in Scotland until recent times—it is less than three hundred years since the Campbells massacred the Macdonalds in Glencoe). Before the people there was the land.

Historians of early Britain have long detected a distinction imposed by geography and climate between the Celts of the easier and softer plain-country of the east and south and those of the more rugged and mountainous highland zone of the west and north, including Ireland and Scotland. Still very relevant are some perceptive and prophetic words about Europe and Britain (with Ireland) written by an Oxford philosopher-historian, R. G. Collingwood, in 1936:

> There has always been a general difference between the richer, more comfortable, and more prosperous life of the lowland zone and the harder, poorer life of the highland; and there have been differences of kind as well, arising out of the same causes. The lowland zone is not only more access-ible to invasion from the Continent, it is also more attractive to invaders; because life is easier there, changes in the way of living are less hard to bring about, and consequently the history of the lowland zone shows from time to time profound changes of this kind, partly through the infiltration of new ideas. The highland zone is unattractive to invaders, hard to invade, and hard to conquer in detail when invaded; its landscape and climate impose peremptory laws on anyone, no matter whence he comes, who settles there; all these causes, therefore, combine to make it a region tenacious of old customs, conservative of temperament, stubborn to resist any kind of change. New peoples and new ideas, when they gain a foothold in it, do so at the price of compromise with the old; and the civilization of the highland zone, analyzed at any given moment in its history, shows a curious blend of the older and newer elements, the old surviving though modified by the new, the new quickly adapting themselves towards conformity with the old.

> In spite of this contrast between the highland and lowland zones, the relation between the two is by no means one of mere difference. The sea which rings them round and holds them together combines them into a single whole with a character of its own. From the point of view of an observer on the European mainland, Britain as a whole is deeply permeated by the characteristics especially belonging to the highland zone; conservatism of temperament, tenacity of customs,

resistance to new ideas except in so far as they modify themselves under the influence of the old; and thus figures as the embodiment of a spirit of compromise, sometimes admired for its cautious and practical common sense and its loyalty to long-tried traditions, sometimes condemned for its backwardness in the march of progress, blind devotion to lost causes, deficiency in logic, proneness to half-measures and hypocrisy. These characteristics of the British spirit arise from the fact that, in its relation to the Continent, Britain in general plays the same part which in particular belongs, within Britain, to the highland zone : cut off from the mainland by sea, it is difficult enough of access to form a melting-pot in which new arrivals, whether of population or of ideas, are assimilated and absorbed, conquering only by being themselves conquered.*

So even when the Romans came to Britain eleven centuries before Henry II brought his Norman adventurers to Ireland, some constant factors in the relationship have already appeared :

1. Britain blocking the way to north-western Europe, but Ireland having much easier access to the Mediterranean and Latin world; British dominant in size and in strategic and commercial importance to mainland Europe.

2. The Celts incapable of uniting against any common enemy, with nothing in their history or geography to give them any sense of nationality or patriotism.

3. The less accessible country assimilating and absorbing its invaders, whether people or ideas, who can conquer 'only by being themselves conquered.'

(iii)

Roman administration and the English landscape worked their unifying and pacifying magic in England, ably assisted by the disorganisation and disunity of would-be rebels. Romano-Celtic civilisation lingered on after imperial Rome, its power crumbling, left the island in AD 410 to fend for itself, in the face of mounting raids by Angles, Saxons, Jutes and Irish. It was a

* R. G. Collingwood and J. N. L. Myres, *Roman Britain and the English Settlements*, Oxford 1936.

Romano-Celtic official, Calpurnius, who early in the fifth century had his fifteen-year-old son kidnapped by Irish slave-raiders —the boy who later became celebrated as Saint Patrick. Both islands gradually became christianised, but the church developed on quite different lines, partly owing to Ireland's lack of contact with Rome from the seventh to the eleventh century, despite her easier access to the Mediterranean. A great racial and cultural divergence had also set in. The Angles, Saxons and Jutes had spread their settlements and trading posts all over England, and by AD 800 England, as distinct from Wales and Scotland, was no longer Celtic but Anglo-Saxon with, presumably, some intermarriage with the Celts. The country congealed into seven kingdoms, usually at war with one another, until in AD 827 they saw the futility of these perpetual wars and combined under a single king, Egbert, to face a new threat: the men from northern Europe known variously as Danes, Vikings, Scandinavians or Norsemen. In the ninth century they overran half England, made raids and then permanent settlements all round Ireland, invaded France as far as Paris and Rouen and in AD 911 took the Duchy of Normandy. A hundred and fifty years later, as Normans, under Duke William of Normandy, they invaded and conquered England.

At this point, then, two more significant factors in Anglo-Irish history have emerged: Celtic Ireland never had contact with the Roman Empire, and therefore had no Romano-Celtic civilisation before the Dark Ages; and Ireland was never invaded or occupied by Anglo-Saxons. The first important foreign impact upon the native Celtic culture, apart from the Christian Church, was that of the Norsemen/Normans.

Since these men had such a crucial impact on the history of both islands, some of their characteristics should perhaps be mentioned here. Coming from northern homelands far removed from the focal areas of civilisation—meaning, above all, Rome and the Mediterranean littoral—they brought little with them but courage, vitality, and military and organisational skill, coupled with a strong and, in view of their methods, a fully justified assumption that any people they encountered would be hostile; and that assumption is embodied in the abiding mark of their presence—the Norman castle. They also brought with them an amazing capacity to adapt, assimilate, absorb, imitate.

What England had to offer, except some of the gentler qualities of the Anglo-Saxons, is open to debate. In Normandy they adopted the French language, architecture and civilisation in general. They penetrated into Italy and Sicily, and there too their architecture became a take-over of what they found. Everywhere they became Christians. And with this power to assimilate they somehow managed to combine a firm belief that, wherever they went, they were the master race, and a strong tendency, once established in a new conquest, to show a marked disloyalty to the sovereign authority 'at home'.

When the Vikings came to Ireland they found no such classical European culture or successor to the latin language to assimilate. They came at first, from 800 AD onwards, as hit-and-run raiders. Their attacks increased in weight and frequency, and by 850 they had established permanent settlements and trading posts. By 900 AD there was extensive intermarriage with the Irish; they were gradually becoming converted to Christianity, and by 950 not only was there a Viking kingdom around Dublin but its kings were principally interested in establishing firm links with another Viking kingdom, in York. And from their settlements in Ireland the Vikings were by now making raids on Scotland—including the capture of Dumbarton in 870. But above all they joined enthusiastically in the main occupation of the pre-Norman Irish—the perpetual feuding and fighting between tribal kings, great kings who lorded it over other tribal kings, and kings of provinces. Whole chapters of Irish history from the time when fairly reliable annals begin seem to comprise nothing but bleak narrative of murder, parricide, fratricide, the killing of sons, cousins, hostages, maiming, blinding, burning, torture, without any discernible effect upon history except the negative one of perpetuating a total inability to combine against any invader. Even the great Brian Boru's last battle, at Clontarf in 1014, is now presented not as an epic victory of the Irish over the Norsemen, but as an episode in an internal power struggle in which the rebellious men of Leinster had some important but secondary support from their Norse allies.* This, then, was the Ireland which King Henry II of England invaded with the full approval of

* Donncha O Corrain, *Ireland before the Normans*, Dublin 1972.

Pope Alexander III; for Henry, having received the Papal Bull making him Lord of Ireland in 1155, sat on it for fourteen years before acting upon it. The reason for the delay demonstrates another of the vital and enduring principles which have governed Anglo-Irish relations. It also shows how a trace of the anticlimactic or absurd tends to appear.

Henry II was not solely or principally King of England. Besides being the son of Duke Geoffrey of Anjou, he had married Eleanor of Aquitaine and thus held vast territories in France which were his primary concern : he was first and foremost a member of the French Angevin dynasty. The Papal Bull of 1155 meant that he could invade Ireland whenever he wanted to; but, in a word, Mummy said no. His mother Matilda was a formidable lady, grand-daughter of William the Conqueror, widow of a German Emperor and later married to Geoffrey, Count of Anjou; and to her, the family estates and interests came first. When the invasion did come, it was an accidental by-product of the interminable feuds between the kings, kinglets and chiefs. In the course of the perpetual power struggle one Dermot Mac Murrough of Leinster broke all the rules of feuding by slipping across to England in 1166 to seek help from over the water. A merchant friend in Bristol, who was on close personal terms with the King, gave him an introduction to Henry II, but Mac Murrough had to spend from August 1166 to the spring of 1167 trailing round the King's Angevin territories to catch up with him. Henry listened politely but was too occupied in France to intervene himself or spare any men. Mac Murrough was given some money and allowed to recruit some mercenaries of doubtful loyalty to the King, and therefore better out of England, with whom he returned to Ireland to join in the free-for-all. Their situation, owing to the constant twists and turns of loyalties and treacheries, soon became precarious and it was not until Henry II personally intervened in strength in 1171 that the conquest began in earnest and, on the face of it, successfully. At any rate Adrian IV's successor, Pope Alexander III, felt able to despatch three letters, in the autumn of 1172, to the Archbishops and Bishops of the Irish Church, to King Henry II and to the Kings and Princes of Ireland. The letter to Henry II is worth quoting in full :

By frequent report and trustworthy evidence and with much joy, we have been assured how that, like a pious king and magnificent prince, you have wonderfully and gloriously triumphed over that people of Ireland, who, ignoring the fear of God, in unbridled fashion at random wander through the steeps of vice, and have renounced all reverence for the Christian faith and virtue, and who destroy themselves in mutual slaughter, and over a kingdom which the Roman emperors, the conquerors of the world, left (so we read) untouched in their time, and, by the will of God, (as we firmly believe), have extended the power of your majesty over that same people, a race uncivilised and undisciplined. It appears that the aforesaid people, as perhaps has more fully come to your knowledge, marry their stepmothers and are not ashamed to have children by them; a man will live with his brother's wife while the brother is still alive; one man will live in concubinage with two sisters; and many of them, putting away the mother, will marry the daughters.

And all from time to time eat meat in Lent; nor do they pay tithes, or respect as the ought the churches of God and ecclesiastical persons.

The literary style of His Holiness, at any rate in the English translation, is, to say the least, explicit. The sources of his information were a little premature about the extent of Henry's conquest of Ireland and the submission of the Irish princes, since it was not until 430 years later that the last of the Irish Earls, Tyrone and Tyrconnell, finally capitulated and fled from Ireland. Nevertheless, nobody can have been left in any doubt that the Norman invasion had the approval of the Pope, and that the reform movement in the Irish Church gave useful cover for England's first, and as it turned out, least successful overseas colonial adventure.

The Anglo-Norman invasion in no way diminished the internal warfare of the Irish kings and chieftains, thus strongly confirming Tacitus's assessment of the Celts of more than a thousand years earlier. Even so, it was not until two reigns later that the English sovereign, King John, having lost nearly all his French possessions, began to devote serious attention to Ireland. From an early stage in the conquest the Anglo-Norman—or,

as they may now more conveniently be called, the English—
kings, tried to extend to Ireland all the institutions of the
monarchy, law, justice and administration as they gradually
evolved in England. Magna Carta, signed at Runnymede beside
the River Thames in 1215, was applied to Ireland in the following year, with certain necessary modifications.

All the English in Ireland had the rights and obligations of
'liege subjects' exactly as in England. But there were two
important limitations in the original colonial policy. First,
English law could only apply where the English ruled, and for
the first three hundred years this meant in practice an area
comprising a few counties around Dublin, which expanded and
contracted according to the resources and effort the English
were able and willing to apply to Ireland. Outside this area,
'the Pale', Irish law (including the laws concerning land tenure
and inheritance), the Irish language and the Irish way of life
continued to prevail. Secondly, even inside the Pale the benefits
of English law applied only to the English, for a reason which
illustrates another recurring theme. Like their Scandinavian
forebears, the settlers showed a marked reluctance to obey their
sovereign authority at home, and in particular were inclined
to obstruct any measures intended to benefit 'the natives'. In
the thirteenth century the King made various attempts to apply
English law to the Irish. But as the following order of 1297
from King Edward I to his Viceroy shows, with a certain lack
of deference to the Irish worthy of Pope Alexander III himself,
it was only an idea for discussion, as it were, and the settlers
did not much care for it. Anyway, the idea was dropped.

As the community of Ireland have offered us 8000 marks if
we will grant them the laws of England to be used in that
country, we wish you to know that, after diligent discussion
and fullest deliberation with our Council in the matter and
inasmuch as the laws which the Irish use are detestable to
God and contrary to all law so much that they ought not to
be deemed law, it seems to us and our Council expedient
to grant them the laws of England, provided however that
in this the common assent of the people, or at least of the
prelates and magnates of that land, who are well disposed,
should uniformly concur.

The prelates and magnates evidently did not concur.

Another recurring theme, already noticed among the Normans in France and Italy, is their readiness to assimilate whatever their newly won land has to offer. In Ireland it took the form of going native, to the considerable annoyance of the King. It was a gradual process, spread over four generations. In 1297 the King's Parliament in Ireland reported:

> Englishmen also, who have become degenerate in recent times, dress themselves in Irish garments and having their heads half shaven, grow the hair from the back of the head, conforming themselves to the Irish as well in garb as in countenance, whereby it frequently happens that Englishmen reputed as Irishmen are slain, although the killing of Englishmen and Irishmen requires different modes of punishment. And by such killing matter of enmity and rancour is generated amongst many. The kindred also, as well of the slayer as of the slain, are often by turns struck down as enemies. And therefore it is agreed and granted that all Englishmen in this land wear, at least in that part of the head which presents itself most to view, the mode and tonsure of Englishmen . . .

All three tendencies—independence from the central authority, unwillingness to share privileges with the natives, and at the same time the tendency to go native themselves—were intensified during the following century. In 1366 the King's Parliament in Kilkenny decided to tidy up the confusion by issuing the infamous statutes of Kilkenny. The Irish living under their own chiefs were excluded from the rights of English law and land tenure, forbidden to hold office in the Church, or state or local appointments, or to own land or trade within the Pale. As for the English, the Statutes are charmingly explicit:

> Now many English of the said land, forsaking the English language, fashion, mode of riding, laws and usages, live and govern themselves according to the manners, fashion and language of the Irish enemies, and also have made divers marriages and alliances between themselves and the Irish enemies aforesaid; whereby the said land and the liege people thereof, the English language, the allegiance due to our lord

the King, and the English laws there are put in subjection and decayed and the Irish enemies exalted and raised up contrary to right. Now therefore . . . it is ordained and established that no alliance by marriage, gossipred, fostering of children, concubinage or amour or in any other manner be henceforth made between the English and Irish on the one side or on the other . . .

. . . every Englishman shall use the English language and be named by an English name, leaving off entirely the manner of naming used by the Irish; and that every Englishman use the English custom, fashion, mode of riding apparel according to his estate; and if any English or Irish living amongst the English use the Irish language amongst themselves contrary to this ordinance and thereof be attaint, that his lands and tenements, if he have any, be seized into the hands of his immediate lords. . . .

And that no difference of allegiance henceforth be made between the English born in Ireland and the English born in England by calling them 'English hobbe' or 'Irish dog', but that all shall be called by one name (viz.) the English lieges of our lord the King . . .

And this racist and elitist legislation, a triumph of the settlers over successive English sovereigns, introduced nearly two centuries before the Reformation, remained the law of the land until 1614; but how successfully even kings can legislate against gossipred and amours is debatable.

It is not surprising that by this time the English and the Irish were describing each other in less than affectionate terms. A complaint from the King's Parliament of 1297:

Frequently also the Irish are stirred up in war by this, that when they are at peace or have had a general truce or armistice for a certain time, or protection of the peace has been granted to them by the Court of the lord the King, some, led by covetousness, others from motives of revenge, envy, or of taking pledges, lying in wait for them, rush suddenly or by night upon them, enter their lands, carry off spoils or take and lead away their cattle or the men found in their marches, who at least in the meantime are committing no mischief against any person; whereby those Irish, as they are excitable, rush instantly to war, and wherever the country is believed to be weakest, there they plunder . . .

Twenty years later the Irish Princes had some things to say about the English, in a long letter of complaint to Pope John XXII :

And as in way of life and speech they are more dissimilar from us and in their actions from many other nations that can be described by us in writing or in words, there is no hope whatever of our having peace with them. For such is their arrogance and excessive lust to lord it over us and so great is our due and natural desire to throw off the unbearable yoke of their slavery and to recover our inheritance wickedly seized upon by them, that as there has not been hitherto, there cannot now be or ever henceforward be established, sincere good will between them and us in this life. For we have a natural hostility to each other arising from the mutual, malignant and incessant slaying of fathers, brothers, nephews and other near relatives and friends so that we can have no inclinations to reciprocal friendship in our time or in that of our sons.

In this same lengthy document there is a very sinister declaration saying in effect that unrestricted guerilla warfare was justified :

Wherefore, if for this reason we are forced to attack that King and our said enemies that dwell in Ireland, we do nothing unlawful but rather our action is meritorious and we neither can nor should be held guilty of perjury or disloyalty on this account, since neither we nor our fathers have ever done homage or taken any other oath of fealty to him or his fathers. And therefore, without any conscientious misgivings, so long as life endures we will fight against them in defence of our right and will never cease to attack and assail them until through want of power they shall desist from unjustly injuring us and the justest of Judges shall take evident and condign vengeance upon them for their tyrannous oppression and other most wicked deeds; and this with firm faith we believe will soon come to pass.

This eloquent communication from the Irish Princes again illustrates the tendency for Ireland to be subordinated to English interests, and for Julius Agricola's 'pawn in the game' to reappear. Before his death in 1307 Edward I had managed to be at war simultaneously in Wales, France and Scotland, and Ireland was ordered to provide 10,000 men for the English armies. Scotland was the biggest problem. In 1306, Robert de Bruyis, best known to English schoolchildren as Robert the Bruce (of spider fame) proclaimed himself King of Scotland. In the ensuing war in 1314, Edward II suffered a disastrous defeat at Bannockburn. The following year Robert's brother Edward invaded Ireland and was proclaimed King of Ireland in 1316. For the next two years, during which Ireland had a Scottish king, most of the country was a battlefield with the Scots and Irish on one side and the Anglo-Irish and the English on the other. Finally in 1318 the Scots were comprehensively defeated and withdrew, Edward de Bruyis being killed. The bitter complaints of the Irish Princes about the atrocities of the English during this war have an element of self-justification. It must have occurred to them that the English king from whom they had just switched allegiance was the Lord of Ireland which, being an island, was in the Pope's gift. And it must always be borne in mind that the mutual antipathy of English and Irish, so eloquently described here, whatever its tribal and political reasons, had nothing whatsoever to do with religion, and that two centuries were to elapse before it did.

Throughout these centuries the English were fully occupied elsewhere. This was the era of the Hundred Years' War with France, the Black Death, and the dynastic Wars of the Roses. The area of Ireland controlled by the English dwindled steadily, and the Anglo-Irish seemed out of royal control altogether. In 1399 the Viceroy and the King's Council reported:

The English families in all parts of the land which are rebels, as the Butyllers, Powers, Gerardyns, Bermynghames, Daltons, Barretts, Dillons and others, who will not obey the law nor submit to justice, but destroy the poor liege people of the land, and take their living from them and rob them, will needs be called gentlemen of blood and idlemen, whereas they are sturdy robbers and not amenable to the law, and

G

will make prisoners of the English, and put them to greater duress than do the Irish enemies, and this from default of the execution of justice.

Item, in addition to this the said English rebels are accomplices of the Irish enemies, and will not displease them, and thus between the one and the other the loyal English are destroyed and injured.

Item, many counties which are obedient to the law are not in the hands of the King, except the county of Dublin and part of the county of Kildare . . .

Finally, as the age of an international feudal Europe was drawing to a close and the first traces of nationalism were discernible, another recurring theme in Anglo-Irish history appeared. This is the ding-dong conflict in the mind of the sovereign power in England over the question of whether the colony, Ireland, should be governed directly from London (direct rule, unionism, integration), or by some form of local government on the sovereign's behalf (Home Rule, devolution, limited independence). Such government as there was took a curious form. The central authority was the King, but there was a separate Irish parliament which by the standards of the day might be called representative. But then, in 1460, when the crippling Wars of the Roses between the houses of Lancaster and York were at their height, a strange episode occurred. The Irish parliament, together with the Viceroy, Richard, Duke of York, issued a unilateral declaration of independence, and because there was no stable government in England a form of Home Rule was maintained in Ireland over many years. There is one close parallel with the Rhodesian declaration of independence: it was a government of the settlers for the settlers, and the native Irish did not participate. And, to use the 1972 phraseology of Belfast and Derry, Ireland outside the dwindling English Pale was, in effect, a no-go area.

The period around 1485 was the lowest point of English authority in Ireland. And as it is a turning-point in European as well as Anglo-Irish history, it is a good moment to take stock. I believe that the salient characteristics of the relationship between England and Ireland were present and discernible in AD 1500, before the Reformation, before Henry VIII established a national Church, before the era of nationalism and the great European wars. All these elements have added their complexities, but they have embellished and not replaced those fundamental factors and basic themes that I have tried to disentangle. The two islands are still islands, each forming a natural political entity. At times of extreme stress the old tribal instincts still emerge, their strength and impact normally much diminished by intermarriage, cultural interpenetration, modern communications, and the complications introduced by religion, property and trade. British governments still do not know how best to govern the part of the island of Ireland that remains British, but the principle that Ireland must be secondary to other British interests is still very much alive. And it took the deaths of thirteen young men in Derry and the burning of an Embassy in Dublin to remind Westminster that an island is a basic political unit.

(iv)

The five hundred years, the fifteen generations between the end of the old mediaeval feudal Europe and the birth of a new economically interdependent and politically ecumenical Europe, comprise the dawn, the high noon, and the dusk of a violent era of nationalism and religious fanaticism. It was also the great era of overseas exploration, trade rivalry, conquest, colonisation, and wars fought at sea. Constantinople fell to the Turks in 1453 and released upon Europe the variegated, vitalising flood of art, literature and philosophy of classical Greece and Rome. But the strongest and most far-reaching influence at the beginning of this age was the Reformation and the rise of the two streams of Protestantism, the teachings of Martin Luther and John Calvin. At first, for reasons of language and geography, neither classical humanism nor the new sects had any marked impact upon Ireland. On the other hand, a third form of Protestantism coupled with nationalism had far-reaching and mainly disastrous consequences. When, in 1534, King Henry VIII was excommunicated on account of his matrimonial and dynastic problems, he broke with Rome, and established a new, Protestant Church of England with himself as its head. Until this time the King of England held the Lordship of Ireland, first granted by the Pope to King Henry II. But in 1541 Henry VIII proclaimed it the Kingdom of Ireland, and so it remained, as a separate realm, with its own parliaments, until 1800. The efficient and ruthless Tudors gradually established centralised control over the whole island, whose institutions continued to be simply replicas of the larger and more solidly established bodies in England.

But it was not the differences between Catholic and Anglican that brought the bitterness and the brutality. It was a problem that had been latent from the beginning, concealed by the very limited degree of English control in Ireland. It was the question of land tenure, property and inheritance, and it was a conflict between English and Irish, not between religions. More precisely, it was a conflict between two systems. By Gaelic law land belonged to the tribe, and chiefs were elected and held their land for life only. The Tudor kings offered them a system of submission whereby they could surrender their lands to the King who would then re-grant them. But this entailed new systems of inheritance, and clashes were inevitable. The savagery with which the Tudors suppressed any resistance was horrifying and the suffering frightful, quite apart from which the lands of those who resisted were confiscated and planted with colonists from England or Scotland. But much worse was to follow, for now religion took a hand.

Calvinism entails a belief in predestination, and the doctrine that redemption is for the elect alone. The Bible is the sole source of God's law; man's duty is to interpret it and preserve law and order in the world. The dominant reforming figure in sixteenth-century Scotland was John Knox, an exact contemporary of Calvin who followed his doctrines with enthusiasm and, as a potted biography says, 'his single-minded zeal made him the outstanding leader of the Scottish Reformation but closed his mind to tolerance'. Now the last stronghold of Irish resistance to the English colonisation was Ulster, and the last stand was that of Hugh O'Neill, the Earl of Tyrone, in 1599. Inevitably his rebellion was defeated. With other Irish earls he fled to exile in Europe in 1607, and his lands were settled with lowland Scots. By 1641 Ireland was full of dispossessed, landless and starving Catholics, and Catholics who refused to accept the King as head of the Church. That year a great rebellion broke out, intended first to regain the lost Catholic lands in Ulster, but then to defend their rights and property under the monarchy (to which they professed entire loyalty). This made matters worse, since by this time the King, Charles I, was at war with his Puritan parliament. Robert Kee describes the sequel* :

> The eleven years of fighting in the civil war that began with the rebellion of 1641 cost the lives of about one third of the Catholic Irish, and many of those who were neither killed or transported by slave-dealers to the West Indies were sentenced in their own country to a life of social ignominy and handicap. Most of the best land of Ireland was now confiscated from its owners and divided among more new Protestant settlers and adventurers, many of them Cromwellian soldiers who were in this way compensated for arrears of pay. Whereas, even after the plantation of Ulster in James I's time two-thirds of the cultivable land of Ireland had remained in the hands of Catholics, now, after Cromwell's settlement, rather more than three-quarters of the cultivable land was to be found in the hands of the small minority of Protestants.

Retribution for these confiscations seemed to have arrived with the accession of the Catholic King James II in 1685 and the passing of an Act to eject the Protestant settlers. But it was James who was ejected and defeated by William of Orange at the Battle of the Boyne, leaving the Protestants free to pass the appalling Act to Prevent the Growth of Popery in 1704, and the Ulster Scots free to retain their usurped lands. With them they also retained a secret fear of ultimate restitution—the siege mentality that resulted from their situation—and the certainty that they were Calvin's Elect, whose duty it was to interpret God's law in the Bible for the preservation of law and order; or, more simply stated, to keep the Catholics in their place.

By this Act and other penal laws, Catholics not only lost most of their lands; by the Act of 1704 they were not allowed to buy land, or own a horse, (the only means of transport) or obtain higher education either in Ireland or at a foreign uni-

---

* Robert Kee, *The Green Flag*, London 1972, 16.

versity. Their trading and commercial activities were restricted. In 1728 they lost their right to vote, and their bishops and regular clergy were exiled. The eighteenth century is considered to be one of the great eras of culture and civilisation throughout Europe, but in Ireland the architecture, literature, learning, drama of the time were exclusively Protestant. There were no talented or educated Catholics. The Penal Laws had seen to that, and they had emigrated in their hundreds of thousands to Europe and America. From the time of this emigration onwards the internal affairs of Ireland could no longer be regarded as an Irish, or an Anglo-Irish affair, in which nobody else was, or had the right to be, concerned.

(v)

The eighteenth century saw the emergence of three new strands in Anglo-Irish history, and a new twist to an old one. Secret societies, gangs of thugs, and paramilitary forces made their physical and political presence felt. A spirit of Irish independence or colonial nationalism as it has been called, began to emerge : The inspiration, or infection of republicanism was spreading from independent America and revolutionary France; and the British government had to take another look at the unsolved and apparently insoluble question of how to rule Ireland. All four elements are still active ingredients in the political chemistry of today.

Life in eighteenth-century Ireland was lived on two levels. The desperately poor and dispossessed, with nothing to live for but the struggle to keep alive, formed secret societies of marauding bands which ranged the countryside robbing, cattle-rustling, rick-burning, and doing what they could to disrupt the life of the landowners. These secret organisations continued to exist in one form or another into the 1880s. They had no coherent political aim. They merely wanted to live. And naturally the landowners produced their own bands of vigilantes to counter them.

The first paramilitary forces were the Irish Volunteers. These were privately organised and financed bodies of men originally recruited to defend Ireland against possible French invasion in 1778 after the regular army had gone to fight the rebel colonists in America. They soon became a well-armed national force some 40,000 strong, almost entirely composed of Protestants. Before long they were to be a significant political force as well, owing to some important developments in the Irish parliament.

As already pointed out, Ireland had had its own parliament of sorts since the thirteenth century. In 1494 the famous 'Poynings Law' was passed in England providing that the right of the Irish parliament (when it met, which was very rarely) to legislate was subject to the prior approval of its Bills by the English parliament. Owing to the Penal Laws Irish eighteenth-century politics were exclusively Protestant politics, and it was among the Protestant ascendancy that the overriding authority of the English parliament was increasingly called into question. To stop this nonsense the English parliament passed what it somewhat bluntly called 'an Act for the better securing the dependency of the kingdom of Ireland', which stated

> be it declared that the said kingdom of Ireland hath been, is and of right ought to be, subordinate unto and dependent upon the imperial crown of Great Britain, as being inseparably united and annexed thereunto, and that [. . . the sovereign in Parliament . . .] had, hath, and of right ought to have full power and authority to make laws and statutes of sufficient force and validity to bind the kingdom and the people of Ireland.

Naturally this fanned the flames. The agitation mounted, and in 1782, with the War of American Independence as good as lost and the alarming possibility of the Irish kingdom or colony going the same way, the British government stood on its head, repealed the 1719 Act and Poyning's Law, and gave Ireland its own parliament, independent under the Crown.

In practice, little changed. Under the unreformed political system in England, and even more so in Ireland, a combination of Crown patronage, the buying and selling of votes and general bribery and corruption, the Irish parliament would always do what its English masters wanted. But even the appearance of independence was only won, after two years of ineffectual parliamentary debate, when the paramilitary Volunteers, now some 80,000 strong, held a delegate conference at

Dungannon, in Co. Tyrone, led by the Ulster Volunteers, and voted unanimously in favour of the Irish declaration of parliamentary independence. The English and Irish parliaments both got the message.

By the end of the century Ireland was in a state of turmoil. The independence of parliament was seen to be a sham, and there was discontent everywhere. The Protestant ascendancy were agitating for reform of the electoral system. The ideals of the American and French Revolutions were spreading fast. The English parliament was distracted by the wars with America and France. The Irish parliament was arousing much discontent by its agricultural policies and the still general, though now relaxed, Penal Laws. The mercantile middle classes, including the surviving Catholics, were demanding a share of political power. The Irish Ministers, who under the prevailing system were in effect the stooges of Westminster, had the classic choice : concession and reform, or repression. Predictably, in March 1796 they passed the Insurrection Act, 'more effectually to suppress insurrections and prevent the disturbance of the public peace'. Predictably, in 1798 the rebellion came, led by the Ulster Protestant idealist Wolfe Tone. Predictably it failed and was followed by hideous reprisals and revolting atrocities. Then, surprisingly, in 1800 the British government stood on its head once more. William Pitt carried through parliament the Act of Union, totally abolishing the Irish parliament or any other form of local autonomy, and merging Britain and Ireland into a single United Kingdom for the first time ever. Henceforward Ireland was to elect Members to the Westminster parliament; but it was still under the unreformed system, and no Catholic could yet be elected. The Act of Union ushered in an epoch of disunity, division, destruction, and death, which continues to this day.

William Pitt's arguments in favour of the Union have been the Unionists' arguments ever since. Briefly :

> The 1782 arrangement, of one Crown and two separate parliaments, demolished the system that held the two countries together.
> Since each legislature has its own power to decide on the great questions of war and peace, alliances and confedera-

cies, what happens if the two parliaments take opposing decisions?

Britain is engaged in her greatest war. The enemy sees Ireland as the weakest area in the British defences. 'Are we not bound then in policy and prudence to strengthen that vulnerable point?'

Ireland's greatest weakness is lack of industry and capital. The only remedy is to unite it with British resources.

Religion must be a problem in a country where the great majority of the people profess a different faith from the general established religion of the Empire, while the property of the country is in the hands of a small number of persons professing that established religion. It is out of the question, while Ireland remains a separate kingdom, to make full concessions to the Catholics without endangering the state. But 'when the conduct of the Catholics shall be such as to make it safe to admit them to the participation of the privileges granted to those of the established religion', the question can be more safely debated in a united imperial parliament than in a separate legislature. In the meantime, Catholic grievances are more likely to be mitigated in a united parliament in Westminster than in Dublin.

Ireland will have the blessings of the British constitution and a stronger defence in the current wars.

With the American colonies lost and the French wars going badly it was probably the defence arguments that counted. Nobody could have foreseen that the Reform Bill and the extension of the franchise, combined with the stages of Catholic emancipation, would end with the Irish MPs holding the balance of power in the Commons and reducing the proceedings of the House to chaos. And forces had already been unleashed which would impel a reluctant England to take notice of the Irish Question and to continue to take notice of it until now. The Union came at a difficult time. Ireland's eighteen years of apparent parliamentary independence had encouraged an Irish patriotism to emerge from all the divisive forces of religion, wealth, land, national and international sympathies. There had been extensive Irish emigration, of Dissenters as well as Catholics, to newly independent America, and many

Catholics had fled to Europe for education and for freedom. Revolutionary and anti-colonial ideas were there for the picking. Among the nursery rhymes and folklore with which this long story began, Irish hopes and griefs were handed down in America even when the tradition became blurred at home. The Industrial Revolution was bringing vast changes, for better or for worse, in economic and social conditions; not least in Ulster, where Belfast was growing in spectacular fashion. And the Union ushered in a century as confused and tragic for Ireland as any that had gone before.

Here I can do no more than sketch out the three main lines along which Irish nationalism developed. The earliest expression of it after the Union was that of Daniel O'Connell, 'The Liberator'. His earliest aim was, very briefly, to raise the living standards of the people, liberate them from their misery and help them to feel that they belonged. Throughout his life he never wavered in his allegiance to the English Crown. His first great parliamentary achievement was the Catholic Emancipation Act, passed in 1829; and his oratory and electioneering tactics in themselves showed the Irish masses the power that they could achieve while remaining strictly disciplined within the law. He then aimed, quite simply, at the Repeal of the Act of Union—but here he had no chance at all. The Electoral Reform Act of 1832 gave Ireland 105 seats in the House of Commons, and only thirty-five Irish members were in favour of repeal. What mattered was, again, the patriotic fervour that he aroused among the Irish people themselves.

In parallel with O'Connell's strictly legal and parliamentary approach, ran another tradition—Irish republicanism, based on conspiracy and the use of terrorism inherited from the secret societies, with the aim of setting up an independent Irish republic. If this had been simply an internal Irish movement it would have been of little consequence. But in fact much of the inspiration, the planning, the money, the weapons and the men came from America, where a huge and embittered Irish community continued to grow. These men and women were the descendants of the refugees from the penal laws of the eighteenth century, later joined by the survivors of the Great Famine of the nineteenth and the victims of the land system in Ireland. Of this, a historian wrote :

Ireland was, and is, a poor country, and in spite of famine and emigration she was still overpopulated. But these misfortunes were greatly aggravated by the policies of the English government. The Irish peasant was crushed by a land system which he hated not only because it put almost absolute power into the hands of the landlord, but also because it rested on the expropriation of land which he considered, by right, to belong to him. His was a fierce, deeprooted enmity. It was not just a matter of material poverty, of life passed in a one-roomed hut on a diet of potatoes. He felt he had been robbed of his heritage. For most of the nineteenth century the English answer was to ignore the hate and crush the crime which it produced. In the forty years before 1870 forty-two Coercion Acts were passed. During the same period there was not a single statute to protect the Irish peasant from eviction and rack-renting. This was deliberate; the aim was to make the Irish peasant a daylabourer after the English pattern. But Ireland was not England; the Irish peasant clung to his land; he used every means in his power to defeat the alien landlords.

It must not be supposed that the Irish picture can be seen from Britain entirely in black and white. The landlords were mostly colonists from England and of long standing; they believed themselves to be, and in many ways were, a civilising influence in a primitive country. They had often had to fight for their lives and their property. The deep hold of the Roman Catholic Church on a superstitious peasantry had tended on political as well as religious grounds to be hostile to England. Ireland more than once since the days of Queen Elizabeth had threatened to become a steppingstone to the invasion of Britain from the Continent. Rickburning, the assassination of landlords, and other acts of terrorism had contributed to a general acceptance in England of the landlord's case. It was hard to grasp that the vicious circle of unrest, heavy-handed repression, and rebellion could only be broken by remedying fundamental grievances.

Irish friends are sometimes surprised to learn that the author of those lines was Winston Churchill (*History of the English-Speaking Peoples, IV*.).

These embittered exiles, united in a love of Ireland and a hatred of England which throve on the folk-memories of the American War of Independence, fostered the Irish Republican Brotherhood, founded the Fenian Movement, and have been closely involved, or even the prime movers, in all the manifestations of Irish republicanism and nationalism outside the law since then. Through the years these movements plotted countless operations, some of which were capable of being carried out, mostly against specific targets or for specific aims, in England and Ireland. They have consistently displayed certain characteristics first discerned in the abortive rebellion led by Wolfe Tone in 1796-9 and the pathetic little rising of Robert Emmet in 1803 : an almost unbelievable lack of planning and political intelligence; inability to distinguish the hard facts from wished-for fantasies; ineptitude in execution; a mystical dedication leading men to certain death, imprisonment or deportation for the sake of Ireland, while others would take smartly to their heels at the first sign of resistance from a few beleaguered constables; the outspoken disapproval of the murders and destruction they caused by the vast majority of those whom they sincerely thought they were serving; the dogged obtuseness and sustained insensitivity of the English authorities in their over-reaction to each outbreak, which, as was intended, made martyrs of the few and enemies of the many who were caught in the aimless net of reprisals; and, in the early days, the evaporation of public support for, and enthusiasm within, the movement itself if a particular operation or campaign was proving unsuccessful or irrelevant.

The confused history of the Irish and Irish-American republican movement, characterised by intrigues and accidents, and a split between those who wanted nothing less than an independent Irish republic and those who would settle for an Ireland independent under the Crown, culminated in the extraordinary story of the Easter Rising in Dublin in 1916. Planned to be part of a general rebellion which had already been cancelled; dependent upon outside aid and arms which never arrived; surrounded by a mildly curious but unimpressed and certainly uninspired populace more interested in going to Fairyhouse Races, it nevertheless ended with the leaders proclaiming a republic from the steps of the general post office and fighting bravely and incompetently on to inevitable defeat and death or capture. It was a form of Irish civil war, for, as in the rising of 1798, many of the police and soldiers against whom the rebels were fighting were themselves Irish. It is idle to speculate on what would have happened if the British had reacted with reasonable clemency and had been seen to have done so. But there was never any possibility of the British authorities, at a desperate moment in a desperate war against Germany, changing the habits of centuries. The death sentences, life imprisonments, and often pointless arrests rapidly swung national opinion, in America as well as in Ireland, behind the rebels, and once again did for the dead leaders the work that they had set out to do.

But when, a month after the Rising, the British Liberal Prime Minister, H. H. Asquith, visited Dublin to survey the damage, it was against a very different political background— not of the repeal of the Act of Union as demanded by Irish nationalists and republicans from O'Connell in the 1830s onwards, but of limited Home Rule for Ireland within the Union, to be achieved by constitutional and parliamentary means.

When the English Liberal, William Ewart Gladstone, had become Prime Minister in 1868, he was the first and perhaps the only British leader to regard Anglo-Irish relations as a matter of overriding importance in itself, and he specifically linked it with Fenian activities outside the law. He said that Fenianism prepared the British population 'to embrace in a manner foreign to their habits in other times, the vast importance of the Irish controversy'. This term combined a number of issues: the disestablishment of the Church of Ireland in 1869, which apart from the shock that it administered to Irish Protestants, also indicated that the Act of Union itself might not be eternally immutable in other respects as well; a Land Bill in 1870 intended to make a start, albeit inadequate, on remedying the evils so eloquently castigated in the passage from Winston Churchill quoted above; Electoral Reform Acts in 1867 and 1884, and the introduction of the Secret Ballot in 1872; all these things contributed to a belated and not wholly welcome discovery in British parliamentary and aristocratic circles of the existence of Ireland.

Gladstone's efforts came to be dominated by the personality, parliamentary genius and opaque aspirations of Charles Stewart Parnell. Although he said, or almost certainly said, at one point, 'None of us, whether we are in America or Ireland, or wherever we may be, will be satisfied until we have destroyed the last link which keeps Ireland bound to England,' he was actually working within the limits of political realism for a very modest form of self-government for Ireland under the overall authority of what was then called the Imperial Parliament in Westminster. It was in fact intended to give Ireland—a united Ireland since nobody had thought of Partition in the 1870s—the constitution which gave Northern Ireland a limited and subordinate local autonomy from 1920 to 1972. Three attempts were made, in 1886, 1892 and 1914, to pass such a Home Rule Bill through parliament, always in the face of strenuous Conservative opposition. The first was defeated in the House of Commons. The second passed the Commons and was defeated in the House of Lords. The third passed the Commons, precipitated a constitutional crisis and the reform of the House of Lords and was then passed by the Lords, becoming law in 1914. But its application was postponed, with the acquiescence of the Irish Parliamentary Party under John Redmond, when the First World War broke out in August 1914.

Such was the situation when Asquith visited Dublin in the aftermath of the reprisals which followed the Easter Rising in 1916. It is not clear what he could achieve. As in the period of death and destruction that resulted from internment without trial in 1971, a 'political initiative' was urgently necessary, and this could only mean Home Rule for Ireland. Asquith appointed Lloyd George as Minister responsible for finding a permanent solution. But Asquith now headed a coalition government whose powerful Conservative and Unionist members were, since the Easter Rising, more and more opposed to any form of Home Rule. These included men who, before the war, had been working to frustrate the will of parliament by dividing Ireland and keeping all or part of the Province of Ulster within the United Kingdom. By personal negotiations devious to the point of dishonesty with Redmond, the leader of the Irish Parliamentary Party, and Carson, representing the Ulster Unionists, Lloyd George persuaded the former that any settlement involving Partition was temporary and the latter that it was permanent. When, as was inevitable, the duplicity was exposed and the Cabinet informed Redmond that the proposed settlement was to be permanent, his party was doomed.

With the continuing arrests in Ireland, the death penalty on Sir Roger Casement for his part in the Easter Rising, and a renewed attempt to introduce conscription in Ireland, it was the Irish nationalists, many of them in English jails, who inherited the political representation of the Irish people. A vague and vast movement, part political and part military, part Republican and part Home Rulers, united only by a deep urge for the whole of the island to be free, swept over Ireland, under the dedicated and elusive leadership of Eamon de Valera. Relations between the nationalists and the British authorities degenerated into a particularly nasty guerilla war, until the summer of 1921 when a truce was agreed on and peace negotiations opened between the British government and representatives of the Sinn Féin administration. During these negotiations Lloyd George manoeuvred the Irish delegates into facing a choice between dominion status for the whole of an undivided Ireland or a republic excluding six counties of Ulster; then further manoeuvring them into accepting a settlement which gave them the worst part of both bargains. In any case the unity issue had been virtually pre-judged the previous year by the Government of Ireland Act, 1920. This provided for two parliaments, one in Dublin and one in Belfast, to which would be delegated limited powers of local government in the Twenty-Six and the Six Counties respectively. With these established, a Council of Ireland would be elected by these two parliaments to deal with all-Ireland matters until such time as they could agree to set up a single parliament for the whole of a united Ireland. The powers of all three hypothetical parliaments would be limited by Article 75 of the Act, which reads :

Notwithstanding the establishment of the Parliaments of Southern and Northern Ireland, or the Parliament of Ireland, or anything contained in this Act, the supreme authority of the Parliament of the United Kingdom shall remain unaffected and undiminished over all persons, matters, and things in Ireland and every part thereof.

It is inconceivable that Lloyd George can have supposed that this modest degree of local autonomy could have satisfied the Irish nationalists. The Northern Unionists seized upon it with alacrity because it gave so little, and conducted themselves for the next fifty years, with the flabby acquiescence of Westminster, as if it gave everything. The Treaty actually signed gave to Ireland, with the Six Counties detached, as it was hoped, temporarily, dominion status, and led to a bitter civil war in Ireland over the acceptance or rejection of its terms.

This war was won by those who were prepared to accept the partition of Ireland as the price for independence; but by most people in the Free State, including many Southern Unionists, it was regarded as a de facto and temporary partition, and the claim that the island is one and undivided was and is upheld by all parties in the Republic. It is possible that if the Government of Northern Ireland, as set up by the 1920 Act, had from the outset governed the Six Counties in the interest of all the people regardless of their religion, the Border might gently have ceased to be an issue. But this is an idle hypothesis. There was never the slightest intention of making it anything but 'a Protestant government for a Protestant people', and those Unionists who from the beginning in 1886 were determined to frustrate Home Rule in Ireland would never have considered governing the North except in the exclusive Protestant interest. In consequence, and because of the events described in earlier chapters, the Government of Northern Ireland has been suspended and the Border remains as live an issue as ever. Fortunately Britain and Ireland have recognised that their wider interests override the problems of the North. Both countries became founder members of the Council of Europe in 1949, and in January 1972 they both joined the European Community. And that should have been the end of the story, with the two sovereign independent and interdependent islands living happily ever after. And so it could have been.

Except for that northeast corner of Ulster.

15

AS AN ordinary modern European-minded Englishman who had no personal ties with Ireland or prior knowledge of it before I was sent here by my government, I can see no reason inherent in Ireland itself why the history of the northeast should have diverged so drastically and disastrously from that of the rest of the island. It cannot be the simple difference between people of the north and people of the south, between Calais and Cannes, Vermont and Virginia, Durham and Devonshire. Normally north-south differences are happily contained within the larger natural political entity; and in any case what is at issue today is not Ulster at all, but only six of the province's nine counties, with the most northerly of all, Donegal, excluded. It cannot be an ancient racial or cultural separatist question, such as that of the Basques and Bretons, or for that matter Scottish or Welsh nationalism, because historically Ireland was always united in its tribal disunity, and the English colonists meted out the same treatment to Ireland as a whole. Nor is the divergence deep-rooted, profound, or complete, which is hardly surprising since the idea of dividing Ireland is less than a century old and the division itself less than sixty years. The structure of the Roman Catholic Church, the Anglican Church of Ireland, the Presbyterian and Methodist Churches, takes no account of the Border, and the headquarters of the Catholic Cardinal and the Anglican Primate of All Ireland are both in Armagh, in Northern Ireland. Much of the cultural and sporting life of Ireland has ignored partition; both parts belong to the same free travel area, and for much of its length the Border, when not obstructed for security reasons on one side or the other, is virtually ignored in the day-to-day life of a rural countryside. Yet when all this has been said, the fact remains that today Northern Ireland is the most violent and hate-ridden parcel of land in Western Europe, where killing and maiming and destruction go on and on, a land where perfect fear casteth out love. And life is not like this in the rest of Ireland, in the Republic and it is not like this in the rest of Britain, of which politically and administratively Northern Ireland forms part. The evils of Northern Ireland can only be eradicated by tracing and neutralising the evils that caused them. It is as pointless to pass moral judgment on the past as to try to change it. But by elucidating it, it may be possible to find some pointers to a rational or even hopeful future.

The alienation of Ulster began when the Earl of Tyrone, who led the last of the Gaelic resistance to English conquest and colonisation, was defeated at Kinsale in 1601 and his lands, comprising six of the nine counties of Ulster, were settled with Scottish Protestants. For several reasons, the events of the next two centuries, during which Catholics throughout Ireland were ruthlessly repressed by the Protestant ascendancy, resulting in enmity between the two groups, acquired a greater significance in Ulster than elsewhere.

Owing to the Jacobean and Puritan plantations, there was a greater concentration of Protestants in the north. Being predominantly Scottish, their Calvinist/Presbyterian outlook made them more rigid and intolerant than their more easy-going and comfortably situated brethren of the Church of Ireland Ascendancy. Their isolation in the midst of angry and dispossessed Catholics forced an independent self-sufficiency upon them, as well as a keen eye for their own self-interest. They had been the leading spirits in plotting the Rebellion of 1798, but when it came to rising and fighting they preferred to side with the government than with the Catholic fellow-rebels. They largely opposed the Act of Union, for fear that a Westminster parliament might be more tolerant than an Irish one in the matter of Catholic Emancipation. But then with the Act of Union Belfast, unlike Dublin, mushroomed into a great British industrial city, based originally upon the linen industry and, later, on shipbuilding. The future now lay in a United Kingdom. Industry, property, wealth, and the material self-interest that accompanied them signified more than religion in the differentiation of Ulster. But if only because the campaigns for

Repeal of the Union and for Emancipation were inspired by Irish Catholics, the distinction between the two faiths had to be stressed and the flames of hatred fanned. And this was very ably done by three clergymen : Messrs Cooke, Hanna, and Drew.

It need never have happened. Towards the end of the eighteenth century the Ulster Presbyterians had formed their Society of United Irishmen who, joined with their Catholic compatriots and inspired as Presbyterians by the democratic and republican ideals of the American and French Revolutions, rebelled against the British in 1798. Their clergy, farmers and merchants suffered as heavily as the Catholics in the savage reprisals that followed. Rapidly growing Belfast was a liberal and ecumenical city, with Presbyterians and other Protestants helping with land and money for building new churches for the growing Catholic population. But one movement, and one man, transformed Belfast from the rising hopeful town of the 1820s to the hopeless shambles of today.

The movement was the Orange Order, and the man Henry Cooke.

During the worst period of the Penal Laws a loosely-knit and semi-secret organisation of desperate Catholics, called the Defenders, had spread over Ireland, united nebulously by anti-British, anti-landowner, and hence vaguely sectarian sentiments. The sectarian element was strongest in the North, where the Protestants were most numerous and most frightened by the progressive relaxation of the Penal Laws and economic competition, and by the crude methods of the Defenders to settle old scores. An equally crude movement, called the Peep o' Day Boys, was formed by the Protestants to counter the Defenders. After a particularly bloody clash in Armagh, known as the Battle of the Diamond, in 1795, the Peep o' Day Boys reorganised as the Orange Society and embarked on a campaign of atrocities against Catholics which earned them a unanimous resolution of condemnation, sent by a meeting of Protestant northern magistrates to the Chief Secretary at Dublin Castle, in which they were described as 'lawless banditti'. Although the Orangemen supported the government in the Rebellion of 1798, their help was not greatly appreciated and for a generation they lay low. It is important to realise that the members of the first Orange Lodges were mainly members of the Established Church of Ireland of English origin, bitterly opposed to Catholic Emancipation in 1829 and to the Reform Act of 1832.

Presbyterianism now stood at the parting of the ways. It could stand for a united Irish non-sectarian radical republicanism, where its traditions and instincts lay; or it could concentrate on being a sectarian and rabidly anti-Catholic, anti-ecumenical, anti-emancipation movement. After an internal power struggle among the Presbyterians, the victor, Henry Cooke, a rigid disciplinarian from a Calvinist and strongly anti-Catholic family, devoted himself to two main aims : as a clergyman, to preaching the gospel of hatred against all men and all things Catholic and promoting violence by incitement from the pulpit; and as a politician, to promoting the interests of the great Protestant landlords. Meanwhile these landlords had through the sympathy of common interests adopted the Orange Order, whose membership by now covered all classes and professions among the Protestants. Thus in north-eastern Ireland a community grew up in the nineteenth century which has survived long after the circumstances in which it originated have ceased to exist. The area bears many striking resemblances to the Pale of the fourteenth and fifteenth centuries, even to the point where it may be said that it now needs the strong hand of a Tudor to call it to order. The interests of the landlords could soon be left safely to the politicians and the Orange Order, while Henry Cooke scattered his supporting poison from the pulpit. As a non-renegade Presbyterian, Henry Montgomery, the loser to Cooke in the politico-religious infighting, said as early as 1829 : 'Political and religious bigotry have mingled together; and those who foment the persecutions amongst us have made it their policy so to conjoin the two principles that scarce an individual is now held orthodox who is not also an enemy to the civil or religious rights of his fellow-men.'

Henry Cooke had a number of able and enthusiastic supporters and successors, both among the Presbyterians and in the Church of Ireland. Among the most notorious of the latter was one Thomas Drew, Vicar of Christ Church in Belfast, and Grand Chaplain of the Grand Orange Lodge of Ireland. It was his inflammatory sermon on 12 July 1857, the text of which can only induce nausea today in all but the mentally diseased, which successfully promoted the bloodiest and deadliest riots ever provoked in Belfast before 1886. Another mob orator with much blood on his hands was a Presbyterian called Hugh Hanna, whose exploits earned him a statue in Belfast until it was blown up in 1970. Oddly enough, or perhaps not so oddly at all, the issue of the *Protestant Telegraph* in which Paisley attacked me also contains his lament about a lack of enthusiasm among Presbyterians and the Orange Order for replacing or resiting this hero.

As the nineteenth century wore on, the triple alliance of property-owning conservatives, Orange Order and militant sectarian clergy grew uneasy. Irish, which to them meant Catholic, nationalism was still very much alive in Ireland and America. The liberal Gladstone had become Prime Minister in 1867. The Church of Ireland had been disestablished in 1869. An Irish Home Rule Movement and an Irish Parliamentary Party had been founded from Dublin in 1873. Then in 1886 Gladstone introduced a Bill intended to grant very limited powers of local government to an Irish administration under the strict overall control of Westminster. The Conservative Opposition led by Lord Randolph Churchill saw in this a means of defeating the government, and he made as the main base of his attack that area of the United Kingdom which after fifty years of conditioning was most hostile to Home Rule : the Province of Ulster. 'Ulster will fight and Ulster will be right' was his slogan, and his political strategy was to 'play the Orange card'. The fact that he succeeded and defeated the Home Rule Bill in parliament diverted attention from the fact that the Orangemen, where they were concentrated and strong, as in most of Ulster, were indeed preparing to fight, and were drilling and arming for the purpose. The same situation arose again in 1892, when Gladstone, still leading the newly-elected Liberals at the age of eighty-three, introduced a second but equally limited Home Rule Bill. This time it was passed in the Commons but, inevitably, defeated in the Lords. And this time the drilling and arming and preparations for civil war were still more strident and more blatant in Ulster, and still nobody in England took them seriously. But the scene was being set for one of the most extraordinary and most disgraceful episodes in the history of British democracy.

From 1895 to 1906 Britain had a Conservative government, and when the Liberals returned they reckoned that Home Rule was not an issue to win or keep votes. In 1910, however, after two elections in quick succession the position in parliament was as follows:

Conservatives (Unionists)	272
Liberals	272
Irish Nationalists	82
Labour	42

So the Liberal Prime Minister, out of no commitment to Ireland but a proper knowledge of parliamentary mathematics, in 1912 introduced a third Home Rule Bill. And this Bill, unlike its two predecessors, had every prospect of becoming law since the power of veto had been removed from the House of Lords by legislation in the previous year.

The response of the Unionist opposition was, to use an ugly but accurate word, treason. For, when a Bill has been properly debated and passed by both Houses of Parliament and received the Royal Assent, it is the law of the land and binding upon all loyal subjects. The Government of Ireland Act became law in September, 1914. It would have set up an elected Irish legislature with an Irish executive dealing only with domestic Irish matters. The entire apparatus of a sovereign state—international affairs, peace and war, the army and the navy, taxation, the unchallenged supremacy of the Sovereign in Parliament—all these things were left untouched and inviolable by the Government of Ireland Act. And yet, to frustrate this modest little measure, which nevertheless gave enough national self-respect to the Irish for Redmond, the leader of the Irish Parliamentary Party, to pledge that his countrymen would accept it as the final settlement, the Ulster Unionists, the Orange Order, and members of the Conservative Opposition in Westminster were prepared to embark on civil war.

Under the leadership of the Senior Member for Dublin University, Sir Edward Carson, and his deputy, James Craig, an Ulster Protestant army was formed and trained and, three months before the obviously predictable war with Germany broke out, was equipped with a massive and illegal importation of German arms. High ranking officers of the British Army were condoning or actively involved in activities which may or may not have transgressed the undemarcated frontiers of sedition. Opposition leaders produced grotesque constitutional arguments to defend the indefensible. Mercifully the question of whether the Liberal leadership had the guts, and the Army the loyalty to the sovereign, to deal with such sedition, had never to be put to the test, as the Great War broke out before the Act was on the Statute Book and the question of Home Rule was shelved for the duration. But the fatal damage had already been done. Asquith, the Prime Minister, had certain proof that the Army could not be relied on if ordered to act against the armed and disciplined forces, the potential rebels, in Ulster. A deal had to be done whereby Home Rule for Ireland would not apply to Ulster (whatever territory the name might cover), and henceforward every Irish nationalist knew that if ever there was to be any sort of independence, however restricted, for a united Ireland, it was not through parliamentary and constitutional means that it was going to be attained. And the Ulster Unionists knew that however unconstitutional, even treasonable, their methods might have been, they had with the support of the Conservative Opposition and the connivance of the Army established, if only temporarily, a separate identity for Ulster.

In 1920 this separate identity became formal. Lloyd George, who had been entrusted with Irish Affairs after the Easter Rising, had himself become Prime Minister, leading a Liberal/Conservative Coalition which included a number of diehards from the days of the Home Rule conflict. The dreary cycle of reprisal and counter-reprisal after the Rising degenerated into guerilla warfare, and descended to such sickening depths that by 1920 Ministers were beginning to question the policy which had failed in Ireland a hundred times before. But the Great War had not removed, but merely postponed, the Ulster threat. We may never know what balance of hope and fear induced Lloyd George to introduce the Government of Ireland Act, as described in the last chapter. The first Prime Minister of the resulting Government of Northern Ireland was Sir James Craig, whose vision was bounded by Ulster pure and simple : in fact very pure and very simple, since it was to be managed by Protestants, through the Orange Order, aided by a sectarian police force, for the benefit of Protestants, for ever.

This system of government was inaugurated when King George V opened the Northern Ireland parliament on 22 June 1921, and ended when formally suspended by the Conservative government under the leadership of Mr Edward Heath on 22 March 1972. As Winston Churchill had once said : 'What ever Ulster's right may be, she cannot stand in the way of the whole of the rest of Ireland. Half a province cannot impose a permanent veto on the nation. Half a province cannot obstruct forever the reconciliation between the British and the Irish democracies and deny all satisfaction to the united wishes of the British Empire.'

16

ALL through this book I have sought recurring themes from the huge tapestry of Anglo-Irish history, and episodes from my own experience that might be relevant to my reading of the Irish scene. The time has come to decide whether these glimpses of the past and events of my own lifetime amount in the end to a mess without meaning, or whether they yield a discernible pattern of the present and offer a wider vision of the future to a blinkered world. Conventionally, such an exercise leaves one a sadder and a wiser man. Whatever about the wisdom, I am assuredly not left sad, because with the aid of a lot of faith and charity I can see some grounds for hope.

One question has first to be cleared out of the way: where does the responsibility lie for the status and structure of Northern Ireland, past, present and future? The answer should be self-evident. It lies with the sovereign parliament of the United Kingdom, which represents the electorate of the entire kingdom. It was a British government that by treaty granted sovereign independence to twenty-six of the counties of Ireland, and a subordinate local administration, under the authority of parliament, to the six counties that remained in the Union. The former action was irrevocable: the latter, as events were to prove, was not.

Yet the answer to this apparently simple question is not crystal clear, for various complex reasons. The granting, first, of local self-government and, later, of independence to only part of the natural and historic unit, the island of Ireland, had been neither desired or contemplated by the British government. The separation of the six counties came about in such a way as to seem to be a victory of Ulster Protestants over parliament, and its administration behaved from the outset as if it were. Secondly, the new Irish Free State was split, to the extent of fighting a civil war, over the question of whether to accept the terms of a treaty which gave freedom to only part of a previously undivided Ireland. The Irish Constitution lays claim to the whole of the island, and since 1972 the British government has formally recognised that the Republic has a legitimate concern in the affairs of the Six Counties. A further element of doubt crept in when, from the earliest days of Stormont, the Westminster parliament seemed to lose interest in Northern Irish affairs. Questions were disallowed, or answers avoided, on the grounds that they were a matter for the Northern Irish government. Moreover, the first Prime Minister of Northern Ireland, Sir James Craig, was almost from the beginning trying to create a new Northern Ireland Army with the connivance of Sir Henry Wilson, the Chief of the Imperial General Staff, until the latter's assassination in 1922; as well as an armed police force (the 'B' Specials), although defence and policing were matters reserved to the British parliament. And in the negotiations with the Free State over whether Northern Ireland should comprise four, or six, or all nine counties of Ulster, Craig was allowed to act almost as an equal party.

But the most important, and at the same time the most understandable derogation from the authority of parliament lay in the decision to allow the inhabitants of Northern Ireland themselves to determine whether to remain part of the United Kingdom or . . . what? The alternative has been variously phrased, but has always been interpreted in the North to mean 'forming part of a united Ireland under a Roman Catholic government in Dublin'. The concept is long out of date but it has remained a phobia in the North, and a complete religious and political system based upon fear has grown up. Constitutionally it would indeed be possible for a British government to repeal the Government of Ireland Act of 1920 if such were the desire of an exasperated electorate, just as it suspended the Northern Ireland government in 1972; and it might still prove necessary to remind Northern Ireland who are the masters. If far-reaching decisions have to be taken concerning a peaceful future for Northern Ireland it is the British government in Westminster that will take them; and it can be assumed that before doing so they would hold detailed discussions with both communities in Northern Ireland, with the Irish government, with the United States government, and with their fellow members in the European Community. Then they would have to decide alone.

Whatever a British government decides to do—and this is a case in which to take no decision would be a very big decision —it will be subjected to great pressures, including, as at present, the threat of illegal force. But this is nothing new. The Six Counties as a separate entity were founded on force and the threat of civil war. The Irish Free State was created by force—the Easter Rising, the reprisals, the guerilla war, the counter-reprisals—resulting in the final truce and peace treaty. The government of the Free State had to use force and fight a loathsome civil war in order to force the Treaty, and Partition with it, upon those who had demanded and expected independence for the entire island. It was by the ultimate sanction of force, in the shape of the B Specials, that the Northern Ireland government hoped to keep the Catholic and Nationalist minority, numbering about one third of the population, in a state of political exclusion. Finally it was by force that a revived IRA operating in and from the Irish Republic, Britain, the USA and Northern Ireland itself, attempted to dominate the political scene and direct the constitutional actions of the British and Irish governments.

It was this same threat of force that determined the size of Northern Ireland. In January 1913 the Ulster Unionist Council decided to raise and arm what today would be called a paramilitary force, the Ulster Volunteers, of 100,000 men trained and commanded by officers retired or released from the British Army. Six months later Sir Edward Carson, MP, the political leader of the movement, informed the leader of the Conservative Opposition in parliament, Bonar Law, 'Everything here is going on splendidly. A difficulty arises as to defining Ulster. My own view is that the whole of Ulster should be excluded from Home Rule, but the minimum would be the six plantation counties. . . .'* Eight years later, when the two questions of Partition and the size of Northern Ireland were being

* The almost verbatim account of these absorbing discussions and revealing admissions will be found in Thomas Jones' *Whitehall Diary*, III, Oxford 1971.

negotiated with the Irish delegates at the peace conference, Lloyd George admitted that the government had been and still was powerless. 'Ulster,' he said, 'would have defeated us . . . They got the whole force of the Opposition concentrated on Ulster. Ulster was arming and would fight. We were powerless. . . . Applying the same arguments of force and fear, Lloyd George thrust, first, Partition, and then a six-county Northern Ireland (as distinct from four or nine counties, for either of which a stronger case could probably be made) upon the Irish negotiators.

To me the saddest item in this catalogue of menace occurred in the spring of 1974 when the Protestants of Northern Ireland, urged on by their politicians and clergy, violently destroyed, by a general strike unresisted by Her Majesty's Government, the delicate instrument that was being constructed to bring justice and peace to the North and friendship to the whole of Ireland. But at least it proved one thing. Northern Ireland, left to itself, was not yet fit to govern itself. Nevertheless, all the possible courses of action have to be weighed up, even with this depressing evidence before us.

The first and seemingly easiest course open to the British government would be to restore the system of government as it was from 1920 to 1972. The objections are overwhelming. Today it would be a complete anachronism. Stormont was created as a temporary expedient until it and its sister parliament in Dublin could jointly form a single all-Ireland government administering limited Home Rule. The deliberate drawing of its borders to guarantee a two-thirds Protestant majority could be justified since Stormont was to have its mirror-image down South. The creation of the Free State made the idea obsolete, but it left the 'Protestant government for a Protestant people' free to be exactly that, and Westminster preferred not to know how it worked in practice. Today the leaders of the Protestant electorate have made it clear that if the former system were restored they would govern in exactly the same way, B Specials and all. In other words, ten years of turmoil, more deaths and destruction than in the years between the Easter Rising and the end of the Irish civil war, the promises of successive British governments to Northern Ireland and the Irish government—all this would be set aside. There would be massive new support for the IRA in America, the Republic, and among nationalists in the North; and so far from making it possible to reduce or withdraw the British Army it would impose on it a much greater and bloodier burden. It could only conceivably happen if a rightwing Conservative party won a massive majority in the United Kingdom and proved that in a century it had learnt absolutely nothing.

The second possibility is total integration in the United Kingdom. A logical case can be made for this. Since the original threat of civil war and sedition was intended by the Unionists to keep the 'plantation counties' of Ulster loyally within the United Kingdom, integration would be meeting the demand. It would indeed call the bluff of the 'loyalists', for what could be a more loyal act than to accept total integration? But the evidence suggests that their loyalty is chiefly to Northern Ireland itself, or more precisely to their own Protestant supremacy in Northern Ireland. Even if the Protestants accepted total integration, it would slam the door on the aspirations and interests of the Catholics and the Republic even more resoundingly and permanently than the restoration of Stormont. The security commitment would, if anything, be increased, since there would be disgruntled Protestant extremists as well as Catholic ones to contend with. And it would be very hard to reconcile with existing understandings with the Irish government. It is possible that integration could be justified as a temporary measure while the whole question of devolution within the United Kingdom is being resolved and a new form of government devised for Northern Ireland in which Catholics are given their proper share of responsibility. But this would leave too many aspirations unsatisfied. That word 'temporary' would be regarded with instant and justified scepticism, and it would not bring peace.

The third possibility is the reunification of Ireland. It is easy to dismiss this idea in three simple sentences. The British government has said that it will abide by the wishes of the people of Northern Ireland. The people of Northern Ireland have said that they do not want to be united with the Irish Republic. Therefore reunification is impossible. But the reality is a great deal more complex and deserves much more thought than this simple little syllogism would imply.

The key statements on this subject are those made by the British and Irish governments in Para. 5 of the Sunningdale Agreements in December 1973 :

> The Irish Government fully accepted and solemnly declared that there could be no change in the status of Northern Ireland until a majority of the people of Northern Ireland desired a change in that status.
>
> The British Government solemnly declared that it was, and would remain, its policy to support the wishes of the majority of the people of Northern Ireland. The present status of Northern Ireland is that it is part of the United Kingdom. If, in the future, the majority of the people of Northern Ireland should indicate a wish to become part of a United Ireland, the British Government would support that wish.

It sounds very fair and reasonable and democratic, and so it is. With one slight flaw, Westminster democracy has always operated faultlessly in Northern Ireland—and that flaw lies in its composition. If the northern Protestants had been willing to settle for Home Rule, there would have been no need for Partition; but having insisted on Partition they had to have a political unit which ensured a Protestant majority big enough to be certain that democratic principles, self-determination, the wishes of the majority, plebiscites, elections, would infallibly produce the same result for ever. So both parties to the Sunningdale Agreements made their solemn declarations knowing perfectly well that no plebiscite or any other form of popular consultation could ever change the status of Northern Ireland so long as the question was posed in the customary terms and the rest of the British electorate was not consulted—which, by the constantly reiterated pledges of successive governments, it cannot be. So reunification *in the terms and manner hitherto contemplated* has to be ruled out. But there are other interesting possibilities.

To look at Ireland in the context of a supra-national Europe has a lot of attraction for anyone with infinite patience and a nice sense of irony; for European integration in practice would mean that Britain would enjoy in an integrated Europe the sort of status that Northern Unionists desire in the United

Kingdom, and these Unionists include some of the more audible anti-Europeans. But there is no need to wait for a latter-day equivalent of the merging of the Seven Kingdoms into one England in AD 827. The European vision, and the European institutions that already exist, can play an important part in Ireland, especially in matters affecting the Border. There are possibilities here that need to be further explored.

The fifth alternative is total independence for Northern Ireland. There are stranger sovereign states in the world, such as The Gambia, whose borders are not only undemarcated for much of their length but tend to fluctuate according to the price of groundnuts in Gambia and neighbouring Senegal. The creation of an independent Northern Ireland would please those who might see in it the longed-for chance to withdraw the British Army and to end British responsibility for the evils of a sectarian society. It might have a certain attraction for the more mindless extremists of both sects who could see in it the chance of a dirty little religious war. But it is ruled out by the solemn declarations at Sunningdale. Independence would be a change of status, a decision on which is left to the people of Northern Ireland. It is most unlikely that a majority of them, after taking a hard-headed look at their situation, would opt for independence.

The sixth possibility can be described uncharitably as a policy of drift, or more realistically as playing it by ear on a day-to-day basis. 'It all seems fairly quiet. No need to stir up trouble. Put up some money to start new factories. Agree to anything they can settle among themselves. Keep pressing the Irish in the South to keep tight control of the Border. The security forces are steadily defeating the IRA'. It is certainly a policy. But it means accepting, as part of the policy, an unending sequence of murdered soldiers and policemen, women and children killed and maimed, beatings, bombings and burnings; in fact, the indefinite continuation of a way of life that an incredulous world has come to regard as normal in the North. And it is we British who get the ridicule and the blame.

That might seem to exhaust the possibilities, leaving only a note of black pessimism on which to end. For myself, I disagree totally. The apparently insoluble problem of Northern Ireland was made by man, and it cannot be beyond the wit of man to solve it—with God's help, and provided we do not go around proclaiming that it is our side that He is on. In various parts of the world I have been involved in difficult situations which became much simpler when certain assumptions which had once been valid had their validity challenged; and when the problem was re-examined in a far wider and deeper context of politics, history, and geography. The only assumption I make is the basic one that Ireland, being an island, forms a natural political entity. This is not an argument for reunification in any form that has so far been discussed; but it places the onus of proving that peace is compatible with Partition upon those who caused it or keep it; that is the British and Irish governments, both of whom have solemnly passed the decision to the one group who can guarantee that Partition will be permanent, but who, left to themselves, brought to an end such peace as there was.

One assumption deeply rooted in British politics two generations ago was that 'Ulster must not be coerced'. It was based on fear of civil war and the party politics of the time. An echo of it was heard in the spring of 1974, when the newly elected Labour government abandoned the vital elements of the Sunningdale Agreements rather than stand up to the political and religious fanatics who forced a general strike upon the Six Counties. It is important to realize what was destroyed :—(i) a coalition mini-government or executive to administer Northern Ireland on a fair and non-sectarian basis, and (ii) a Council of Ireland, as described in Appendix II and outlined in Chapter 10. The destruction of this most hopeful initiative for Ireland was not 'coercing Ulster'. It was a tiny part of the British electorate, living in Northern Ireland, coercing the rest and being allowed by the government to get away with it. I am convinced that the sabotaged political structure was, is, and will remain right. I believe also that the British electorate of all parties saw that it was right, and has become sick and tired of seeing its wishes thwarted, and a bloody guerilla war prolonged, by a minority living in Northern Ireland, for reasons that are decades, even centuries, out of date. As a loyal British taxpayer I would hope that the British government can take a new look at the Irish Question. As a friendly resident and taxpayer in the Irish Republic, I would hope that the Irish government would play a constructive part in such a re-appraisal. As a European I hope that Ireland, the island, can be brought into its European context.

I believe that there is a peace package to be prepared if we start by unwrapping the Sunningdale parcel and removing half of it—the local government part. All parties are agreed that this is an internal British matter, the Northern Irish have destroyed what they had, and so long as the Six Counties remain British territory the British government is free to conduct its foreign relations as it thinks right. Attention can therefore be focused on the Council of Ireland.

There is nothing wrong with the role proposed at Sunningdale for a Council of Ireland, nor with the principles on which it was designed. But it suffered from two fatal flaws, or one flaw which can be viewed in two ways. The very idea of a political body in which the Six Counties would be expected to cooperate with the Republic in matters of common interest scared the wits out of the Northern Protestants. It was so obviously intended to be the first step down the perilous slope at the end of which sat the nominee of the Pope ruling their Ulster from Dublin Castle. Secondly, its composition was a curious throwback to the days of Home Rule and Partition controversies, when the status of the northern and southern parts of Ireland was planned to be identical. In 1974 one party would have been a local administration subordinate to the British government and the other an independent state, a full member of the European Community. I doubt whether such an asymmetrical arrangement would have been workable. On the other hand I doubt whether even today, when the integration of the Community has advanced so far, any two of its member states have a frontier so nebulous and at the same time so prolific of problems. I think there is a very strong case for setting up, within the framework of the Community, an Anglo-Irish Council exactly on the lines of that agreed at Sunningdale, except that one of the parties would not be Northern Ireland but Britain. The British participation would of course include a high proportion of Northern Irish, but this would not be in any way essential if they did not want to take part. If the setting up of such a body posed problems within the Community, machinery exists for setting it up within the Council of Europe;

H

but the problems which it would need to tackle are more germane to the European Community.

Prominent among these problems is that of the Border, not in the sense of an international frontier or a security zone but of an area which breeds the crimes associated with smuggling. As it is, the Border is virtually uncontrollable. If all taxes, duties, levies, and all other revenue and fiscal matters could be harmonised, even at the cost of differentiating Northern Ireland from the rest of Britain, the criminals would vanish with the crimes, the forces of the law would be freed for graver matters, and the border between two member states of the European Community would have made an important advance in the European process of withering away.

An Anglo-Irish Council could do a great deal more than this. For many of the matters which concern the European Community the Border is an irrelevance, for it would make more sense to treat north-western Ireland as a whole; in other cases the interests of Northern Ireland may be closer to those of Ireland as a whole than to those of the rest of Britain. To have a bilateral Council administering these matters with a watchdog assembly debating its work would surely lighten the load on Brussels considerably. It has already been agreed at Sunningdale that the Council should concern itself with agriculture, commerce, industry, forestry, fisheries, tourism, transport, sport, culture, the arts, the police, crime, violence, and human rights; and that the two elected bodies should 'legislate from time to time as to the extent of functions to be devolved to the Council of Ireland. If Northern Ireland is reluctant to re-establish its own assembly and executive, the British half of the components of the Council could, as I have suggested, include Northern Irish representatives who would be prepared to cooperate in this venture.

It should be borne in mind that if suggestions such as these were adopted, by the time the Council was functioning the Irish electorate, North and South, would have elected members to a single parliament, the European parliament. There could also, much later, be a European Passport. I am sometimes asked whether, since I live in Ireland, I have thought of acquiring Irish nationality. The answer is no, because the only passport for which I would consider surrendering my British one would be European. There are plenty of British citizens and dual nationals living in the Republic, just as there are hundreds of thousands of Irish living, working, and voting in Britain on the same terms as the British. In Northern Ireland the hard core of sectarian and political bigotry, of which both communities are guilty, is being very slowly but inexorably eroded. We live in an age of religious and political ecumenism, and I do not believe that we can separate the one from the other; nor should we try to. Of course there are, and always will be, those who are solidly resistant to all change. But when an immovable obstacle lies in the way, surely the right course for the ingenious and ambitious person is to find a way round and bypass the blockage. I have very little sympathy for those who stand wringing their hands and saying, 'We'll never change anything', because it is perfectly obvious that many things are changing in Europe, and changing for the better. And this leads to the question of Irish unity.

Today's European is bound to ask what Irish Unity means. We have listened for so long to the attitudes and resulting policies of Northern Ireland being described as ossified, or petrified, or fossilised, that it is incumbent on the rest of us, who believe that innovation is the only way to peace, to make sure that our own thinking is flexible and up-to-date. Those who are opposed to Irish unity are clear what it is that they are against: a single government, in Dublin, governing all of Ireland. There are a number of very frightened men in the North, and much of the bombast and bluster from parliament and pulpit is a cry of fear lest the slightest move from a totally rigid posture should be a step in the dreaded direction. They have therefore to insist that they alone must take the decisions. The British and Irish governments having conceded this point, it is going to be very difficult for either to repudiate their undertakings about a change of status in the North. So the question is whether the unity of Ireland can be reinterpreted in such a way as to heal the deep wounds and cure the ancient ills. I am not Irish, and I cannot fathom the depths or explore the workings of the Irish mind, still less the Irish heart. Moreover, during the last ten years the issue of unity has become inseparable, in the eyes of most Irish people, whether in the Republic, the North, Britain, or the United States, from that of the rights and the treatment of the Catholics in Northern Ireland. Here is what Jack Lynch, as Taoiseach, said at his party convention eight years ago, when the bad times had begun and the signs of hope had not yet appeared :

> Partition is a deep throbbing weal across the land, heart and soul of Ireland, an imposed deformity whose indefinite perpetuation eats into the Irish consciousness like a cancer. As I have said, it is impossible for true Irishmen, of whatever creed, to dwell on the existence of Partition without becoming emotional. But emotionalism and the brand of impetuous action or demands that it leads to cannot possibly solve, or even help in dealing with, such a problem. The reasons for the distrust, the enmity, the hatred that exist in the Six Counties are far older than Partition. Partition's crime is that it gave them an official stamp and official backing and cemented them into a way of life.

Now eight years later, we can look out upon a very different prospect.

What Jack Lynch called Partition's crime, the official stamp and official backing, are gone. Sectarian government in Stormont has been removed, and it would take an act of unparalleled cowardice in Westminster to restore it. A start has therefore been made in removing 'the reasons for the distrust, the enmity, the hatred. . . .' In the Republic, I doubt whether attitudes have changed much since Jack Lynch gave expression to them some eight years ago in such terms as the following (my italics) :

> I need not explain or justify the fundamental desire of the overwhelming majority of the people of this island for *the restoration in some form* of its national unity . . .
>
> The unity we seek is not something forced but a free and genuine union of those living in Ireland based on mutual respect and tolerance and *guaranteed by a form or forms of government authority* in Ireland providing for progressive improvement of social, economic and cultural life in a just and peaceful environment . . .
>
> Let me make it clear, too, that in seeking reunification our aim is not to extend the domination of Dublin. We have

many times down the years expressed *our willingness to seek a solution on federal lines* and in my most recent statement I envisaged the *possibility of intermediate stages* in an approach to a final agreed solution.

To all these ideas and advances the classical Northern Protestant answer is, 'No, we are British subjects and all we want is our Stormont system of government back exactly as it was before'. To which all parties in the Westminster parliament have answered no.

So the deadlock and the deaths and destruction continue. And yet for those who are prepared to go back to the beginning, as I have done, and look at Ireland as it is today and at Europe as it hopes to be tomorrow, a new pattern emerges clearly enough to prove to those who openly or secretly condone the killing how stupid they are. It does not offer a final solution because until all parties concerned are mature enough to display a spirit of compromise there cannot be a final solution. Nevertheless it can do no harm to examine this new pattern.

The thinking behind the Taoiseach's words quoted above is still valid and constructive but it needs to be moved into its up-to-date context. As he said, the reasons for the distrust, enmity and hatred in the North are far older than Partition. But the arrival of the Scottish Calvinist settlers twelve generations ago is only one divisive episode in an island that has never been united in depth. The first character to appear in my hurried review of Irish history was Agricola's guest, the prince on the run from a rebellion. The first Normans arrived as mercenaries in one of the interminable wars that kept Ireland divided for five centuries. It was Irish militia, Catholic as well as Protestant, who were most ruthless in suppressing the Radical Rebellion of 1798. In the 1830s Belfast Protestants were subscribing funds to help in building new churches for the growing Catholic population. The unifying influence has always been the island itself, gently absorbing its Vikings, Normans, English, and most recently its Scots. They have all come, as Collingwood said, 'conquering by being conquered'. Partition originated in English politics when Lord Randolph Churchill saw in the sectarianism artificially whipped up in the North a chance for the Conservative Party to oust the Liberals. The Taoiseach was right in saying that Partition gave the old enmities an official stamp and backing. But now, eight years later, there are, *or could be*, some important changes:

Whether through direct rule from Britain, or by delegation to a coalition administration, there will be no more sectarian government in Northern Ireland.

The monolithic Protestant-Unionist block is not as solid and flawless as it was. It cannot yet be said that the winds of change are blowing very hard, but enough to make the flagpoles quiver.

If there is an Anglo-Irish Council, and the European Community's policies are helpful, the Border will for all practical purposes wither away.

With direct elections to a European Parliament, and with countries becoming more and more integrated and surrendering more and more of their traditional sovereignty, there will virtually be a federal solution to the Northern Ireland-Britain-Republic relationship.

I am not pretending that these developments would solve the question of Partition or bring instant peace to the North. Nor do I suppose that if the authorities tried to make them happen they would work out exactly as I have suggested. Nevertheless I believe that somewhere in this area there is a constructive programme to be worked out on which serious moderate people, and their leaders, could agree. If they have to choose and to follow new leaders, that is their right. There is certainly no place in the scheme for men with guns or for those who urge them on in the press and from the pulpit. And is it out of place to suggest that those patriots overseas, who in all innocence have subscribed to corrupted causes, should form United Irish Appeals through which to serve peace and reconstruction in their own country?

And there, in hope, I must leave it, since I can neither foresee nor help to shape the future. It has been a long journey through many countries and many centuries, with many trusted friends along the way. The pattern that I have traced in my own life and through history may exist only in my own mind, and others may not see it my way at all. But no matter. I can only say what I believe to have happened. In the secret depths we are, in any case, each and every one of us, alone; and it has all been a labour of love.

CHRONOLOGY

AD 77-83   Julius Agricola Roman Governor of Britain.

AD 81   Agricola considers but decides against invading Ireland. Entertains fugitive Irish prince in Britain.

AD 410   Romano-Celtic Britain left to fend for itself against raids by Angles, Saxons, Jutes, Irish.

Early 5th C. Son of a Romano-Celtic official kidnapped and enslaved by Irish raiders. (Later became St Patrick.)

5th-8th C. English settlements (Angles, Saxons, Jutes) spread over south and east England.

9th C.   Norsemen (Vikings) raid and settle in N.W. France (Normans), England and Ireland.

9th-10th C. The Seven Kingdoms of England unite (AD 827). Extensive intermarriage of Norse and Irish. Norsemen in France are given Duchy of Normandy. Dublin powerful state in Norse world. Extensive Norse settlements in Wexford, Waterford, Limerick. Norse settlements subjected to Irish rule. All Ireland, including Norse areas, christianised. Reform movement begins in Irish Church.

1066   Duke William of Normandy invades England.

1154   Henry II, son of Duke of Anjou and husband of Eleanor of Aquitaine, accedes to English throne.

1155   Papal Bull of Pope Adrian IV makes Henry II Lord of Ireland and grants him permission to invade.

1166-7   Dermot MacMurrough of Leinster seeks help in Irish struggle from Henry II in Aquitaine. Money and a few mercenaries granted.

1171   Henry II intervenes personally and Norman conquest of Ireland begins.

1172   Conquest confirmed by Pope Alexander III.

1216   Magna Carta extended to Ireland.

1246	Henry III orders that all the laws of England shall be obeyed in Ireland (i.e. by the Church, earls, barons, knights, and all free tenants).
1277	Qualified consent to extend English laws to the Irish race granted by Edward I but withdrawn in face of Anglo-Irish opposition.
1297	Parliament of Ireland complains that the English in Ireland are adopting native dress and hair-styles, and describes them as 'degenerate English'.
1300	Edward I at war in Wales, Scotland and France. Irish have to contribute 10,000 men for English armies.
1306	Robert de Bruyis (Robert the Bruce) proclaims himself King of Scotland.
1314	Total defeat of English by Scots at Bannockburn.
1315	Edward de Bruyis, brother of Robert, invades Ireland and is proclaimed King of Ireland.
1316-18	English and Anglo-Irish at war with Scots and Irish throughout most of Ireland.
1317	Protest by the Irish Princes to Pope John XXII about English atrocities.
1318	Edward de Bruyis killed, Scots heavily defeated and withdraw from Ireland.
1337-1453	Hundred Years War between England and France.
1366	The Statutes of Kilkenny ban marriage etc. between English and Irish, and place pure Irish outside the protection of English law and liberty.
1399	King's Council of Ireland reports massive disaffection of great English families throughout Ireland.
1455-85	Dynastic Wars of the Roses in England.
1460	Declaration of Independence by Irish Parliament under Viceroy Richard, Duke of York.
1453-1500	Constantinople falls to Turks, Renaissance spreads across Western Europe. Birth of European nationalism.
1485	Accession of Tudor dynasty in England.
1494	Poynings' Law subordinates Irish parliament to parliament of England.
1517	Martin Luther opens attack on doctrines and authority of Catholic Church.

1534	Henry VIII signs Act of Supremacy and establishes Protestant Church of England with himself as its Head.
1536	John Calvin preaching in Geneva. Calvinism spreads rapidly, especially in Netherlands, Scotland, and England.
1541	Henry VIII abolishes title of Lord of Ireland and styles himself King of Ireland.
c. 1540-1600	Tudors impose centralised government in Ireland to replace traditional tribal systems. Fierce resistance from Gaelic Irish and Old English.
mid 1500s	First colonisation of central Ireland from English counties of Ireland.
1601	Defeat of resistance of Earl of Tyrone, aided by Spaniards at Battle of Kinsale.
1607	'Flight of the Earls', Tyrone and Tyrconnell, to Europe. Plantation of Tyrone lands, i.e. six of the nine counties of Ulster, with Scottish Protestants.
1641	The Great Rebellion. Catholic Confederation of Kilkenny set up.
1652	Final Suppression of the Rebellion by Cromwell. One third of Irish Catholics estimated killed, others deported.
1685	James II becomes King.
1688	'Glorious Revolution'. William of Orange replaces James II.
1690	William of Orange defeats James II at Battle of Boyne.
1691	French and Irish defeated by William at Aughrim.
1704	Act to prevent the Growth of Popery passed. British trade restrictions on Irish goods.
1711	First recorded appearance of secret societies in Ireland.
1719	The Declaratory Act proclaims total subordination and dependence of Ireland upon Britain.
1776	American Declaration of Independence.
1778	Formation of the paramilitary Irish Volunteers. Catholic Relief Act.
1782	Dungannon Convention of Irish Volunteers. English government accepts Declaration of Independence of

	Irish parliament. Declaratory Act of 1719 repealed. Further Catholic Relief Act.
1785	First sectarian secret societies in Ulster.
1789	French Revolution.
1791	Formation of United Irishmen in Belfast.
1792	Defenders' (Catholic peasant) activity intensifies.
1793	Outbreak of war between Britain and France. Enfranchisement of Irish Catholics.
1796-97	French invasions of Ireland planned.
1798	Wolfe Tone's United Irishmen rebellion savagely suppressed by Army and Militia. French expedition lands in Mayo and is routed.
1801	Act of Union.
1803	Emmet's Rising in Dublin.
1815	Battle of Waterloo. Exile of Napoleon.
1829	Catholic Emancipation Act.
1832	Reform Act.
1835	First sectarian riot in Belfast.
1843	Hillsborough political rally. Northern Ireland. Orange Order/Tory/Presbyterian links formed.
1845	The Great Famine.
1848	The 'year of revolution' in Europe.
1858	Irish Republican Brotherhood founded to link American and Irish movements.
1867	Fenian Rising in Ireland and terrorist acts in England.
1868	Gladstone becomes Prime Minister.
1869	Church of Ireland disestablished.
1873	Dublin Convention founds Home Rule Movement and Irish Parliamentary Party.
1879	Irish National Land League formed.
1886	Gladstone's first Home Rule Bill defeated in House of Commons. Lord Randolph Churchill 'plays the Orange card'. Savage sectarian rioting in Belfast.
1900	John Redmond becomes leader of Irish Parliamentary Party.
1905-08	Sinn Féin organisation formed by amalgamation of existing societies.
1911	Parliament Act limits powers of House of Lords.

1912	Home Rule Bill passes Commons and Lords. Ulster Covenant against Home Rule.
1913	Ulster Volunteer Force formed. Irish Citizen Army formed. Irish Volunteers set up.
1914	Threat of mutiny by British Army Officers at The Curragh. Gun-running from Germany in north and south. First World War breaks out. Home Rule Bill becomes law but is suspended with Redmond's consent.
1916	Easter Rising in Dublin. Death penalty on fifteen leaders.
1917	Sinn Féin declares for a Republic. De Valera elected President.
1919	Serious fighting with Royal Irish Constabulary. 'Black and Tan' War.
1920	Government of Ireland Act.
1921	Northern Ireland Parliament opened by King George V. Truce in Ireland (July). Irish Agreement signed (December).
1922	Ireland, except for the six counties of Northern Ireland, becomes an independent state within the Commonwealth. Boundary Commission set up.
1922-3	Irish Civil War.
1925	Boundary Commission finally constituted, meets, and draws up report. Boundary Commission disbanded and report suppressed.
1939-45	Second World War.
1949	Irish Free State leaves Commonwealth and becomes a Republic.

APPENDIX I

JOINT DECLARATION OF AUGUST 1969

Following a meeting at 10 Downing Street on 19 August 1969, a Declaration was issued by the United Kingdom Government and the Northern Ireland Government in these terms:

1. The United Kingdom Government re-affirm that nothing which has happened in recent weeks in Northern Ireland derogates from the clear pledges made by successive United Kingdom Governments that Northern Ireland should not cease to be a part of the United Kingdom without the consent of the people of Northern Ireland or from the provision in Section 1 of the Ireland Act 1949 that in no event will Northern Ireland or any part thereof cease to be part of the United Kingdom without the consent of the Parliament of Northern Ireland. The Border is not an issue.

2. The United Kingdom Government again affirm that responsibility for affairs in Northern Ireland is entirely a matter of domestic jurisdiction. The United Kingdom Government will take full responsibility for asserting this principle in all international relationships.

3. The United Kingdom Government have ultimate responsibility for the protection of those who live in Northern Ireland when, as in the past week, a breakdown of law and order has occurred. In this spirit, the United Kingdom Government responded to the requests of the Northern Ireland Government for military assistance in Londonderry and Belfast in order to restore law and order. They emphasise again that troops will be withdrawn when law and order has been restored.

4. The Northern Ireland Government have been informed that troops have been provided on a temporary basis in accordance with the United Kingdom's ultimate responsibility. In the context of the commitment of these troops, the Northern Ireland Government have re-affirmed their intention to take into the fullest account

at all times the views of Her Majesty's Government in the United Kingdom, especially in relation to matters affecting the status of citizens of that part of the United Kingdom and their equal rights and protection under the law.

5. The United Kingdom Government have welcomed the decisions of the Northern Ireland Government in relation to Local Government franchise, the revision of Local Government areas, the allocation of houses, the creation of a Parliamentary Commissioner for Administration in Northern Ireland and machinery to consider citizens' grievances against other public authorities which the Prime Minister reported to the House of Commons at Westminster following his meeting with Northern Ireland Ministers on May 21 as demonstrating the determination of the Northern Ireland Government that there shall be full equality of treatment for all citizens. Both Governments have agreed that it is vital that the momentum of internal reform should be maintained.

6. The two Governments at their meeting at 10 Downing Street today have re-affirmed that in all legislation and executive decisions of Government every citizen of Northern Ireland is entitled to the same equality of treatment and freedom from discrimination as obtains in the rest of the United Kingdom, irrespective of political views or religion. In their further meetings the two Governments will be guided by these mutually accepted principles.

7. Finally, both Governments are determined to take all possible steps to restore normality to the Northern Ireland community so that economic development can proceed at the faster rate which is vital for social stability.

APPENDIX II

TEXT OF SUNNINGDALE AGREEMENTS

THE TEXT of the agreed communiqué is:

1. The conference between the British and Irish Governments and the parties involved in the Northern Ireland Executive-designate met at Sunningdale on 6th, 7th, 8th and 9th December, 1973.

2. During the conference, each delegation stated their position on the status of Northern Ireland.

3. The Taoiseach said that the basic principle of the conference was that the participants had tried to see what measure of agreement of benefit to all the people concerned could be secured. In doing so, all had reached accommodation with one another on practical arrangements. But none had compromised, and none had asked others to compromise, in relation to basic aspirations. The people of the Republic, together with a minority in Northern Ireland, as represented by the S.D.L.P. delegation, continued to uphold the aspiration towards a United Ireland. The only unity they wanted to see was a unity established by consent.

4. Mr Brian Faulkner said that delegates from Northern Ireland came to the conference as representatives of apparently incompatible sets of political aspirations who had found it possible to reach agreement to join together in government because each accepted that in doing so they were not sacrificing principles or aspirations. The desire of the majority of the people of Northern Ireland to remain part of the United Kingdom, as represented by the Unionist and Alliance delegations, remained firm.

5. The Irish Government fully accepted and solemnly declared that there could be no change in the status of Northern Ireland until a majority of the people of Northern Ireland desired a change in that status.

The British Government solemnly declared that it was, and would remain, its policy to support the wishes of the majority of the people of Northern Ireland. The present status of Northern

Ireland is that it is part of the United Kingdom. If, in the future, the majority of the people of Northern Ireland should indicate a wish to become part of a United Ireland, the British Government would support that wish.

6. The Conference agreed that a formal agreement incorporating the declarations of the British and Irish Governments would be signed at the formal stage of the conference and registered at the United Nations.

7. The conference agreed that a Council of Ireland would be set up. It would be confined to representatives of the two parts of Ireland, with appropriate safeguards for the British Government's financial and other interests. It would compromise a council of ministers with executive and harmonising functions and a consultative role and a consultative assembly with advisory and review functions. The council of ministers would act by unanimity, and would comprise a core of seven members of the Irish Government and an equal number of members of the Northern Ireland Executive, with provision for the participation of other non-voting members of the Irish Government and the Northern Ireland Executive or administration when matters within their departmental competence were discussed.

The council of ministers would control the functions of the council. The chairmanship would rotate on an agreed basis between representatives of the Irish Government and of the Northern Ireland Executive. Arrangements would be made for the location of the first meeting, and the location of subsequent meetings would be determined by the council of ministers.

The consultative assembly would consist of 60 members, 30 members from Dail Eireann chosen by the Dail on the basis of Proportional Representation by the single transferable vote, and 30 members from the Northern Ireland Assembly, chosen by that Assembly and also on that basis. The members of the consultative assembly would be paid allowances. There would be a secretariat to the council, which would be kept as small as might be commensurate with efficiency in the operation of the council.

The secretariat would service the institutions of the council and would, under the council of ministers, supervise the carrying out of the executive and harmonising functions and the consultative role of the council. The secretariat would be headed by a secretary general.

Following the appointment of a Northern Ireland executive, the Irish Government and the Northern Ireland Executive would nominate their representatives to a council of ministers. The council of ministers would then appoint a secretary general and decide upon the location of its permanent headquarters. The secretary general would be directed to proceed with the drawing up of plans for such headquarters. The council of ministers would make arrangements for the recruitment of the staff of the secretariat in a manner and on conditions which would, as far as is practicable, be consistent with those applying to public servants in the two administrations.

8. In the context of its harmonising functions and consultative role, the Council of Ireland would undertake the important work relating, for instance, to the impact of E.E.C. membership. As for executive functions, the first step would be to define and agree these in detail. The conference, therefore, decided that, in view of the administrative complexities involved, studies would at once be set in hand to identify and, prior to the formal stage of the conference, report on areas of common interest in relation to which a Council of Ireland would take executive decisions and in appropriate cases, be responsible for carrying those decisions into effect. In carrying out these studies and also in determining what should be done by the Council in terms of harmonisation, the objectives to be borne in mind would include the following:

(1) To achieve the best utilisation of scarce skills, expertise and resources.

(2) To avoid in the interests of economy and efficiency, un- necessary duplication of effort.

(3) To ensure complementary rather than competitive effort where this is to be advantage to agriculture, commerce and industry.

In particular, these studies would be directed to identifying the purposes of executive action by the Council of Ireland, suitable aspects of activities in the following broad fields:

(*a*) Exploitation, conservation and development of natural re- sources and the environment. (*b*) Agricultural matters (includ- ing agricultural research and animal health and operational aspects of the Common Agriculture Policy), forestry and fisher- ies. (*c*) Co-operative ventures in the fields of trade and industry. (*d*) Electricity generation. (*e*) Tourism. (*f*) Roads and transport.

(*g*) Advisory services in the field of public health. (*h*) Sport, culture and the arts.

It would be for the Oireachtas and the Northern Ireland Assembly to legislate from time to time as to the extent of functions to be devolved to the Council of Ireland. Where necessary, the British Government will co-operate in the devolution of functions. Initially the functions to be vested would be those identified in accordance with the procedures set out above and decided at the formal stage of the conference to be transferred.

9. (I) During the initial period following the establishment of the Council, the revenue of the Council would be provided by means of grants from the two administrations in Ireland towards agreed projects and budgets, according to the nature of the service involved.

(II) It was also agreed that further studies would be put in hand forthwith and completed as soon as possible of methods of financing the Council after the initial period which would be consonant with the responsibilities and functions assigned to it.

(III) It was agreed that the cost of the secretariat of the Council of Ireland would be shared equally, and other services would be financed broadly in proportion to where expenditure or benefit accrues.

(IV) The amount of money required to finance the Council's activities will depend upon the functions assigned to it from time to time.

(V) While Britain continues to pay subsidies to Northern Ireland such payments would not involve Britain participating in the Council, it being accepted nevertheless that it would be legitimate for Britain to safeguard, in an appropriate way, her financial involvement in Northern Ireland.

10. It was agreed by all parties that persons committing crimes of violence, however motivated, in any part of Ireland should be brought to trial irrespective of the part of Ireland in which they are located. The concern which large sections of the people of Northern Ireland felt about this problem was in particular forcefully expressed by the representatives of the Unionist and Alliance parties. The representatives of the Irish Government stated that they understood and fully shared this concern.

Different ways of solving this problem were discussed : Among them were the amendment of legislation operating in the two jurisdictions. On extradition, the creation of a common law enforcement area in which an all-Ireland court would have jurisdiction, and the extension of the jurisdiction of domestic courts so as to enable them to try offences committed outside the jurisdiction.

It was agreed that problems of considerable legal complexity were involved, and that the British and Irish Governments would jointly set up a commission to consider all the proposals put forward at the conference and to recommend, as a matter of extreme urgency, the most effective means of dealing with those who commit these crimes.

The Irish Government undertook to take immediate and effective legal steps so that persons coming within their jurisdiction, and accused of murder, however motivated, committed in Northern Ireland, will be brought to trial, and it was agreed that any similar reciprocal action that may be needed in Northern Ireland be taken by the appropriate authorities.

11. It was agreed that the Council would be invited to consider in what way the principles of the European Convention on Human Rights and Fundamental Freedoms would be expressed in domestic legislation in each part of Ireland. It would recommend whether further legislation or the creation of other institutions, administrative or judicial, is required in either part or embracing the whole island to provide additional protection in the field of human rights. Such recommendations could include the function of an ombudsman or commissioner for complaints, or other arrangements of a similar nature which the Council of Ireland might think appropriate.

12. The conference also discussed the question of policing and the need to ensure public support for and identification with the police service throughout the whole community. It was agreed that no single set of proposals would achieve these aims overnight, and that time would be necessary. The conference expressed the hope that the wide range of agreement that had been reached and the consequent formation of a power-sharing Executive, would make a major contribution to the creation of an atmosphere throughout the community where there would be widespread support for identification with all the institutions of Northern Ireland.

13. It was broadly accepted that the two parts of Ireland are

to a considerable extent inter-dependent in the whole field of law and order, and that the problems of political violence and identification with the police service cannot be solved without taking account of that fact.

14. Accordingly, the British Government stated that, as soon as the security problems were resolved and the new institutions were seen to be working effectively, they would wish to discuss the devolution of responsibility for normal policing and how this might be achieved with the Northern Ireland Executive and the police.

15. With a view to improving policing throughout the island and developing community identification with and support from the police services, the Governments concerned will co-operate under the auspices of a Council of Ireland through their respective police authorities. To this end, the Irish Government would set up a police authority, appointments to which would be made after consultation with the council of ministers of the Council of Ireland. In the case of the Northern Ireland police authority, appointments would be made after consultation with the Northern Ireland Executive, which would consult with the council of ministers of the Council of Ireland. When the two police authorities are constituted, they will make their own arrangements to achieve the objectives set out above.

16. An independent complaints procedure for dealing with complaints against the police will be set up.

17. The Secretary of State for Northern Ireland will set up an all-party committee from the Assembly to examine how best to introduce effective policing throughout Northern Ireland with particular reference to the need to achieve public identification with the police.

18. The conference took note of a reaffirmation by the British Government of its firm commitment to bring detention to an end in Northern Ireland for all sections of the community as soon as the security situation permits, and noted also that the Secretary of State for Northern Ireland hopes to be able to bring into use his statutory powers of selective release in time for a number of detainees to be released before Christmas.

19. The British Government stated that, in the light of the decisions reached at the conference, they would seek the authority of parliament to devolve full powers to the Northern Ireland

Executive and Northern Ireland Assembly as soon as possible. The formal appointment of the Northern Ireland Executive would then be made.

20. The conference agreed that a formal conference would be held early in the new year, at which the British and Irish Governments and the Northern Ireland Executive would meet together to consider reports on the studies which have been commissioned and to sign the agreement reached.

INDEX